Making R Work

How Smart Schools Are Reforming Education Through Schoolwide Response-to-Intervention

Wayne Sailor

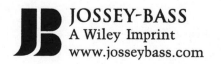

JOSSEY-BASS
A Wiley Imprint
www.josseybass.com

Published by Jossey-Bass

A Wiley Imprint

989 Market Street, San Francisco, CA 94103-1741—www.josseybass.com

Jossey-Bass books and products are available through most bookstores. To contact Jossey-Bass directly call our Customer Care Department within the U.S. at 800-956-7739, outside the U.S. at 317-572-3986, or fax 317-572-4002.

Jossey-Bass also publishes its books in a variety of electronic formats. Some content that appears in print may not be available in electronic books.

Library of Congress Cataloging-in-Publication Data

Sailor, Wayne.
  Making RTI work: how smart schools are reforming education through schoolwide response-to-intervention / Wayne Sailor.
      p. cm.
  Includes bibliographical references and index.
  ISBN 978-0-470-19321-1 (pbk.)
  1. Remedial teaching. 2. School improvement programs. I. Title.
  LB1029.R4S235 2009
  371.9'043–dc22

                                                                2009023236

Printed in the United States of America
first edition

PB Printing   10   9   8   7   6   5   4   3   2   1

Contents

Figures & Tables

Figures

Tables

Foreword

Wayne Sailor writes that the three domains of teaching are science, relationships, and inspiration. I would say that the book he has produced is about those same three themes. Let me explain.

First, the book is about the science of assessing the differences between learning and performance, which Dr. Sailor is well grounded in both theoretically and practically. He offers examples from teachers, principals, and superintendents as they come to see the differences. In a clear, concise, and painstaking way, he provides the theoretical and structural foundation for understanding response to intervention (RTI). Most books on this subject eschew the structural, yet it is collaboration and the integration of resources that make RTI happen in schools.

Dr. Sailor combines his science, the theoretical underpinnings of this presentation, with multiple school-, district-, and state-level examples of how this policy has largely remained a special education initiative. The fact that this policy is aligned with special education could, if it so remained, prove to be an insurmountable barrier to its success in local schools.

His science is not limited to teaching and learning. He provides examples of successful systems change as well. He also wisely takes time in this book to note the limitations of rational-technical approaches to any structural change initiative, and then speaks to the importance of relationships. This should make all readers engaged in this topic smile with appreciation in recognition of the limitations of research.

Second, teaching and learning is about relationships. The importance of first establishing meaningful relationships preceding anything else is a widely accepted practice. Coming to know the other is the starting point for teacher and learner alike. Dr. Sailor emphasizes instructional coaching through the work of James Knight and explains how coaching and the relationships formed are an instrumental part of changing the nature and type of teaching practice. Dr. Sailor shows teachers how to use data to inform instruction formatively to improve student learning and performance. Formative assessment is part of the continuing cycle of the teaching-learning process and building the teacher-to-student relationship. Without feedback on performance students cannot improve in their learning. Data are the vehicle for deepening the relationship between teacher and student.

Third, Dr. Sailor offers a story of both relationship and inspiration about a fourth-grade teacher who knew how to engage a precocious and gifted but bored child. This book is inspirational because the author as researcher is also a social activist who has conducted research in complex schools filled with poverty, ethnic division, conflict, and poor school performance—Ravenswood, California; Kansas City, Kansas; New Orleans, Louisiana; and, most recently, the nation's capital—to take up the cause of school reform. He tells inspiring stories with data of how these cities are coming to understand how they can change their thinking and structures to support the academic and social development of all their students.

The methods Dr. Sailor outlines include collaborative practices that integrate students, teachers, and systems of support for all students. In these challenging times, he writes of empowerment, not separate silos of people, resources, and ideas. He writes as well of collaboration and integration of effort, not continued fragmentation and separation of expertise, and for ownership of all students and the engagement of families and communities, especially for very needy students.

Much work is revealed and effort displayed at every level of our educational system. This book is the result of a lifetime of effort, and we should all be grateful to Dr. Sailor's fourth-grade teacher. She created an inspiration for us all.

Leonard Burrello
Professor and Chair of Educational
Leadership and Policy Studies
University of South Florida, Tampa, Florida

Acknowledgments

My heartfelt thanks to my good friends Lou Brown and Leonard Burrello and my long-standing colleague Elizabeth Kozleski for their helpful suggestions on the first draft of this book. I acknowledge my federal government colleagues Lou Danielson (now with the American Institute for Research-AIR), Rene Bradley, and Jennifer Doolittle from whom I have learned much about positive behavior support and RTI (response to intervention). My Louisiana State University friend and colleague, Alan Coulter, furthered my education on RTI.

I thank my Kansas colleagues, Alexa Posny, schools chief for Kansas, and S. Colleen Riley, state special education director, for helping me understand Multi-Tiered Systems of Support, the Kansas state RTI initiative. Thanks also to Amy Jenks of the New Hampshire Department of Education, Dawn Miller of Shawnee Mission School District in Kansas, and Christie Whitter, principal of Madison Elementary in the Gardner-Edgerton School District in Kansas.

Particular thanks to Maria De La Vega, superintendent of Ravenswood City School District in California, and to the principals and teachers of Ravenswood who have taught me much about how schools change and to principal David Herrera of Cesar Chavez Academy in Ravenswood whose leadership somehow made it all seem easy. Thanks to Lisa Pruitt, Lena Van Haren, and April Stout in Ravenswood who, together with my University of

Kansas colleague Jim Knight, have helped me to understand the power of instructional coaching.

I also thank Linda Rohrbaugh, Elissa Salas, and Richard Nyankori of Washington, D.C., Public Schools for helping me to stay tethered in reality as I continue to learn from day-to-day experience.

Finally, I thank my schoolwide applications colleagues Blair Roger in Oakland, California; Amy McCart, Nikki Wolf, and Jeong Hoon Choi at the University of Kansas; and especially Mariann Graham, without whom this book would never have made it to press.

Many others assisted in this project, and I ask forgiveness from others I should have named and offer my sincere apologies. I plead fading memory.

The Author

Wayne Sailor graduated from the University of California, Berkeley, in 1964, and earned his M.A. and Ph.D. in clinical psychology at the University of Kansas in 1967 and 1969, respectively. He taught in the Special Education Department at San Francisco State University and in the joint doctoral program with the University of California, Berkeley, for seventeen years. He moved to Lawrence, Kansas, in 1992 and has taught in the Special Education Department as a professor since 2001. Together with his colleague Blair Roger in California, he created the schoolwide applications model school reform process to assist schools in fully implementing schoolwide response to intervention (RTI), which is operational in schools in Kansas, California, and, most recently, Washington, D.C.

This book is dedicated to Wendy, my soulmate and my constant source of inspiration. Thanks.

Preface

The children, as they gained in strength and capacity, were gradually initiated into the mysteries of the several processes. It was a matter of immediate and personal concern, even to the point of actual participation. We cannot overlook the factors of discipline and of character-building involved in this kind of life.

John Dewey

November 2008 was a momentous year in the history of the United States. Against all odds, an African American man, who ran on a platform of change and hope against a grim backdrop of worldwide financial calamity, was elected president. It was also a fascinating year of change and hope in America's public schools: the era of accountability ushered in by the Bush administration succeeded in moving science from university research centers directly into measurement of the classroom teaching-learning process and, more important, pupil progress. The results of this overlay of scientific assessments, however, have been discouraging for the most part. America's schools for the first time have been held measurably accountable for student learning. The problem is that they are being held accountable for producing something they do not know how to do given the realities.

U.S. schools, like most other public institutions, are products of a bygone age of specialization, where goals could be segmented into discrete targets of opportunity and specialists could be trained to address those targets. Specialized resource systems tend to grow into small industries, ever expanding their own discourse communities and communities of practice—but also moving away from the original enterprise. If the whole is only as good as the sum of its parts, then the next step must be to reconnect the parts.

This book offers one pathway to achieving that next step, the reframing of educational resources to focus on a common goal: the improvement of academic achievement for all students. Response to intervention (RTI) as a schoolwide endeavor offers a potential breakthrough by moving science in the classroom beyond accountability assessment and into the direct improvement of the interactive processes engaged in teaching and learning. As such, it is a good fit with the ethos of change and hope.

I wrote this book from the standpoint of nearly three decades of research in public schools. Most of my work has been in urban schools, my particular passion, but the conclusions I have drawn from that work, as well as from the work of many colleagues around the country and in Canada, from whom I have learned much, are applicable to all of America's schools—urban, suburban, and rural. Why shouldn't a high-performing suburban school be able to move to the next level and become a much higher-performing school? Why shouldn't an inner-city low-performing school become a high-performing school? We know from published examples from all over the country that we can no longer blame the children, or their parents, or their race, culture, or neighborhood if those children fail to learn. The lessons from the outstanding successes of the few schools that moved from poor to great need to be made widely available. This book is thus designed to reveal a potential framework for success. As such, it is offered as a resource to school and district leaders, teachers in both general and specialized educational support systems such as special education, Title I, etc., and to parents, and researchers who are ready to engage the difficult task of undertaking systems change by working from a blueprint of educational reform grounded in science, on the one hand, and steeped in hope, on the other.

The book is divided into three parts. Part One lays out in three chapters the essential framework for change that is embodied in RTI. Part Two, which consists of Chapters Four to Six, offers a step-by-step process for putting the various components of RTI into motion in the school and in the classroom. The final chapters, in Part Three, show what RTI looks like at the individual school, district, and statewide levels. The Conclusion offers a glimpse of the potential future of schoolwide RTI in helping to take American education to the next level.

I have sought throughout this book to provide examples of key points and to guide readers to useful books, Web sites, and other tools. New resources on RTI are emerging at a fast pace, a hopeful sign.

Hope and promise for the future are in the air. No longer can any child—black, brown, or white; rich or poor; girl or boy—say, "Why make the effort? I can never reach the highest levels of power and make a true difference in the world." It is up to us to give America's young people the educational tools for success to reach their own personal aspirations. Schoolwide RTI may provide the catalyst to begin to realize that goal in all of our nation's schools.

Wayne Sailor
Lawrence, Kansas

Part I

The Origin and Design of Schoolwide RTI

1

Defining RTI

Response to intervention (RTI) is best understood as a model used to guide efforts to teach (intervention) based on measures of pupil progress (response) and grounded in the idea of prevention. The phrase, "little kids, little problems; big kids, big problems," captures the idea. Suppose we could collect some relatively simple data on a kindergarten class that could be a powerful predictor of which children would succeed in the third-grade curriculum and which would be likely to fail. What if, based on these data, we could structure specific decisions about our teaching approach directed to the children determined to be at risk for failure that could greatly improve their chances of succeeding in the third grade? Of course, we would need to carefully monitor the progress of these students to ensure we are on the right track and make needed teaching adjustments if indicated. If we do these things, which I show in this book are not particularly burdensome, we will be using schoolwide RTI to raise the power of the teaching-learning process to boost academic achievement and prevent academic failure downstream for all kids.

> *Suppose we could collect some relatively simple data on a kindergarten class that could be a powerful predictor of which children would succeed in the third-grade curriculum and which would be likely to fail.*

Features of RTI

Current definitions of RTI have several features in common as well as several that diverge. The common features, which this book examines in some detail later, are these:

- A three-tier system of matching interventions to assessed student academic and behavioral needs
- Systematic screening of young children using scientifically acceptable measuring instruments
- Interventions that have solid grounding in research and for which there is scientific evidence that they improve behavior or academic achievement, or both
- Progress monitoring of students identified as being at risk for low academic achievement, again using scientific measures
- Decision rules concerning levels of support provided through intervention

Features of RTI that diverge across various published definitions have mainly to do with the uses to which RTI is addressed. We look at standard protocol RTI, problem-solving, RTI, and school-wide RTI.

Standard Protocol RTI

Many of the systematic investigations of RTI processes that have appeared to date have been focused on disability determination (for a summary of this research, see *Handbook of Positive Behavior Support*, which I edited with Glen Dunlap, George Sugai, and Rob Horner). This standard protocol RTI refers to sets of research-validated decision rules with which to guide specific interventions at each of three tiers that are formulated through assessment. Tier 1 refers to universal interventions, applicable to all students. Tier 2 refers to *more intensive* interventions targeted to groups of students on the basis of assessed need. Tier 3 refers to *individualized highly intensive* interventions directed to a few students for whom secondary tier interventions are insufficient. Progress monitoring results are then used to determine if a specific learning disability is present that would require a more scientifically valid method of identification than psychological testing, the more prevalent method of disability determination. The breakthrough in standard protocol RTI is in the addition of scientifically valid and reliable measures that are curriculum based rather than referenced against normative distributions that are divorced from the immediate curriculum, such as IQ tests.

RTI and Special Education

Credit for introducing the RTI model into schools goes to special education, which has sought ways to bring greater scientific rigor to the process of determining who should be eligible for supports and services under the Individuals with Disabilities Education Act (IDEA). Readers interested in the origins of RTI in special education and its implications for public policy are directed to a 2006 landmark publication of the National Association of State Directors of Special Education (NASDSE), *Response to Intervention: Policy Considerations and Implementation*. The National Research Center on Learning Disabilities has made available a detailed manual for implementing standard protocol RTI, *Responsiveness to Intervention (RTI): How to Do It* (it can be downloaded from www.nrcld.org).

Problem-Solving RTI

Other viewpoints about uses of RTI extend beyond the standard protocol definition. The second popular conception of RTI that emerged at about the same time (circa 1990) extended the model to children placed at risk for academic failure due primarily to behavior problems (see Bergan & Kratchowill, 1990). Rather than using RTI for disability determination, the model was employed to determine the level of intervention in a behavioral consultation approach with children whose behavior was impeding their response to efforts to teach them. This extension of RTI to determination of the level of intervention to address a social-behavioral problem came to be known as *problem-solving* RTI.

The advent of problem-solving RTI presented an opportunity for two important expansions of the approach beyond the disability determination grounding of standard protocol RTI. First, the application of RTI logic to remediation of behavior problems affecting learning set the stage for a full-blown prevention model, addressed to social and behavioral development, to emerge. Called *positive behavior support*, this evidence-based system of interventions at three tiers enabled the emergence of a broader definition of RTI that integrates both behavioral and academic measurements and interventions.

In the next chapter, I examine the dramatic interplay of forces that came about during the early years of the administration of George W. Bush and the launching of the educational accountability movement that provided the spark that made possible the explosion in RTI research and development. RTI is, after all, not a new idea. Stanley Deno, Doug and Lynn Fuchs, Don Compton, Dan Reschley, and others at Vanderbilt University have been conducting careful scientific studies of RTI processes for over two decades. It took a shift in public policy, the launching of No Child Left Behind (NCLB), with its strong focus on educational accountability, to put RTI into wide spectrum use, beginning with special education, and in the last few years making the leap into school-wide applications.

Schoolwide RTI

The first major publication on RTI addressed to the professional community of general education appeared in Rachel Brown-Chidsey and Mark Steege's 2005 book, *Response to Intervention*. They pointed out that not all researchers in special education thought an extension to general education was a good idea. We have all witnessed the meltdown of promising educational practices in the translation from research to practice. Scientific studies involve rigor and careful measurements, but clinical practices often do not follow research-prescribed specifications. When things go badly as a result, one often hears, "We tried such-and-such approach. It didn't work." Just one or two reported failures of application can cause a promising practice to be relegated to the shelf of history while newer practices are put into play. A number of social scientists have pointed out that much more rigorous research is needed before federal and state policy shifts set the stage for RTI to be put into widespread practice.

Schoolwide RTI as an extension of problem-solving RTI is advancing apace with federal and state policy initiatives paving the way. Brown-Chidsey and Steege, to their credit, made a strong case for preserving the processes of careful measurement and decisions, based on reliable data, that are germane to applications of RTI in practice. Since teachers increasingly are bombarded with demands of educational assessments, the rigorous screening and progress monitoring requirements of RTI will likely face a hard sell, at least initially. Brown-Chidsey and Steege addressed this issue:

> Schoolwide RTI as an extension of problem-solving RTI is advancing apace with federal and state policy initiatives paving the way.

In order for RTI to become a routine part of general education, teachers, administrators, and specialists will need to learn how to implement and interpret RTI methods and data. Some teachers may not have received much, if any, training in data analysis. Others may worry that RTI is another "add-on" to what they are already doing and fear that there are not enough hours in the school day to incorporate RTI practices. Importantly, RTI does not require "adding on" to what is already being done in the classroom. Instead, it involves reviewing current classroom practices to identify those that yield evidence of effective instruction as well as those that do not. RTI methods call for teachers to *replace* those practices that do not yield student improvement with those that do. When using RTI, general education teachers will remain the most important part of students' school success [p. 10].

The advent of problem-solving RTI and, more recently, schoolwide RTI reveals an important conceptual distinction from standard protocol RTI. The latter views RTI as a more scientifically advanced process to identify the presence of a disability, in particular a learning disability (LD). This concept puts emphasis on identifiable limitations that are a characteristic of the individual child (that is, the disability) rather than focusing on environment limitations. Problem-solving RTI shifts that focus to the context in which limitations arise. Behavior problems, for example, may be situational, and the best intervention may prove to be directed more to ecological factors than to the individual. Schoolwide RTI advances this theme by extending RTI processes to all factors that screening assessments may reveal to be impeding the learning process.

The next major publication to appear on schoolwide RTI was John McCook's *The RTI Guide: Developing and Implementing a Model in Your Schools* in 2006. This book offers the advantage of providing what is essentially a manual on how to do schoolwide RTI with illustrations of specific applications of the approach in Knox County, Tennessee. The manual provides useful examples of scoring forms, sample parent information letters, and other materials. For schools getting started with an RTI conversion, this manual affords a very user-friendly training guide.

Another recent schoolwide RTI book to appear is *RTI: A Practitioner's Guide to Implementing Response to Intervention* (2008) by Daryl Mellard at the University of Kansas and Evelyn Johnson of Boise State University. Although it is not as prescriptive as McCook's manual, it does an excellent job of anchoring schoolwide RTI in educational policy initiatives and statutes and providing a well-integrated summary of critical RTI features.

Evolving Definitions of RTI

Thus far, I have provided a sketch of the origins of RTI and its rapid emergence in American public education. Some view it as a major conceptual breakthrough, while others regard it as a runaway train. From my point of view, both are possibilities. Everything will hinge on the importance of adherence of the process to data. Without careful measurement at each step of the way using scientifically acceptable instruments for screening, progress monitoring, and fidelity of application of interventions guided by decision rules grounded in scientific research, the breakthrough will evaporate. It is all the more likely to evaporate because it is labor intensive and requires extensive professional development in order to be successful.

My own experience with RTI thus far leads me to opt for the viewpoint that it is an immense conceptual breakthrough that can move American education to the next level if it is followed carefully and prescriptively. That is the reason for this book. But it is important first and foremost to understand the logic of RTI and its evolving definitions as we begin to put it to the test in our nation's schools.

Standard Protocol Definitions

RTI originated in special education as an effort to bring child performance data into the eligibility determination process. From there it rapidly moved into broader applications in both general and special education to focus on prevention of potential failure in, first, reading and then, more recently, in math. In the discussion that follows, I examine in detail definitions of RTI that emerged during this transformational period.

The following definition, supplied by Evelyn Johnson, Darryl Mellard, Douglas Fuchs, and Melinda McKnight in their 2006 book, *Responsiveness to Intervention: How to Do It*, applies to standard protocol, where disability determination is the primary target for the implementation of RTI:

> RTI is an assessment and intervention process for systematically monitoring student progress and making decisions about the need for instructional modifications or increasingly intensified services using progress monitoring data. The following is the fundamental question of RTI procedures: Under what conditions will a student successfully demonstrate a response to the curriculum? Thus, interventions are selected and implemented under rigorous conditions to determine what will work for the student [p. i.2].

They continue:

> RTI can be used as a process that is one part of the evaluation for the determination of SLD [a specific learning disability]. A strong RTI process includes the following critical features:
>
> - High-quality, scientifically-based classroom instruction

- Student assessment with classroom focus
- School-wide screening of academics and behavior
- Continuous progress monitoring of students
- Implementation of appropriate research-based interventions
- Progress monitoring during interventions (effectiveness)
- Teaching behavior fidelity measures [p. i.2].

Around the time of reauthorization of the IDEA in 2004, the U.S. Office of Special Education Programs launched a broad national conversation on the general topic of eligibility determination, in this case for LD. Called the LD Initiative, this multiyear effort involving large numbers of stakeholder groups, public testimony in hearings around the country, and symposia on evidence from research culminated with the following 2007 definition by Renee Bradley, Lou Danielson, and Jennifer Doolittle of the Office of Special Education Programs:

> RTI has been conceptualized as a multi-tiered prevention model that has at least three tiers. The first tier, referred to as primary intervention, consists of high-quality, research-based instruction in the general education setting, universal screening to identify at-risk students, and progress monitoring to detect those students who might not be responding to this primary intervention as expected. Within this multi-tiered framework, decisions regarding movement from one level to the next are based on the quality of student responses to research-based interventions. Subsequent levels differ in intensity (i.e., duration, frequency, and time) of the research-based interventions being delivered, the size of the student groupings, and the skill level of the service provider [p. 9].

Daryl Mellard and Evelyn Johnson in their 2008 book have provided a concise and readable extension of the standard protocol conception of RTI for school practitioners. In clarifying their understanding of the utility of RTI, they wrote:

> RTI can serve three distinct applications: screening and prevention, early intervention, and disability determination. Within this text, we emphasize RTI in a general education setting for prevention and early intervention of students' learning difficulties. Strong evidence supports the RTI components and principles to improve instruction and related student outcomes. The research does not, to date, support the use of RTI as an exclusive component to disability determination. However, the research foundation may be used in incorporating RTI as *one* component of disability determination. As such, RTI provides documentation that the student has received appropriate and high-quality instruction in the general classroom, but more thorough assessment is required to determine the nature and extent of the student's disability if a special education referral is made [p. ix].

Combined Standard Protocol and Problem-Solving Definitions

Combining standard protocol and problem-solving definitions, NASDSE published a remarkable document in 2006, *Response to Intervention: Policy Considerations and Implementation*, that signaled a major shift in the traditional special education policy arena. Prior to 2006, the field of special education had seemed content with pursuit of an expansion agenda. Characterized by the rapid creation of new disability categories (among them, autism spectrum disorder and attention deficit hyperactivity disorder), the field was becoming a growth industry, with increasing numbers of scientific journals, new organizations, and ever increasing federal and state budgets. The 2006 publication made clear that the state director's group now views RTI as a potential pathway to the reduction of numbers of students identified for special education and as a potential bridge between NCLB and IDEA. At a time when some in the field of special education, on the basis of scientific conservatism, were for confining RTI to a status of providing one source for disability determination, the state directors were creating a window of opportunity for integrating special and general education policy with RTI as a principal driver in the process. The NASDSE definition of RTI thus reflects a blend of standard protocol and problem-solving RTI conceptions. More important, it advanced the problem-solving RTI case by fully integrating social and behavioral interventions with academic interventions under a single RTI logic model. Here is the NASDSE (2006) definition of RTI:

> Response to Intervention (RTI) is the practice of providing high-quality instruction and interventions matched to student need, monitoring progress frequently to make decisions about changes in instruction or goals and applying child response data to important educational decisions. RTI should be applied to decisions in general, remedial and special education, creating a well-integrated system of instruction/intervention guided by child outcome data. Child outcome data are essential to:
>
> - Making accurate decisions about the effectiveness of general and remedial education instruction/interventions;
> - Making early identification/intervention with academic and behavioral problems;
> - Preventing unnecessary and excessive identification of students with disabilities;

- Deciding eligibility for special programs, including special education; and
- Determining individual education programs as well as delivering and evaluating special education services [p. 1].

The theme of combining standard protocol and problem-solving RTI approaches for school applications was discussed in John McCook's implementation manual for practitioners. He suggests defining a set group of interventions to be used throughout the system. Which interventions are to be used with individuals or groups of students are then decided by problem-solving teams. Specific interventions are chosen from lists of scientifically based research methodologies that were identified to address particular areas of concern.

Schoolwide Definitions

In my view, RTI is a carefully researched system of specific applications that is evolving as a model as the system interacts with public policy at federal and state levels. It began as standard protocol RTI, an improvement in the overall process of determining the presence of a specific learning disability, with part of the initial research directed to problems in reading. The national organization of special education state leaders set the stage for moving into schoolwide applications of the RTI logic system by incorporating applications of the system to social and behavioral problems impeding learning, which had been a principal feature of problem-solving RTI.

The next stage of RTI evolution appears to be delineation of a fully integrated behavior and academic risk prevention system with three tiers, characterized by decision rules for matching interventions to measured student need, with fidelity of application at each level of engagement. Such an integrated RTI model offers the distinct advantage of bringing general and special educators together to pursue a common agenda of matching resources and professional expertise to identified student need on the basis of scientific data. There is a cautionary note, however. Although careful research has identified some useful measurement tools and applications of RTI have led to some useful decision rules for matching interventions to student needs, applications of schoolwide RTI go far beyond the available necessary tools to maintain the evidence-based feature of standard protocol RTI. That said, there is no stopping a rapidly accelerating train. Maintaining the rigorous scientific basis for RTI logic, its hallmark, will require a substantial investment of federal, state, and philanthropic resources directed to research and professional development in guiding the emergence of schoolwide RTI.

> *Maintaining the rigorous scientific basis for RTI logic, its hallmark, will require a substantial investment of federal, state, and philanthropic resources directed to research and professional development in guiding the emergence of schoolwide RTI.*

The best, and certainly the most concise, definition of schoolwide RTI that I found is that provided by Brown-Chidsey and Steege: "Response to Intervention (RTI) is a systematic and data-based method for identifying, defining, and resolving students' academic and/or behavioral difficulties" (p. 144). Brown-Chidsey and Steege elaborated:

> RTI methods focus on a new problem definition in which the problem is measured by the distance between what is expected and what is occurring. Instead of the student being the problem, the problem is a phenomenon resulting from student-environment interactions. Traditional approaches to dealing with students who struggle in school have included reducing what is expected of them with curriculum modifications. RTI methods call

for a different problem-solving approach in which each student's response to specific teaching procedures is tracked with *data* and reviewed *systematically* to determine whether other instruction is needed. Certainly there are educators already using some, or all, components of the RTI method. However, in order for RTI to be maximally effective for all students, all educators must understand and employ consistent procedures [p. 139].

Brown-Chidsey and Steege's comments, written primarily for general educators, provide a close fit with the RTI model that my colleagues and I have been investigating using a comprehensive school reform approach as the driver. Called the Schoolwide Applications Model (SAM), the approach offers the advantage of providing a reliable and valid fidelity estimation tool, the SAM Analysis System, that permits the careful evaluation of the extent to which each of fifteen critical features of the model are being implemented at each stage of enculturation of the systems change approach. This process enables an evaluation of the effects of specific schoolwide interventions such as schoolwide positive behavior support on student social or academic achievement as measured by scientifically validated instruments. As new models of schoolwide RTI emerge, it will be of paramount importance to have validated fidelity estimation tools. Validated here means measurement tools that have been subjected to rigorous psychometric evaluation and have been shown to have predictive validity with regard to student achievement. Without these, our ability to replicate highly successful models will be impaired.

Comprehensive Schoolwide RTI

I elaborate more on how schoolwide RTI operates within the SAM school reform model in later chapters, including some examples from a participating school district. Figure 1.1 illustrates the RTI

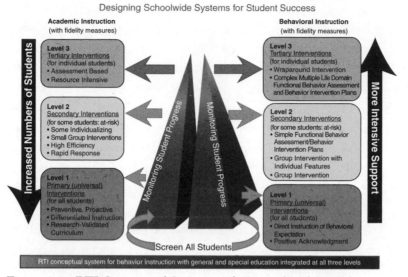

Figure 1.1   RTI Conceptual System with General and Special Education Integrated at All Three Levels

model that characterizes SAM and other schoolwide RTI applications. (It should be noted that similar figures appear in McCook's 2006 book and NASDSE's 2005 book.)

The figure casts the RTI model as a pyramid. Horizontal lines bisecting the pyramid illustrate the three levels reflecting the intensity of interventions. Conceiving of RTI as a three-tiered system is really just a matter of convention. The original public health prevention model from which RTI emerged in education was cast as having primary, secondary, and tertiary tiers, and that tradition has carried forward. In practice, there will quite likely be tiers within tiers, and future RTI models will likely reflect multitiered systems of support rather than the three-tiered model. Schools implementing SAM, for example, use color codes to reflect levels of support. Although Figure 1.1 does not appear in color here, in use the darker blue toward the base reflects universal applications, and shifts toward yellow and orange toward the middle reflect greater intensity of supports. Red toward the top of the pyramid signals individualized levels of support, while dark red at the tip can reflect wraparound, such as the comprehensive approach developed by Lucille Eber and her colleagues in Illinois (see www.pbisillinois.org). Wraparound, the most intensive level of individualized support, can involve school, community, and family participation in a complex educational and treatment plan. With repeated measures over time, the SAM RTI pyramid can reflect changes in levels of intensity at district, school, grade, and classroom levels; specified groupings of students (for example, English Language Learners and special education students); and individual students. The goal at all levels is to increase the percentage of the pyramid that is shifted downward toward the blue end.

Color shifts on the pyramid can vary on the left and right halves, showing academic levels of intervention and social and behavioral interventions on the right. For example, a student may be in grade-level universal instruction for academics, but be monitored for progress in social or behavioral risk factors on the basis of office disciplinary referrals, and be in a "check in/check out" schoolwide positive behavior support secondary-level intervention. Check in/check out here refers to a supervised self-monitoring procedure that has demonstrated success in helping students to learn pro social behavior. The pyramid software would show this student solidly in the blue area on the left side of the pyramid but in a corresponding pale yellow color designator on the right side (social and behavioral side).

The reason for using the color designation in SAM is to encourage teachers and administrators to think of levels of intervention and support as a continuum rather than as discrete categories. We have already encountered some school districts that purport to have an RTI model in place but conceive of secondary-level interventions as a "resource room" where "the secondary kids" spend their day and tertiary-level interventions as being where special education enters the picture. In these cases, the "tertiary kids" are usually in special education classrooms.

The strength and great advantage of schoolwide RTI is its capacity to integrate school resources (such as general and special education functions and supports) and its dynamic quality of applying greater levels of intensity where indicated, and scaling back extraordinary interventions where indicated, by data from progress monitoring. As I elaborate in Chapter Two, schoolwide RTI affords the opportunity for educators to reframe problems of the teaching-learning process more from the perspective of social sciences and away from the more categorical medical (i.e., diagnostic/ prescriptive and focused on problems located in the individual) model that exists in most schools today.

> *The strength and great advantage of school-wide RTI is its capacity to integrate school resources (i.e., general and special education functions and supports), and its dynamic quality of applying greater levels of intensity where indicated, and scaling back extraordinary interventions where indicated, by data from progress monitoring.*

The arrows at the left and right sides of the figure indicate the direction within the model of more intensive supports and services moving up from the base (right arrow) and the direction of increasing numbers of students requiring fewer intensive supports and services toward the base (left arrow). Some RTI pyramid schematics include percentages of students at each of the three levels, usually depicted as 80 to 85 percent in level 1, 10 to 15 percent in level 2, and 1 to 5 percent in level 3. My colleagues and I feel that on the basis of our data from urban core schools, these figures can be misleading. We have worked with schools, for example, where fewer than 40 percent of the students were functioning under universal levels of support and where as many as 30 percent required individual levels of support for behavior or academics, or both.

Figure 1.1 provides a few examples of instructional interventions for both behavior and academics at each of the three traditional levels of RTI. For example, level 1, universal instruction in social/behavioral development, includes teaching school expectations of personal deportment and providing a measurable system for acknowledging students who reflect learning of and performance on school expectations ("catch 'em being good"). On the academic side, level 1 (or universal) educational interventions include differentiated instruction matched to student learning characteristics and teaching within a research-validated curriculum, particularly in the areas of reading, writing, and math subject areas.

Figure 1.1 indicates the need of careful screening to identify students at younger grade levels or early in the school year who may be at risk for learning impairments due to processing problems (academics), social or behavioral problems, or combinations of the two. Furthermore, the pyramid reflects the requirement to monitor the progress of students (at all positions) who have been identified as being at risk for failure to progress at grade-level expectations on the basis of cognition, behavior, and the presence of a disability.

Finally, the caption reflects the intent of this schoolwide RTI approach to fully integrate educational resources, technology, services, and supports.

To Sum Up

RTI is a contemporary manifestation of an earlier public health prevention model. In education, its debut was manifest in extensive research into why students fail to learn to read; whether those who so fail should be classed automatically as LD; and whether data on how students respond to intervention strategies at different levels of intensity should be added to psychological test data as a basis for diagnosing LD and determining eligibility for services under IDEA. This conception of RTI is called *standard protocol RTI*.

A parallel form of RTI with applications in education and school psychology is directed to determining levels of intervention required to ameliorate academic or behavior problems. This form of the RTI model, which relies on team processes within schools for screening progress monitoring and level and type of intervention, is not particularly concerned with eligibility determination for special education; rather, it is directed more to matching school resources with identified student need on the basis of ongoing assessments. This form of RTI is called *problem-solving RTI*.

The national organization for state directors of special education, NASDSE, put forward a set of policy recommendations in 2006 that advanced an agenda of combined standard protocol and problem-solving RTI that has set the stage for *schoolwide RTI*, which is now emerging as a major conceptual advance in both the general education and special education professional and research communities. Advances in schoolwide RTI have now set the stage for the emergence of a comprehensive model of RTI grounded in school reform, the shape of which is the substance of the rest of this book.

All forms of RTI are characterized by three levels (sometimes called tiers) of educational support, or interventions: primary (universal), secondary (targeted group), and tertiary (individual). The process begins with early screening for academic or behavioral risk factors that may impede learning due to the presence of disability or other factors. Students determined to be at risk undergo monitoring to determine if increased levels of support are merited, if the student is responding to interventions, and if more intensive levels of support can be withdrawn. Data from both screening and progress monitoring assessments must emerge from the use of measurement tools with strong psychometric properties.

2

Schoolwide RTI

Why Does It Matter?

Policy analyst Terry Deal, now at the University of Southern California, and his colleagues Purrinton and Waetzeos have written about the importance of framing as a major consideration in comprehending, advancing, and analyzing public policy. Framing is a simple but elegant concept, and its importance is immediately recognizable to dealers in fine art. The way that a particular painting is framed is an important consideration in its prospective sale. Art dealers are skilled in selecting frames that show pictures to advantage. The frame, in other words, becomes an integral part of the work of art and how that work of art will come to be understood by the buyer.

By Deal's analysis, a similar relationship exists for elements of social policy and how each might be framed. Take disability, for example. The concept of disability has formed the basis for a wide range of social policy initiatives around the globe. In the United States, disability policy is at the heart of the Individuals with Disabilities Education Improvement Act (IDEIA), the special education amendments to the omnibus education law that funds a percentage of all public education in our nation's schools. Another sweeping example is represented by the Americans with Disabilities Act of 1990, which many regard as a cornerstone in extending the civil rights movement in America to persons with disabilities.

Framing these significant issues in social policy around the concept of disability may have made associated costs and other reasons for concern to the general populace more palatable and thus more likely to be enacted into law. In the case of the special education law, what if the social policy had been framed differently? For example, educators, families, and their constituent organizations and lobbyists might have framed social policy around a concept of a need for extra services and supports for some students to be able to benefit from schooling. We can call this alternative frame *resource enhancement*. Is it likely that a resource enhancement social policy initiative would receive the same favorable response from the "prospective buyer," the general public and its representatives in government, as has the "disability" frame? I think not. As a nation, we have historically advanced social policy that is generally consistent with values expressed in the Constitution and reflected in the Bill of Rights. This whole trend in 250 years of social policy itself is a frame: civil rights.

The Frame of Disability

To better understand the importance of framing in social policy, it may be useful to examine in some detail the frame of disability and its niche in the public policy arena. The concept of disability can be thought of as a change of frame that began to occur around 1970. The earlier frame was "handicap." The term *handicap* appears to have originated on the streets of London sometime in the eighteenth century. People with afflictions of one sort or another would stand on street corners with their caps in hand to receive small donations from sympathetic passersby. The element of sympathy and recognition that misfortune can befall any of us at any time morphed into an industry to provide goods and services to those in need, including "the handicapped." Special education law emerged as a piece of the overall developing welfare state agenda directed to the concept of "education of the handicapped." The original 1974 version of IDEIA was the Education of the Handicapped Amendments of 1974. The amendments were to the omnibus education funding bill: Elementary and Secondary Education Act.

The framing shift from handicap to disability emerged from a maturing of the social policy agenda away from a sympathy logic and toward a more compensatory idea. Instead of extending educational opportunities to the handicapped because it is the right thing to do (that is, civil rights), the concept became more tuned to what people so identified might accomplish if given the opportunity through the right resources and supports. The frame of disability appears to have represented an effort to extend the frame of pathology or disease state, and its promise of cure, that characterized the explosion in medicine, and in particular psychiatry, during the 1960s and 1970s. Framed this way, the idea of disability lent itself to a diagnostic and prescriptive logic that almost exactly mirrored psychiatry.

> *The framing shift from handicap to disability emerged from a maturing of the social policy agenda away from a sympathy logic and toward a more compensatory idea.*

In traditional medical practice, a "mentally ill" patient undergoes extensive psychological testing performed by a clinical psychologist. Treatment in the form of psychotherapy is then extended to the patient by the psychiatrist, tailored to the implications of the particular disease-state category ascribed to the psychologist's diagnosis. Psychiatry continues to be practiced to this day in accordance with the American Psychiatric Association's copious *Diagnostic and Statistical Manual*, which is updated from time to time and contains ever newer categories of mental illness.

The educational counterpart to the clinical psychologist in medical practice is the school psychologist, and the special education teacher is in the counterpart role of psychiatrist, but the logic model represented by the "disability" frame is essentially the same: referral, diagnosis, categorical label, and treatment (teach). Thus, in the 2004 version of IDEIA, we are confronted with a wide variety of disability categories, such as specific learning disability, autism spectrum disorder, and emotional and behavioral disability.

The frame of disability is thus a medical frame. Sometimes called the medical model, this take on educational policy has served its purpose well, as witnessed by the enormous growth in federal and state expenditures for special education since 1974. The field of special education is not only itself a growth industry of remarkable dimensions, it has spun off smaller growth industries producing adaptive technologies and publishing. Because IDEIA contains language that empowers families to seek due process in the event schools are deemed to be recalcitrant in providing an education as specified in the law, a legal growth industry has emerged, with legions of lawyers and advocacy organizations, all peripheral to special education.

The "handicap" frame was largely based on public sympathy for a disenfranchised segment of the populace. The evolution to "disability" became predicated on the trust in a medical model and the real or implied science that underpins it. It has unquestionably been an important frame for its period and has allowed an enormous advance of social policy, but as a frame, it has flaws. Some of these flaws have come under intense scrutiny in recent years, and the frame may be on the verge of being replaced again, at least in the field of education.

One flaw in the disability frame is the term itself. The term *handicapped* came to be viewed as demeaning, if not downright pejorative, but the term *disability* is not much of an improvement. Its "dis" prefix converts a generally favorable noun to an unfavorable, or at least less favorable, connotation. Consider some examples: approval—*dis*approval, like—*dis*like, and satisfied—*dis*satisfied. Ability is a favorable trait in our culture. Disability reduces ability to a quasi-disease state. Some persons labeled "disabled" are becoming increasingly dissatisfied with that descriptor, yet most accept it because the term is tied to needed goods and services as framed in social policy. The earlier term, *handicap*, of course, lives on in parking space designators and access markers for elevators, ramps, and so forth as contemporary artifacts of earlier social policy conceptions.

A deeper flaw in the disability frame is rooted in its medical model underpinnings. The diagnostic and prescriptive model for ongoing supports and services would probably continue to enjoy public admiration if the underlying science provided some evidence for its validity. Here is where the frame encounters some serious shortcomings: it simply does not work according to most reckonings. A child who is referred, diagnosed, labeled, and taught in accordance with a prescribed approach tailored to that disability label, and fails to enjoy enhanced academic achievement, stands as a contradiction to the frame. The argument that we simply need more research begins to lose its luster as we enter the fourth decade of IDEIA implementation.

The first real exposure of the framing problem confronted by the medical model came with the publication of *Rethinking Special Education for a New Century*, a critique of special education by the Thomas B. Fordham Foundation and the Progressive Policy Institute, headed up by conservative education policy analyst Chester Finn in May 2001. This collection of papers, edited by Finn, Andrew Rotherham, and Charles Hokanson, was timed to inform the forthcoming policy hearings in Congress that would lead to the proposed reauthorization of IDEA (as it was called at the time) in 2002. The act was not actually reauthorized until 2004, largely because of the contentiousness of the debate that ensued. Consider this quote from the editors:

> Even as important reforms began to sweep through regular K–12 education, the IDEA program was becoming set in its ways. Not every change it brought about turned out to be positive, and, although it has surely helped address many education challenges, it has created some, too.

For too long, most politicians, policymakers, and others involved with the IDEA and the special education system that law has helped to construct considered it taboo to discuss these problems and challenges. It seemed at times as if anything less than unadulterated praise for the IDEA was indicative of hostility towards its goals or—worse—towards children with special needs. Thus, the IDEA has come to be viewed as the "third rail" issue of education policy: It's fine to support more spending, maybe even suggest some incremental changes along the program's margin (generally by way of expanding it and closing loopholes), but it has not been okay to probe its basic assumptions and practices, much less criticize them. Well-intentioned people who have attempted to highlight deficiencies, inequities, and problems with special education have been criticized as interlopers with bad motives or political agendas and told to leave such matters to the "stakeholder community" [p. v].

Having spotlighted the sacred cow status afforded to special education within its disability frame, the editors challenge the medical model underpinnings more directly in their summary remarks at the conclusion of the volume: "Different rules for disabled children foster a 'separate but unequal' education system. It strikes us as ironic or worse that laws meant to break down barriers and open doors now serve to promote separatism and inequality" (p. 341). A bit further on they write, "Rather than today's 'one-size-fits-all' IDEA mandates and procedures, policymakers should consider creating two or possibly three categories of students within the special-needs population" (p. 343). And finally, they ask:

Exactly what gives students with specific learning problems an entitlement to greater education resources than their peers who simply are slow learners and/or struggling for other reasons? As policymakers struggle to correct the chronic dysfunction plaguing many of the nation's largest school districts serving high concentrations of poor and minority students, this difficult question needs a full airing [p. 346].

With a newly elected neoconservative president, George W. Bush, in the White House, and both houses of Congress having Republican majorities, this voluminous critique from the conservative Fordham Foundation found a warm reception in the congressional debates from those in the majority. The message of the volume was straightforward: If the medical model as a basis for special education works (and is therefore worth the taxpayer expenditure), where is the scientific evidence to back it up? What finally happened after the rancorous debates from 2002 to 2004 was a reauthorized version of IDEA that essentially weakened due process provisions for families but left the medical model undamaged.

RTI as a Potential Frame for Educational Policy

One of the papers in the Fordham volume found legs that carried far beyond the 2004 reauthorization and may well be the publication that, more than any other one of the period, set into motion the beginnings of what may prove to be the third frame for organizing and understanding public policy, at least in education, directed to those who require extra services and supports to successfully engage the teaching-learning process in America's schools.

The paper I refer to is "Rethinking Learning Disabilities" by G. Reid Lyon and colleagues who were, at the time, immersed in the conduct of research on literacy and how it is learned and best taught, particularly for students with the learning disabilities (LD) label. Lyon, who has at various times served as a general education (third grade) teacher, a special education teacher, a school psychologist, and a developmental neuroscientist, was head of the

Division of Child Development and Behavior of the National Institute of Child Health and Human Development, National Institutes of Health. From this position, Lyon launched a major change in how children who fail early on to learn to read should be addressed as an alternative to automatic referral to special education, particularly under the categorical label LD. It was this "assault" on LD eligibility determination in 2001 that, I argue here, simultaneously weakened the disability frame as a basis for education policy, while advancing an "accountability" (outcomes) conception. The accountability movement, in my view, ultimately set the stage for the emergence of a schoolwide RTI frame.

> *The accountability movement, in my view, ultimately set the stage for the emergence of a schoolwide RTI frame.*

A Focus on Literacy

Consider this quote from Lyon and his coauthors (2001): "We estimate that the number of children who are typically identified as poor readers and served through either special education or compensatory education programs could be reduced by up to 70 percent through early identification and prevention programs" (p. 260). Seventy percent is a big number. If Lyon and his coauthors prove to be correct with this assumption, the field of special education will certainly undergo significant downsizing. His basic argument is that the psychological testing formula used to diagnose LD lodged a failure to achieve expected grade-level progress in reading squarely with the child and paid no attention to environmental circumstances that could explain all or at least a portion of that failure. Elsewhere, Lyon argued publicly that LD may in many cases be "TD" (teaching disability). While such comments caused controversy and irritated many in special education, Lyon may well have been speaking prophesy: the dawning of a new frame for consideration of the policy requirements of matching resources to identified pupil needs, starting with special education.

Summarizing a large body of rigorous research in the area of children learning to read, Lyon and his colleagues stated, "Teachers must be provided the critical academic content, pedagogical principles, and knowledge of learner characteristics that they need in order to impart systematic and informed instruction to their students" (p. 280).

A Shifting Perspective

The question for policymakers is, On what basis do we allocate additional resources to public education to address the unmet needs of a sector of the general population of students? Under the original handicap frame, with its inherent appeal to emotion and sympathy and to its fit with the civil rights movement, the idea of special education was born: special resources for special children.

Then the kaleidoscope shifted patterns, and the frame became disability. A new way to consider a sector of the population was to view the resource need-match as a quasi-medical issue and introduce science as a basis for advancing public policy directed to this issue. Now that frame is increasingly being challenged by its lack of demonstrable progress, particularly within a framework of scientific investigation; discontent with the label disability; and the increasing recognition that failure to respond at expected levels to the curriculum may have a lot to do with factors other than those that reside within the individual so labeled.

> What I think we know so far is that any new frame on education resource need-match policy will likely move away from an exclusive focus on various limiting characteristics of the individual, in favor of greater attention to the ecology of the individual's learning situation and life circumstances.

The kaleidoscope is turning once again. The new pattern may begin to come more fully into focus as we once again near the process of reauthorization of IDEIA presently slated for 2010. What I think we know so far is that any new frame on education resource need-match policy will likely move away from an exclusive focus on various limiting characteristics of the individual, in favor of greater attention to the ecology of the individual's learning situation and life circumstances.

An important question to be addressed is, To what extent is there a scientific basis for perpetuating the quasi-medical disability categories? Or, put another way, do students with special education labels have more in common with those who have no labels than has been previously assumed? We know, for example, that African American children in many states are way overrepresented in special education. Under the disability frame, we would have to assume that the incidence of disability is much higher for African Americans than for European Americans. Yet many would regard such an assumption as inherently racist. In Connecticut, for example, in 2003, an African American child was four times as likely to be assigned the label *intellectually disabled* as a white child, a finding that emerged in the context of a special education law suit, *P.J. v. Connecticut Board of Education*.

Research is showing us that failure to progress at grade level can arise from a number of considerations, including poverty, discrimination on the basis of ethnic identity, discrimination on the basis of primary spoken language, weak instruction, poor curricula, and a host of other factors that are seldom addressed in formulating educational policy. Since most of these factors lie outside the child, it does not require a quantum leap of judgment to see the need for a new organizing framework for policy in education that can move beyond disability.

RTI as a Basis for Educational Policy

As a nation, our approach to public policy tends to be reactive rather than proactive (or preventive). We generally do not allocate taxpayer dollars to address a problem until it becomes significant.

People were dying at an alarming rate in San Francisco before the city, state, and federal branches of government began to advance policy directed to AIDS, for example.

The problem with prevention policy is that the tangible results are pretty far into the future, yet private and public funders of policy initiatives want to see results quickly. The advent of early childhood education programs has helped to counteract that tendency. Significant decreases in social and learning problems by the fourth grade have been mathematically linked to targeted interventions by early childhood educators during the preschool years. The developmental psychologist Esther Thelan at Indiana University, for example, has used the mathematical predictive capability of chaos theory software to reveal similar relationships.

The argument that a dollar spent at age three will save a hundred dollars at age ten is persuasive to conservative lawmakers only if it is backed up by incontrovertible scientific evidence. It is only relatively recently, with the advent of sophisticated computer technology, that these longitudinal effects can be mathematically assessed.

All of this has set the stage for the current explosion of interest in RTI. RTI has all of the key ingredients with which to reframe policy directed to matching resources to identified needs. As a schoolwide problem-solving model, it embraces in a single system:

1. Prevention
2. Problem identification with scientific precision
3. Targeted interventions directed reliably to the problem
4. Accountability for tracking results of interventions
5. A focus on sociobehavioral factors that contribute to the problem
6. A focus on organismic factors such as sensory or cognitive deficits that contribute to the problem
7. Transdisciplinary problem-solving teams to match resources to measured needs

8. Development of decision rules grounded in scientific evidence that can help educators to select particular interventions (curriculum and instruction) with which to address specific identified problems

Where the frame of disability led to most of the assessments undertaken to address an emerging problem in, say, reading, RTI directs most assessments toward environmental factors. More important, RTI examines the interaction of personal factors with environmental circumstances. Assessments of a child who has a problem learning to read, increasingly informed by breakthroughs in neuroscience, yield information that has direct implications for selecting curricula and type of instructional interventions. This leads us to the possibility of formulating some general decision rules, grounded in evidence from rigorous investigations, that will assist teachers to better match learning resources to identified needs.

We have a major shift of focus underway that is fueled by scientific breakthroughs in both personal attributes (for example, brain theory) and in environmental modifications (for example, schoolwide positive behavior support, the subject of Chapter Three). The question becomes: Is RTI, as we know it today, a suitable organizing system that can bring all of the elements together needed to take American education to a new level? Consider each of these key components and see if you think an answer in the affirmative may be warranted.

> *The question becomes: Is RTI, as we know it today, a suitable organizing system that can bring all of the elements together needed to take American education to a new level?*

Prevention

In their 2006 book *RTI and the Classroom Teacher*, Beth Hardcastle and Kelly Justice capture the prevention idea as a mind-set: "The change in mindset moves *away* from a process that waits for a child to fail before it responds and moves *toward* a process that responds *before* a child experiences significant delays" (p. 8). An effort to stimulate a prevention mind-set through public policy is witnessed in the inclusion of the three-tiered intervention model in the No Child Left Behind Act (NCLB). Focused on reading as the place to start, NCLB requires a core curriculum in reading, grounded in science, and directed to all students as a primary-tier intervention. NCLB includes a requirement for moving to more intensive instruction, a secondary-tier intervention, when ongoing measures indicate that a child is not responding adequately at tier 1.

There is an obvious early childhood focus in the literature of RTI. It is preferable in all cases to intervene as early as possible when behavior or learning problems emerge. Problems that go unchecked can gradually worsen and become much more resistant to remediation. A behavior problem that is not addressed when it is noticed in kindergarten can evolve into a severe behavior disorder by the fifth grade.

Because of economies of scale, tier 1 interventions are also the least expensive. As more intense interventions are needed and we move further up the RTI pyramid, costs rise proportionately. Tier 3 interventions can be very expensive since they can require numerous professionals and a wide range of extraordinary assessments and interventions.

Finally, the prevention orientation of RTI helps us to move away from the automatic nature of many referrals to special education. By focusing on the interaction of person factors and environment factors, a child who has a physical affliction and is in a wheelchair, for example, may require some physical adaptation to his immediate learning environments but no services through IDEIA. Reducing unnecessary referrals to special education can allow funds required for eligibility determination, often an expensive and time-consuming series of assessments, to be redirected to environmental adaptations to accommodate the child.

Such redirection of resources, however, may require change in policy.

Problem Identification

The traditional way of deciding if a child has a learning or behavior problem has largely been a matter of teacher judgment. A second grader who incessantly distracts the children around him by drumming on his desk and making vocal sounds, after failing to respond to directives from his teacher and one or two office referrals, may be thought to have a disability and therefore be a candidate for referral to special education. A teacher may decide that such a child "probably has ADHD" and is therefore a good candidate for removal to a different educational environment. The problem is that one teacher's "wild child" is another's "burgeoning genius."

Suppose instead that the teacher in this case had available a valid and reliable measuring device that would enable him to make more precise observations of and conclusions about such a student by considering the student's behavior in relation to the rest of his peers in the classroom. In fact, such a tool exists and was developed for exactly this purpose, and I discuss it in some detail further in this book, but for now, consider that it is an example of a systematic process that is valid and reliable for screening a class of children for risk of behavior problems that impede learning. Under RTI, screening tools enable teachers to make a case for involving others in determining whether a particular child merits closer examination and, perhaps, some different or additional educational interventions.

Such screening instruments also exist on the academic side of the pyramid. Valid and reliable methods of screening for risk of behavior problems as well as for reading or mathematics problems currently exist and are coming into more widespread use, particularly in the early grades. Some screening instruments are tied directly to the reading or math curriculum used in the school. These are called curriculum-based measures (CBMs), and I examine these in some detail later in the book. Still other screening measures exist but stand independent from the particular curriculum being taught. These norm-referenced measures have been standardized across thousands of students in different geographical areas within and across ages and grade levels.

The advantage of a CBM is that it is aligned directly with the curriculum being taught and with other assessments at grade level. Norm-referenced screening tools are useful when there are no CBMs associated with the curriculum and when students move from school to school where specific curricula may vary. Such screening tools are also called "universal screeners" or "stand-alone" screening assessments. The advantage of screening within an RTI framework is that it helps to remove some of the subjectivity in teacher judgments as to whether a problem exists and whether, if it does, it requires special attention.

Targeted Intervention

Screening for risk usually takes place early in the school year, often in September. The result of screening is usually determination of a percentage of children in a classroom who are at some level of risk for failure to respond to measured grade-level expectations of performance on high-quality instruction using a science-grounded curriculum directed to all of the children in the classroom. For some of the identified children, a simple adjustment at tier 1 instruction may suffice to remove the child from risk consideration. This might include differentiating instruction, for example, or withholding attention for inappropriate behavior.

For some children at risk, a tier 2 intervention may become warranted on the basis of careful monitoring of the child's progress in the risk-determined area. In a few cases, even a tier 3 intervention may become warranted. A researcher at the University of South Florida,

George Batche, has estimated some gross percentages of children who are likely to require interventions at each of the three tiers. Percentages at any one school, however, or for any single classroom may be strongly tied to community factors such as demographics, family income, or population density.

The most critical element in selecting the right intervention is the fidelity with which any particular intervention, at any level, is implemented. RTI requires a fair test of an effort to solve a problem with a child who has been determined through screening to be at risk for failure to progress at grade level.

I return to consideration of educational interventions under RTI in later chapters, but for now, consider a child who has been determined to require a tier 2 intervention for first-grade reading. Whether a particular approach will succeed, say instruction on a content enhancement, will be determined to a degree by whether a teacher delivers the instruction faithfully in accordance with the procedures for which the intervention was scientifically validated. Implementing an intervention correctly—what is called *fidelity of implementation*—increases the degree of confidence that a teacher or other staff member may have that the progress monitoring data accurately reflect the child's response to this particular intervention. This is a key element in the scientific grounding of RTI.

Accountability

A key feature of schoolwide RTI is accountability. If a particular intervention or set of interventions is set into motion on the basis of screening for risk, how will we determine when and if success has resulted from the effort? For this purpose, a number of scientifically grounded tools have been developed, and more are undergoing research. The process of collecting data on accountability for interventions carried out with fidelity is called *progress monitoring*.

If a particular tool lends itself to both initial screening and progress monitoring, it has been demonstrated through research to be reliable and valid for repeated measures assessments. As we will see later, particular tools with this advantage exist for early-grade reading and are beginning to emerge for early math. On the behavior side, different standardized assessments are needed for screening versus progress-monitoring functions.

The Importance of Fidelity

The goal of strict adherence to fidelity of implementation of educational interventions is to be able to make accurate judgments for determining the levels of intervention required to enable a child to engage the grade-level curriculum with as much success as possible. If a particular curriculum enhancement strategy is carried out faithfully (that is, with fidelity) and the progress-monitoring measures indicate the procedure is not working, the teacher or child study team is then in position to move to the next decision point about type and level of intervention to be engaged next with the child. Or progress monitoring may show that the second-tier intervention was successful and the student can now keep up with the rest of the class in grade-level reading.

A Focus on Sociobehavioral Factors

Schoolwide RTI brings the particular advantage of carefully examining social and behavioral influences that may place a child at risk for larger behavioral problems or academic problems (or both) later. In the next chapter, I deal with the behavioral side of the RTI pyramid in detail, but suffice it here to say that screening for both sides is essential under an RTI-driven system.

A child found to be at risk for reading failure at the second-grade level may have a cognitive problem or may be anxious or depressed. Without considering the behavioral screening results together with the literacy screening data, we may misinterpret the nature of the problem and select an inappropriate intervention to address the problem. A behavioral screening tool should be able to identify a child with either externalizing behavior problems, which are readily observable instances of problem behavior, or internalizing problems, which are often not so easily observed. Depression, anxiety, and situational or posttraumatic stress disorders are examples of internalizing behavior problems that may impede the learning process. In this case, the academic screening tool would turn up a child at risk for grade-level failure in reading, but the primary source of the reading problem may well be an internalizing behavior problem rather than a cognitive issue. Selection of an appropriate intervention might be medical, or pharmaceutical, or counseling, or some combination of these, rather than a secondary-level reading intervention.

Without considering the behavioral screening results together with the literacy screening data, we may misinterpret the nature of the problem and select an inappropriate intervention to address the problem.

Organismic Factors

RTI has made dramatic progress in recent years on the development of screening and progress monitoring instruments directed to reading. Many of these developments are directly attributable to the influence of the focus on early reading, and in particular, the Reading First initiative in NCLB.

Reading First and Early Reading First

These two initiatives were written directly into subsections of NCLB and were intended to ensure that previous research reflecting success from specific reading interventions directed to students who seem to be having difficulty would be implemented ahead of referrals for special education. The Early Reading First grant program provides funding to successful applicants to begin reading instruction using evidence-based methods, in preschool and kindergarten settings.

Recipients of Reading First grants establish Reading First Academics at their schools which adhere to complex guidelines to ensure a seamless web of evidence-based reading instruction across the grade levels. Readers interested in more detail about these two initiatives should consult the U.S. Department of Education Reading First Guidelines document available from www.ed.gov/programs/readingfirst/guidance.doc.

Propelled by advances in brain theory and a resultant enhanced understanding of the role cognitive deficits play in processing symbolic information, researchers have been able to develop and test screening and progress monitoring tools that, combined with evidence-based interventions at the level of curricular and curriculum enhancements, as well as advances in high-quality instruction, enable a much greater degree of precision to occur in overcoming obstacles in learning to read at early grade levels.

Similar breakthroughs are occurring in math screening, progress monitoring, and curriculum and instructional enhancements, but progress in math has been slow relative to reading. Much less funding, for example, has been available for research and development of RTI tools for math than for reading. Other curricular content areas such as writing and science are in their infancy in the development of RTI tools and strategies.

Transdisciplinary Problem-Solving Teams

If a single grade-level teacher had sole responsibility for implementation of RTI, the job would quickly become untenable. This is why it is called *schoolwide RTI*: the school, not the classroom, is the unit of analysis.

One of the innovative features of schoolwide RTI is reliance on multiple perspectives, training histories, and professional identities in implementing RTI. The process by which this is typically accomplished is through use of transdisciplinary teams. The term *transdisciplinary* in this context refers in part to diversity of team membership within a school (special educator, school psychologist, parent, general educator, and social worker, for example). It goes beyond simply having different professionals on a team to conduct and evaluate RTI processes, however. It also implies that members of such teams share knowledge and a common language system across the various professions and disciplines represented and are in conceptual agreement where RTI is concerned.

The value of transdisciplinary team implementation lies in the enhanced problem-solving value of the different perspectives each member brings to the process. The structure and functions of these teams will be examined in greater detail further on. For now, it is important to recognize that the burden for implementing RTI is distributed in the school rather than borne solely by a classroom teacher. As we shall see, different schools use different team configurations to implement RTI, and it will fall to future research to reveal the relative efficacy of one approach over another.

Decision Rules for Selecting Interventions

The final component of RTI to be considered in moving to school-wide practice is the use of decision rules for directing specific interventions to identified problems. In my opinion, we will never get to the point of a cookbook teaching approach that allows, say, a computer program to read screening data and tailor a particular intervention to address an identified problem. Special educators, for example, went through a period in the 1980s when psychological test protocols were entered into a computer program for an identified child, which would then generate a suggested individualized education program (IEP) to become the basis for the IEP meeting. (It seems to me that "computerized IEP" is a contradiction in terms.)

More realistically, the advent of scientifically grounded screening and progress monitoring tools will likely lead to emergence of a set of general decision rules particularly for determining when a child, on the basis of data, can move across any of the tier boundaries on the RTI pyramid. For example, a child determined to be at risk for cognitively based failure to read at grade level is determined to require a secondary-tier intervention. Progress monitoring data over a period of months determines, through use of a data-based decision rule, that the child can now return to tier 1 instructional engagement and reflect grade-level expected progress. This level of precision in the emergence of general decision rules is starting to become attainable for reading at early grade levels. Most decision rule emergence awaits further research.

To Sum Up

In this chapter I advanced the theoretical conception for school-wide RTI grounded in the framing analysis put forward by policy analyst Terry Deal. I addressed the question of whether a new model for special education is called for by first challenging the assumptions that underlie the more traditional referral process for special education supports and services. Using framing as a theoretical perspective, I questioned the relevance of special education categories and challenged the concept of disability itself as a useful predictor of what a person can accomplish, particularly from schooling.

From there, I identified eight core components of RTI and showed how each represents an example of educational innovation that can potentially take schools to the next level, both academically and economically. My conclusion is that RTI offers a new and fresh approach to K–12 education, and it does so by more fully integrating environmental as well as personal factors in the teaching-learning process and anchoring the needed systems change endeavors in rigorous scientific standards and procedures. In the next chapter, I explore the social and behavioral side of the RTI pyramid and its implications for assessment and instruction.

3

The Social-Behavioral Side of RTI

He [the assistant principal] did not think it was his responsibility to keep the child from following a path that would lead to prison. In fact, he informed me that he was preparing to put this child on an indefinite suspension from school. This was an extreme form of punishment used in a small number of cases for children with persistent behavior problems. It allowed the school to remove difficult children to be schooled at home while still collecting funds from the state for their average daily attendance. Under the plan, work would be sent home, and occasionally a teacher or counselor would make visits to monitor the academic progress of the student. I asked if he thought that such a plan would work for this child given what he had said about the difficulty of his situation at home (the child was being raised by an elderly grandmother). He responded by telling me that there was nothing more the school could do: "Kids like him just can't be helped. They take up so much of my time and keep teachers from serving the needs of other children who are here to learn. It may not be the best thing for him, but right now, it's the best thing for the school" [Noguera, 2008, p. 112].

With this brief vignette, the urban sociologist Pedro Noguera paints a grim but familiar picture of how one school regards troubled youth. In bygone times, unruly children were made to sit in a corner of the classroom with a dunce cap on. Others were made to sit at the "trouble desk" behind a partition that screened them from the other children. Catholics who are my age will likely remember the pain of sore knuckles from the days when nuns patrolled the classroom with rulers.

School Discipline

School discipline has become yet another growth industry in American education. My team's research on the topic has led us to the conclusion that schools approach problem behavior and the related issue of social development in one of two ways: use of either exclusionary or inclusionary tactics to address problems. Unfortunately, from our point of view, the majority of schools in our experience pursue the former rather than the latter strategy.

The Tactic of Exclusion

Interview administrators in exclusionary schools, and they are likely to tell you that the job of the school is to educate the children who came to learn. Disruptive children, they say, detract from the teachers' ability to deliver the curriculum to the "good kids" and need to be removed from the grade-level classroom until such time that they can "demonstrate appropriate self-control." If their disruptive behavior continues beyond a certain point, such children may need to be educated "elsewhere."

> *Interview administrators in exclusionary schools, and they are likely to tell you that the job of the school is to educate the children who came to learn.*

"Elsewhere" may take a variety of forms. Referral to special education may achieve a label of behavioral disability, for example, in which case the child is removed to a classroom where children with similar labels are congregated under the supervision of a special education teacher.

If a child is not identified for special education, other possibilities exist. Some schools maintain detention rooms where a child goes to work on homework as a punishment for disruptive behavior. Schools may have an in-school suspension area, where a child may spend large portions of the educational day and where the suspension may last for weeks. I visited one school in Pennsylvania where so many students were in in-school suspension that they used the high school auditorium as the setting and screened educational films all day under the supervision of an assistant principal.

Finally, exclusionary schools may move to exclude children through out-of-school suspension, expulsion, or, as in the case of Noguera's vignette, home schooling. How many parents have had to lose their jobs in order to stay at home and educate their child when that was the only remaining option left to them?

Some school districts set up alternative schools for students who have been excluded for disciplinary reasons from their neighborhood or assigned school. I have visited a number of these in various urban settings around the country and have been struck with the extent to which they resemble prisons, with security guards throughout the building and locked doors. Pedro Noguera points out in his book *The Trouble with Black Boys* that visitors to alternative schools in urban areas may be struck by another common feature: most, if not all, of the students are African American or Latino/a. Are these bad kids (personal characteristics)? Or do circumstances of their schooling, and perhaps their communities, play a role in their disruptiveness (external characteristics)?

Noguera points out that as students mature in the school system, they begin to understand and internalize the viewpoints of the adults (and the labels they use) directed to them. They become cynical and retaliate against the school for what they perceive to be a clear violation of an implicit social contract to provide them with an education. When this turning point has been reached, things begin to get much worse, and the road to prison begins to take on reality. Exclusionary tactics applied to children for social reasons set a process into motion for exclusionary tactics to be applied by society at large when the child reaches adulthood. After all, this social pattern may be all the young person has ever known.

Teachers in exclusionary schools are likely to be evaluated on the basis of how the children in their classes perform on annual, grade-level standardized assessments required by the state. One teacher summed it up for me by stating: "Dr. Sailor, I need this job! If [J.A. and R.S.] can't get their acts together and pay attention to the point where they are moving up in their weekly test scores in math, then they need to be somewhere else. I have to show that my class is helping the school to make AYP [adequate yearly progress] this year, or I run the risk of a decision to nonreelect [that is, be fired]."

Under No Child Left Behind, teachers are under unrelenting pressure to contribute to their school's measured performance on a common yardstick across the state. If academic mastery on the part of students is the primary measure of teaching adequacy, then incentives for exclusion of children who do not fit in are sizable. Where discipline is at issue, the primary and most frequently used line of defense is the office disciplinary referral. Students are directed out of class to the principal's office, the guidance counselor, the detention room, in-school suspension, and even, in some cases, to a chair in the hallway outside the classroom. An implicit assumption of schools that pursue exclusionary tactics is that children's social and behavioral development is not the business of the school. It is a problem to be addressed by the family and the community, but not the school.

The Tactic of Inclusion

John Dewey, in his book *The School and Society*, published in 1915, provided an alternative philosophy of education. Dewey's idea was that education is essential for perpetuating a democratic society.

Furthermore, citizenship, a crucial component of a democratic society, is an essential part of schooling. Even further, Dewey felt that a failure to address democratic citizenship in pedagogy could eventually undermine the foundations of a democratic society and set the stage for the eventual possibility of tyranny.

Dewey spoke of the school as a social center—an integral part of an evolving community with close ties to the families of its children and oriented to lifelong education. He realized over a century ago that as life in communities, particularly in the cities, became more complex, "pure intellectual instruction" would soon result in a lack of faith in schools as social institutions. He was concerned with the possibility of a "relaxation of social discipline and control," suggesting that "moral education" would increasingly become a necessary ingredient in the education of children. One can only imagine what Dewey would have to say about so many of America's schools today where progress on a norm-referenced state test is the sole measure of efficacy for schooling and where children who do not fit the common mold of grade-level expectancy for both achievement and deportment are sent packing.

We can, by today's standards, characterize Dewey's educational philosophy as essentially inclusionary. If a child comes to school unprepared to engage and respond to the teaching-learning process, then it is the responsibility of the school to analyze the situation, link to family and community institutions if needed, and direct pedagogy to the remediation of the problem. In other words, citizenship is part of the curriculum. Dewey anticipated the consequences of increasingly complex circumstances in managing life in urban communities, but at the turn of the twentieth century, he could not in his wildest dreams have imagined the extent of moral, physical, and social decay that is commonplace in our cities today.

Sadly, schools that are reflective of Deweyian inclusionary philosophy are in the minority, particularly where they are most needed: in inner-core urban neighborhoods. From my own work in engaging urban school districts in the process of implementing comprehensive school reform, I estimate that at most, 20 percent of American schools in 2009 are pursuing inclusionary practices. As a formal system of practice on a large scale, only the community school movement truly reflects Deweyian philosophy (see www.communityschools.org).

Community Schools

Community schools, popularized by Lizbeth Shorr in her book *Common Purpose*, operate around the country in full partnership with health and social services systems within their communities. In these schools, families (or other primary caregivers) are considered the unit of analysis for educators. Community schools often open early to provide breakfast and social opportunities for students before instruction begins. They remain open at night for students to attend after-school programs and for adults to attend adult literacy class, further their learning in other ways, gain computer skills or Internet access, and take up other community learning options such as parenting newborns, vocational education, etc. Michael Kirst, professor of education at Stanford University, has written extensively as far back as the 1980s of the need for "twelve-hour schools" to adequately address the increasingly negative implications of life in urban America for children. The community school movement is a strong step in that direction. Such schools are usually regular public schools rather than charter or private schools and can be found at all regional and demographic configurations. They tend to arise out of the response to a community need in combination with enlightened leadership at both the district and site levels.

Community schools are pursuing an inclusionary philosophy. Rather than shuttling students in and out of classrooms for infractions that echo their substandard living circumstances, these schools gather information on the nature of problems that students present and then seek resources both in and outside the school to address the problems in the context of ongoing instruction. Rather than removing a child from instruction for problem behavior, instruction directed to social learning is provided within the overall teaching-learning context.

Schoolwide Positive Behavior Support

Beginning in the mid-1980s, researchers Rob Horner and George Sugai at the University of Oregon became interested in whether a formal, structured approach to dealing pedagogically with difficult, atypical behavior could be developed through careful scientific investigation. If it could, their goal ultimately was to package it so that professionals engaged in serving people with problem behavior could have strategies for teaching alternative socially desirable repertoires that would simultaneously replace the deviant behavior. Together with colleagues in universities around the country, they were successful in attracting government funding to engage a fifteen-year sustained program of research and development directed to what is now called positive behavior support (PBS). When PBS becomes part of the pedagogical orientation of schools, it is called *schoolwide positive behavior support* (SWPBS). PBS has now emerged as a major field of research, development, and professional practice, with its own scientific journal, the *Journal of Positive Behavioral Interventions and Support*, and its own international association, the Association for Positive Behavior Support.

In recent years, the U.S. Office of Special Education Programs has provided support for a National Technical Assistance Center on PBS (see www.pbis.org). The Technical Assistance Center provides support to about twenty-five states as of 2009, through extensive material development and the provision of professional development to schools and state personnel on implementation

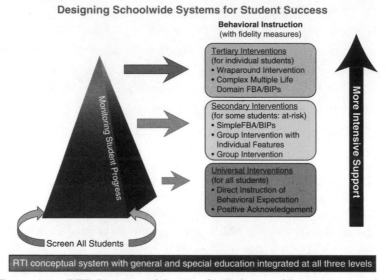

Figure 3.1   RTI Conceptual System for Behavioral Instruction with General and Special Education Integrated at All Three Levels

of SWPBS. As an inherently inclusionary strategy for confronting issues of disciplinary infractions and as a three-tiered prevention strategy with instruction at its heart, SWPBS is a perfect fit for the more recent emerging agenda of schoolwide RTI. Figure 3.1 presents the left side of the conceptual schoolwide RTI figure that appears in Figure 1.1.

Although under schoolwide RTI, behavioral and academic interventions are conceptualized to work together, for the purposes of this chapter, we examine the components of the SWPBS first. To understand why SWPBS is inherently inclusionary as educational philosophy and thus is a perfect fit for schoolwide RTI, it is useful to examine in some detail its definition, and, in particular, why the word *positive* is part of it.

Many teachers and administrators are used to the idea that students they identify as "problem children" mainly need a firm hand. They may assume that a student with disruptive behavior is that way because of neglectful parenting and that the school can make up for the assumed bad parenting practices by taking a strict approach with such students, including the use of punishing consequences for episodes of problem behavior.

PBS grew out of a large number of research findings that cast serious doubt on the efficacy of punishment as a way to control difficult behavior and certainly on the value of punishment as a way to teach desirable social behavior. First, punishment directed to those behaviors by teachers sometimes models exactly the kind of antisocial response that the teacher wishes to eliminate. A teacher who yells at a child who is misbehaving, for example, should not be too surprised to see the same child yelling at another child during an episode of problem behavior.

A second problem with punishment as an approach to discipline arises from another large body of findings from scientific research that shows outcomes from punishment stop short of eliminating the target behavior that produced the punishing consequence. Consistent punishment at best serves to suppress a particular problem behavior. Not only does the behavior tend to reoccur with increasing frequency when the punishment stops; a different, and potentially even more disruptive, behavior may emerge to replace the problem behavior through a process that is like the medical phenomenon of symptom substitution, wherein treating one symptom of a virus such as a runny nose may lead to emergence of another such as a cough, etc.

The term *positive* in PBS was introduced to emphasize the importance of focusing on teaching alternatives to problem behavior through positive, self-affirming, and otherwise motivational tactics while moving punishing circumstances to the back burner. PBS does not conclude that there is never a role for mild punishment, particularly when it serves as a cue to remind a person that an infraction has occurred, but it is certainly not the main intervention.

> *The term positive in PBS was introduced to emphasize the importance of focusing on teaching alternatives to problem behavior through positive, self-affirming, and otherwise moti-*

vational tactics while moving punishing circumstances to the back burner.

Understanding SWPBS

Major advances in K–12 education often emerge from different, and sometimes differing, theoretical perspectives. Two dominant perspectives that have informed the profession of teaching for decades are cognitive psychology and behavioral psychology. These two are contrasting models for many applications in educational practice but come together to a large extent in SWPBS. Although much of the early research in the 1980s on PBS was firmly grounded in applied behavior analysis, a decidedly behavioral perspective, more recent scientific investigations have incorporated cognitive and biological findings into a larger theory of change that informs practice in the schools.

SWPBS assumes that behavior is learned for the most part and involves a combination of biological (organic), sociological (societal), and anthropological (cultural) factors that are subject to change as a function of teaching in a context of supportive, nurturing, and caregiving professional practice in schools. It is characterized by four defining features:

1. *Evidence-based practice* It is an applied science. Its practices are guided by evidence obtained from rigorous investigations whose findings are published in peer-reviewed journals.

2. *Practical multicomponent interventions* It integrates a variety of interventions in order to provide a good fit for the context in which teaching occurs so that such teaching is practical and efficient.

3. *Lifestyle outcomes* Interventions are guided by values that seek broad and durable lifestyle changes for children that will help them to become prepared to function effectively in a broad social and societal context.

4. *Sustainable systems change* Interventions are directed to both children and their environments, including their social context, in order to help them achieve sustained effects from the teaching practice.

When these four defining features are combined in a three-tiered, prevention-oriented, professional delivery model, SWPBS becomes a nearly perfect complement to the academic intervention side of schoolwide RTI.

Evidence-Based Practice

Professionals using punishment-oriented exclusionary tactics are essentially asking a *what* question: What should I do about this child's behavior? Practitioners of SWPBS are asking a *why* question: Why is this student behaving this way? If we can understand why a problem behavior is occurring, then we should be able to teach a replacement behavior that is more socially acceptable.

Scientific investigations have provided a small mountain of evidence that behavior that seemingly requires a disciplinary intervention occurs for one or more reasons that can be discovered and understood in the context in which it occurs. In other words, behavior, whether desirable or undesirable, occurs for a reason, and discovering that reason opens the possibility of teaching an alternative behavior that achieves the same function.

Erminda, for example, at times engaged in a noisy and repetitive vocal behavior that served as a distraction to the whole class. When this behavior occurred, the usual procedure was first a stern warning from the teacher that was soon followed by a referral to the principal's office. Over a period of weeks, her instances of periods of loud vocalizing increased rather than decreased. A PBS consultant who began to explore the possible reasons for Erminda's problem behavior discovered that the episodes tended to coincide with the beginning of math instruction. This process of exploring the context of problem behavior to discover its function under positive behavior support has a formal name: functional behavior assessment (FBA). Simple FBAs can be conducted by teachers who have been trained in SWPBS and can occur at level 1 (universal support—that is, for all students) or at level 2 (selected group support). Complex FBAs at level 3 (individual support) require extensive investigations and are performed under guidance from a transdisciplinary team within the school and including, perhaps, representation from the community and home.

A simple FBA at level 1 uncovered that Erminda vocalized in order to get out of having to engage the math lesson—an escape-avoidance function. The very act of referral out of class was strengthening her tendency to engage in disruptive vocalizing. The consultant and the teacher decided that Erminda should be taught to raise her hand when she needed a break from the lesson, in which case she could draw, a preferred activity for her, for a few minutes before returning to the lesson. Coupled with praise and attention from the teacher for working on her lesson, this procedure succeeded in a relatively short time in eliminating Erminda's inappropriate vocalizations and even led to improvement in her math skills.

Much problem behavior in schools can be found through the FBA process to be serving one of three functions: escape-avoidance, attention seeking, or sensory issues such as rocking, for example, to produce vestibular stimulation. The element of science, or evidence-based practice, comes in with reliance on a substantive base of knowledge from research to guide the FBA process and match a particular strategy for teaching (interventions) with the identified function from the FBA. In Erminda's case, the function was escape-avoidance, so the selected intervention was to teach her a nondisruptive, and thus socially acceptable, way to achieve the same function. Paired with skillful and positive teaching methods, her new replacement behavior of raising her hand to get brief breaks allowed her to spend increased time on her math lesson, which led her to achieve increases in measures of her academic progress in math. In the broader context of RTI, this procedure at level 1 on

the behavioral side of the pyramid interacted with a level 1 engagement on the academic side, differentiated instruction, to enable
Erminda to improve socially and academically. In this example, science provided a more powerful strategy than the exclusionary tactic
of standard office disciplinary referral.

Practical Multicomponent Interventions

Schoolwide positive behavior support is designed to fit a teaching
model that occurs in the natural context of the school (levels 1
and 2) and in the school, home, and community (levels 2 and 3).
For Erminda, a simple FBA produced a relatively simple teaching
modification that produced a powerful outcome for the student, the
teacher, and even the class. Some challenges presented by students,
however, are not so simple and may require a chain of structured
interventions to deal with one problem at a time.

Erminda's teacher was able to determine that the selected
teaching intervention was working by keeping data records, which
provided progress monitoring. The teacher kept a simple ongoing
record of the number of times Erminda raised her hand and, from
the paperwork, a record of Erminda's progress on the lessons. The
vocalizations (the "problem") did not even have to be monitored
in this case. The teacher soon noticed that as the number of problems Erminda correctly solved on the math lessons increased, her
vocalizations were becoming less frequent and distracting.

The guiding principle of multicomponent interventions is the
design of effective and efficient FBAs, followed by selection of
the most effective and efficient interventions with which to
address the findings from the FBA, and finally, selection of the most
effective and efficient method of progress monitoring with which
to assess the success or failure of the teaching plan. Effectiveness in
this case depends on careful reliance on evidence-based practice.
Teachers can become effective practitioners through their preservice preparation and ongoing professional development. In the case
of more complex level 2 or level 3 FBAs and multicomponent

interventions, a highly trained consultant working in concert with a transdisciplinary team at the school may be required.

Lifestyle Outcomes

Exclusionary teaching practices when addressed to issues of discipline primarily reflect a concern for the school, the classroom, or even the teacher rather than for specific learning outcomes for the child. The question, "Whose problem is it?" applies. If a socially undesirable problem behavior is the child's, then he or she needs help with it. If the problem is the school's, the class's, or the teacher's, then simply removing the child provides the solution to the problem.

SWPBS is rooted in a pragmatic philosophy and so addresses the "Whose problem?" question from the standpoint of a values perspective. The particular values to be addressed are those of the individual receiving support, as well as those of the individual's family or advocates. This means that SWPBS interventions are designed to be sustained lifestyle changes over time.

SWPBS is thus directed to more than just solving a problem of challenging behavior. It also includes attention to teaching prosocial behavior, such as citizenship and character, that will better equip the student to have enduring friendships and enjoy enhanced self-esteem in order to gain a higher quality of life. In Erminda's case, teaching her to raise her hand to realize a brief escape-avoidance function provided her with a much better match of her behavior with that of her classroom peers than vocalizing; thus, it increased the possibility of greater peer acceptance, more friendships, and greater self-esteem—all lifestyle changes.

Sustainable Systems Change

The K–12 teaching profession is primarily informed by the discipline of psychology: the science of understanding the individual human being, whether in isolation or a social context (social psychology). But some of the body of knowledge that informs teaching comes from other corners of the social sciences, particularly from sociology and anthropology.

SWPBS is professional practice that reflects the contributions of the sciences of sociology and anthropology as well as psychology. Sociology is the study of collectives of human beings such as groups, schools, organizations, and teams. If a child's behavior seems quite different in one classroom compared to her behavior in another classroom, some component of the FBA may need to involve the collection of systems-level data. What, for example, are the features of one classroom over another that might contribute to particular aspects of the student's behavior?

Excellent examples of sociologically grounded interventions within SWPBS can be found in published reports of classroom management interventions (level 2). I once observed a high school geography class in an urban school setting that was being taught by a teacher newly graduated from a nearby university's teacher education program. She went through an entire lesson plan with her back to the class, never noticing, despite the level of noise, that virtually no one was paying attention and several students had left the classroom. Students had formed into several small groups and were talking and joking around with each other while completely ignoring the teacher. After the bell, I asked the teacher for her opinion on what had taken place and learned that she had defined her role as teaching to whomever might be paying attention while trying hard to ignore those who were uninterested in the lesson.

That teacher would clearly have benefited from a SWPBS level 2 classroom management professional development experience, in which she would learn to engage students (and use peer pressure) in group classroom projects to create a positive and engaged classroom climate. The professional development activity would be informed in part by sociological studies of secondary school classroom management.

When the team at the school engages in person-centered planning as part of a level 3 intervention, both the functioning of the team as an entity (its process) and its product (the plan) are likely to display characteristics that are familiar to, and perhaps might be predicted by, sociologists. A person-centered plan has a strong lifestyle focus and considers interventions that may be directed to a group of students with the desired outcome of helping the target student gain a social network of support. In this case, the team-governed decision-making process reaches far beyond matching a particular teaching strategy to a single behavior. It engages the entire social nexus of the individual in order to support lasting behavioral change directed to an enhanced lifestyle.

Anthropologists are concerned with culture, a broader concept than system, group, or organization, and one that includes history to a large extent. A school, for example, can have a pattern of organization and function as a system, all of which would be of interest to scientists trained in sociology. We might find that five schools in a district had essentially the same pattern of organization and as systems functioned pretty much the same way. Each school, however, is likely to have its own unique culture, and each is likely to be quite different from school to school, a phenomenon known to and studied by anthropologists.

One of the reasons that so many efforts to reform schools fail is likely a result of neglect of school culture factors by school reformers as they begin implementation. School culture is a powerful factor in predicting student achievement, a finding that stems from scientific research published by educational anthropologists. A closely related concept, school climate, can be reliably assessed through measurement tools to provide evidence of changes at the level of school culture. SWPBS is a powerful change agent for shifting schools with a negative or depressed culture to begin reflecting a positive culture. A comprehensive school reform model that follows a standard protocol that is mandated to schools by their district on a top-down basis, for example, might result in enhanced academic achievement in one school that undergoes systems change in accordance with the model, but another otherwise similar school in the same district might realize no measured gain from the process. In the first case, the model was a good fit with the particular culture of the school. In the second case, it was not, and the professional community of the school resisted the systems change efforts.

> *SWPBS is a powerful change agent for shifting schools with a negative or depressed culture to begin reflecting a positive culture.*

Summing Up Schoolwide Positive Behavior Support

Schoolwide positive behavior support encompasses the respective bodies of knowledge (that is, the evidence) contributed by all three processes of engagement: assessment (FBA), intervention (positive behavior support plan that may include a person-centered plan), and progress monitoring (data collection geared to decision making). It is precisely this transdisciplinary aspect of SWPBS that enables it to provide a good fit to a schoolwide RTI approach. Under schoolwide RTI, academic assessments, interventions, and methods of progress monitoring are also products of transdisciplinary team processes. Later in this book, I will examine specific measurement tools that can be applied within each of the three levels of SWPBS as well as within levels of reading and math interventions.

To Sum Up

This book presents a model for schoolwide RTI that encompasses the three levels of academic intervention as well as three levels of social-behavioral intervention. This chapter focused on the social and behavioral side of the conceptual pyramid. The traditional school model for discipline was reviewed as a case of pursuing exclusionary strategies and tactics for dealing with disciplinary infractions and problem behavior. As a three-tiered prevention system for dealing with individual problem behaviors as well as classroom management and school climate, SWPBS was discussed as an inclusionary approach that is a good fit for schoolwide academic RTI.

SWPBS, the social-behavioral side of the schoolwide RTI pyramid, was examined in terms of its four primary defining features: evidence-based practices, multicomponent interventions, lifestyle outcomes, and sustainable systems change. Finally, SWPBS was discussed as a transdisciplinary approach to social and behavioral risk prevention and intervention. As such, it is applied scientific professional practice that is informed by the disciplines of sociology and anthropology as well as psychology.

Part II

How Schoolwide RTI Works

4

Universal Screening for Prevention

Thus far, I have discussed theoretical and structural issues in setting up schoolwide RTI. This chapter is concerned with the first operational aspect of the process called *universal screening*.

RTI is a dynamic and systematic framework for matching school, and perhaps community, resources to identified student need in order for the student to successfully engage the teaching-learning process. The general unit of analysis is the curriculum as taught in the grade-level classroom. Some, perhaps many, students will successfully engage the curriculum with no extraordinary interventions beyond the standard instructional practices of the classroom teacher. This chapter is about how to apply techniques of universal screening for academics and behavior to determine which students may need additional interventions to achieve success.

Determining Success Criteria

Any discussion of screening must necessarily begin with a criterion reference in order to know what determines success. Since scores on any measures of student mastery can be expected to be normally distributed on any good test of a portion of the curriculum, the decision to move to more intensive interventions is not an easy one. Suppose in a class of twenty-five students taking a test on the material covered in Chapter Six of the geography textbook, we find the following: out of twenty questions, three students got eighteen to twenty items correct; six got a score of thirteen to seventeen; five scored between nine and twelve; four scored six to eight; and two produced fewer than six out of twenty correct scores on the test. One definition of a good test is that it adequately discriminates among levels of performance. Very few, if any, students should get all of the answers correct (the ceiling in this case is too low) and all students should get at least some answers correct (there is an adequate floor).

Scores on the Chapter Six test approximated a bell-shaped curve, that is, they were normally distributed within the class. Is this an indication that the students who scored in the bottom category should be considered at risk for academic or social failure? Not if the chapter-level geography test is the only screener. It is, however, one source of information available in conducting risk assessment.

A more significant source of information would be to examine student rankings on all six chapter tests to date. Are the same students scoring in the bottom percentile of the class distribution—or do students tend to move up and down in the rankings so that their performance is variable from test to test? A consistent pattern of poor performance can be a source of risk assessment for a student.

The goal in universal screening under RTI is to compile information from a number of sources to gain the clearest possible picture of student performance under the best possible circumstances of level 1 differentiated instruction. "Best possible" means we are using the best available curriculum grounded in what No Child Left Behind (NCLB) refers to as scientifically based research.

Students who reveal a clear pattern of performance on curriculum or social indicators that establish a downward trend deviation from the norm will be identified for consideration of extraordinary interventions associated with level 2 of RTI. Similarly, upward deviations from the trend of the class norm can provide an indication that a student (perhaps a "gifted" student) has the potential to engage an accelerated program, which may also be a level 2 intervention.

The term *norm* in this context refers to a normative (or normal) distribution of scores on some measure. There are generally two types of norms against which screening assessments are referenced: internal and external norms. The example of the chapter test is an internal norm: scores on the test are evaluated in terms of how the class as a whole performed. Students in the grade-level classroom are compared to each other on performance measures referenced against internal norms. Internally normed tests used as screeners offer the advantage of providing teachers with information from students they know well and can offer judgments based on consistent grade-level performance on a variety of curriculum components.

Externally referenced measurements indicate how a student has performed on a test compared to hundreds or even thousands of students from all over the country who comprise the research sample on which the test was standardized. The Dynamic Indicators of Basic Early Literacy Skills (DIBELS), for example, is an externally normed screener that assesses components of early reading skills in younger childrens' grade levels. Since one of the tenets of RTI implementation is setting high expectations for all students, use of either internal or external screeners alone for making a decision to engage level 2 interventions is not recommended. Schools have their unique cultures, and sometimes schools serve students representative of a broader encapsulated culture. A school in South Central Los Angeles, for example, with a high percentage of Latino students may be expected to be normatively different from a school in New Orleans serving mainly African American students. A good external screener should have been standardized on samples of students representing different cultures, and so should be relevant to all schools.

Suppose the example of the geography test occurred in a school in a high-poverty area with a history of substandard performance and failure to demonstrate adequate yearly progress gains as required under NCLB. Students who scored in the upper ranges on the internal screener might still score in the low ranges on an external screen. The requirement of high expectations for all points to the need for both types of information.

The issue of determining who is at risk of failure to achieve academic success has no easy solution under problem-solving schoolwide RTI. My recommendation is for teachers and grade-level teams to use both internal and external screeners to assess risk. A decision to apply level 2 interventions to particular student-assessed needs is important and certainly nontrivial. Secondary-level interventions are expensive, can be time-consuming, and in many cases may not be needed. When collaborative teaching is in place involving the general education teacher supported by a special education, Title I, or English Language Learning teacher, and instruction is decentralized, with small groups in a class, many challenges presented by students can be addressed through joint problem solving and differentiating instruction under level 1 circumstances.

My recommendation is for teachers and grade-level teams to use both internal and external screeners to assess risk.

Behavioral Screening Under RTI

Problem behavior is best defined here as behavior on the part of a student that impedes that student's ability to benefit from the teaching-learning process. Such behavior comes in two types: internalizing and externalizing. Approaches to screening can be school based, standardized, or both school based and standardized.

School-Based Screeners for Behavioral Risk

The most widely used screener for risk of academic achievement failure resulting primarily from social or behavioral problems is the frequency of office disciplinary referrals (ODRs). Referrals out of class for disciplinary reasons are more or less the standard. School discipline codes are nearly always punishment oriented and link an increasing series of infractions, usually in the classroom, to a series of warnings such as check marks after the student's name on the board, to exclusionary consequences ranging from class removal to a "quiet room," through being sent to the principal's office, detention, in-school suspension, out-of-school, time-limited suspension, and expulsion.

Schools implementing schoolwide positive behavior support (SWPBS) shift disciplinary code strategies to inclusionary tactics, so one way to evaluate the success of a systems change process to establish SWPBS in a school is to track frequencies of ODRs at individual, classroom, grade, and school levels and to expect a steady month-to-month decreasing trend. There is a significant problem, however, with using ODRs as either a screener or a formative assessment of the schools' success in putting SWPBS in place: ODRs are really a measure of teacher behavior, not that of the student.

ODR: Questionable Metric

Research shows that the same student can receive numerous ODRs from one teacher but none from another. It has also shown that reasons provided for making referrals tend to vary from classroom to classroom and even from time to time within the same classroom for occurrences of the same problem behavior. All of this means that ODRs are a questionable metric for assessing individual student risk factors. That said, however, it should be noted that ODRs have been shown to be a valid predictor of a school's progress implementing SWPBS as measured by the correlation of reductions in the frequency of ODRs with other external assessments of outcomes associated with SWPBS implementation.

Schools implementing schoolwide RTI should track ODRs at all levels as one measure of system change progress. I recommend, however, that ODRs not be a primary indicator in risk assessment screening. Disciplinary referrals are largely a product of teacher variables, such as skill level in classroom management, personal philosophy and style, extent of preservice training or professional development exposure to SWPBS, and interactive history with particular students, in addition to social and behavioral challenges presented by individual students.

Internalizers or Externalizers

The issue of social and behavioral screening is complicated by an important distinction that should be drawn between students who are at risk for academic achievement failure due to externalizing behavior problems and those at risk for reasons of internalizing conditions. Reports of individual students who are at risk for or exhibit both types of risk factors are rare, although they have appeared. These are students who, for example, exhibit bipolar disorders.

Students with externalizing problems present the usual circumstances for risk assessment. The term *problem* as used here refers to the likelihood that a particular behavior or pattern of behavior will impede a student's progress in the teaching-learning process. It is a problem for the child, not the teacher, by this definition, so we can potentially measure it at the level of the child regardless of a particular classroom or adult-child interaction. Typical externalizing problems that can dramatically affect learning (and thus performance) are hyperactive behavior, out-of-seat occurrences, talking inappropriately, bothering other students, dress code violations, repeatedly being late, and aggressive acts toward property or others. Some more dramatic examples of externalizing behaviors may be indicative of an emerging disability or symptomatic of an actual disability. Screening for problem behavior is not the same as screening for disability but may include the same measures. NCLB makes it clear that RTI measures can be one indicator of the need to engage supports and services under IDEA but cannot be the only indicator. When RTI behavioral screening suggests the presence of disability, usually in combination with other sources of evidence, a referral for further assessments by a school psychologist, social worker, or the school mental health counselor should be considered.

> *The term* problem *as used here refers to the likelihood that a particular behavior or pattern of behavior will impede a student's progress in the teaching-learning process.*

Students with internalizing problems that place them at risk for potential academic achievement failure are harder to identify. These are students who are often social isolates, victims of bullying, or victims of sexual or physical abuse (in some circumstances) and who may be chronically anxious or depressed. Their problem behavior almost never disrupts the class or is a major distraction for the teachers. These students nevertheless can be in the early stages of developing significant mental health problems that can have deleterious effects on their academic achievement. More important for schools, there is evidence that internalizers, if left alone when there are early signs, may become capable of extraordinarily violent antisocial acts.

Standardized Screeners for Behavioral Risk

Ideally a screening tool for the detection of high-risk externalizers is objective (it is administered by an outside trained assessor); has good psychometric properties (it is reliable and valid); and is based, at least in part, on direct observation of students in a variety of school environments, including the classroom. A reliable instrument produces about the same scores with repeated measurement opportunities (test-retest reliability) and with different assessors (interrater reliability).

Also ideally, a separate screening tool for internalizers is a reliable and valid questionnaire, filled out by the student, with perhaps a separate form to be completed by the teacher or a parent, or both. The results of such an assessment enable a skilled mental health professional to provide recommendations to the teacher concerning risk assessment.

Unfortunately there are numerous problems with introducing these kinds of ideal standardized measurement tools for screening within an RTI framework. Screening needs to take place early in the school year particularly for grades pre-K through 3, but ultimately for all students. The cost in terms of assessment personnel and time is out of reach of most schools and school districts. In addition, teachers are not always responsive to data on students collected by outsiders, particularly when such findings may not be a good fit with the teacher's own understanding of particular students.

Systematic Screening for Behavior Disorders

In our work with participating school districts using our RTI-based comprehensive school reform model, the Schoolwide Applications Model (SAM), which I describe in detail further on in the book, we prefer to use systematic screening for behavior disorders (SSBD), a combination standardized and school-based screener that addresses both externalizing and internalizing behavior problems. This instrument is administered by teachers on students in their classrooms and has now been extensively researched in primary and secondary school populations.

Screening for behavioral risk presents some challenges for RTI. RTI is a framework for direct extrapolation from scientific research to classroom practice—the interventions. To adhere to rigorous scientific standards, screening assessments should employ psychometrically sound instruments and trained, skilled assessors. Researchers consider teacher-generated data to be potentially unreliable and therefore invalid for the purposes of assessment because teachers are seldom trained in psychometrics and rigorous assessment procedures. But rigorous and scientifically acceptable standardized assessments are often prohibitively expensive and out of the reach of many school district budgets. So for behavioral screening assessments, we are caught somewhat between teacher clinical judgment and the demands of rigorous scientific measurement.

My decision to use SSBD, a combination screener, has to do with its value in assisting teachers to focus more intensively on individual students in their classrooms and become more attuned to the need to differentiate instruction (a level 1 RTI intervention). SSBD accomplishes this by asking teachers to focus on students and then rank-order them on sets of characteristics that define externalizing and internalizing behavioral risk.

SSBD provides a teacher with a three-stage set of operations for determining the risk of externalizing behavior and then of internalizing behavior. In stage 1, teachers study definitions of patterns of problem behavior that may place students at risk for impaired learning. They rank each student in their class, producing a list of up to ten externalizers and ten internalizers. The top-ranked student on each list is considered the best fit for the risk profile and the number 10 ranked (or last one) is the least for that group of students.

In stage 2, teachers fill out a pair of brief actual events and frequency checklists on each of the identified students in both columns. The result is a small wealth of teacher-generated information on students who may exhibit risk factors in their classrooms. In our screening practices, we use only the first two stages to conserve teacher time and because, for screening purposes, enough information is generated to enable team decisions to be made regarding a need for level 2 or level 3 interventions, the need for progress monitoring, and whether particular level 1 enhancements are warranted. In our experience, inner-core urban schools may turn up as many as three or four externalizers with this tool who will require progress monitoring and at least level 2 interventions. Expectancy rates for internalizers are lower, turning up one or two students on average. Middle-class suburban schools can be expected to turn up fewer externalizers with SSBD and perhaps more internalizers than inner-city schools do, but these percentages are largely speculative.

SSBD is, not surprisingly, somewhat of a hard sell to busy teachers who already feel overwhelmed by burdens of assessment and paperwork. In our experience, once a teacher has acclimated to SSBD, usually by about the third student in stage 2, the process moves swiftly and averages about ten minutes per student. Teachers who have been using SSBD as a behavioral screener for two or three years feel that it is of genuine value in detecting and focusing on high-risk students, and that value outweighs the time constraints in collecting the data.

> *Teachers who have been using SSBD as a behavioral screener for two or three years feel that it is of genuine value in detecting and focusing on high-risk students, and that value outweighs the time constraints in collecting the data.*

Academic Screening Under RTI

The purpose of academic screening is the same as for behavioral screening: to determine, as accurately as possible, which students, beginning with kindergarten, may be at risk for failure of academic achievement in curricular content areas such as reading and math. Academic screening processes differ somewhat from behavioral screening because much more research has appeared to date on RTI processes applied to academics, particularly reading. The difference between school-based screeners (ODRs in behavioral screening) and standardized screeners (SSBD) is less of an issue in academic screening because of the ready availability of well-researched and scientifically rigorous measuring tools available for reading and now beginning to emerge in math. Since some evidence suggests that students determined to be at risk in both math and reading will likely also be at risk for most, if not all, other content areas, screening and progress monitoring in these two areas may be sufficient under RTI.

Universal Academic Screening

In the early stages of development in schoolwide RTI, it was thought that academic risk assessment screening should be confined to grades K–3 since the early grades were where reading problems could be caught in time to provide interventions that would prevent later risk from developing. More recently, researchers have argued on the basis of evidence that screening should be universal: it should occur across all students at each grade level in a school. Moreover, recent evidence suggests it should be relatively frequent—no fewer than three times per year.

Fortunately, there are factors that allow frequent and universal screening to occur without placing an undue burden on teachers. First, results of screening inform instruction, so teachers find the process helpful. Second, unlike behavioral screeners where there is much less evidence from research, screening instruments overlap with progress monitors, so there is no duplication of effort in many cases. Third, academic screeners are often baseline measures of students' progress as they begin a new phase of the content curriculum. Universal academic screeners are often accessed through technology, and the data can be formatted in different ways. For example, a particular student's baseline data for grade-level reading can be compared with the average scores of his class, his grade level, or some other grouping of interest such as English Language Learners. It should be noted that rigorous academic screeners at the high school level have yet to be identified from published research.

Screening Accuracy and Efficiency

Two dimensions are of particular concern to academic screeners: Is the instrument accurate in timely identification of students at risk for academic achievement failure in a given content area? Is the instrument efficient—that is, can it be administered quickly and easily and thus not add to a classroom teacher's burden in any significant way?

Accuracy is important so as not to waste precious time and resources on students who may simply be slow starters or may be going through a disruptive period in their lives. Identifying such students as at risk for failure reduces the accuracy of the tool by overidentifying (referred to as *false positives*). The accuracy of a screener may also be compromised by failure to identify students who are at risk for failure (referred to as *false negatives*).

Efficiency has much to do with costs associated with screening assessments and with maximally productive use of teachers' valuable time. Furthermore, as assessment factors, accuracy and efficiency tend to be in a positively correlated relationship with one another. If screening measures lacked accuracy, we would need to expand the breadth and scope of assessments to become more accurate, but the trade-off would be in efficiency in terms of cost and teacher time. A tool identified with evidence that it is accurate for its purpose is likely to also be high in efficiency, as long as it is easily accessible, low cost, and not a burden on teacher time.

Accuracy is also correlated with assessment frequency. Researchers have been able to show, for example, that universal screening carried out at the beginning, the middle, and near the end of the school year significantly reduces the incidence of false positives and false negatives.

Normative and Criterion-Referenced Screeners

Just as the school-based versus standardized source of data is one dimension to be considered with behavioral screening tools, the normative-criterion-referenced dimension is another factor to be considered in selecting an academic screener. A normative screener compares a student's performance on a measure with a particular grouping, usually within the school such as the student's classroom or other classrooms at the same grade level. The problem for normative screeners is that too low a standard may result if the class or school is heavily affected by circumstances that tend to suppress academic performance in general. RTI requires an educational standard of setting high expectations for all students.

Criterion-referenced screeners are preferable because they are more likely to have been extensively researched, be both accurate and efficient, and are usually tied to state standards for the content area to which they are addressed and, in many cases, tied directly to the curriculum of the class or grade level. Criterion-referenced measures are usually standardized on thousands of students from many geographical areas of the country.

Discriminant Validity

The degree of sophistication emerging in the development of academic screeners enables schools to not only identify which students are at risk for academic failure but to begin to hone in on the specific features of the deficit that has been identified. Daryl Mellard and Evelyn Johnson in their 2008 book, *RTI: A Practitioner's Guide to Implementing Response to Intervention*, refer to the discriminant validity of an instrument as its ability to discriminate among various content-related deficits. In reading, for example, screening instruments not only identify students at risk for reading failure but also provide data helpful to teachers in pinpointing the source of the reading problem. These data can enable teachers in level 1 RTI to differentiate instruction and perhaps solve the problem early in the identification process. Success can then be tested by seeing if the same student is identified for risk at a later screening period.

Curriculum-Based Measures

Curriculum-based measures (CBMs) have emerged as the preferred method for academic content-area screening. A major advantage is that some of them can serve both screening and progress-monitoring functions, so they are very efficient. For content areas lacking strong, commercially available CBMs, there are normative CBMs such as a writing test administered three times a year at grade level and designed by the teacher. Finally, there are commercially available universal CBMs. These screening and progress monitoring tools are standardized against a general set of content indicators that can apply to any specific curriculum in a given content area at all grade levels. Since different school districts and even schools within districts often use different published curricula, universal CBMs permit comparisons on grade-level performance across schools, districts, states, and other units.

Universal CBM

John McCook, in his 2006 book, *The RTI Guide: Developing and Implementing a Model in Your Schools*, presents a good example of universal screening using probes as a part of the RTI model employed in Knox County, Tennessee. In this model, teachers administer CBM probes that range from one to four minutes per child three times per year. The probe for reading is a measure of words read correctly per minute. Each probe is administered three times in a single session, and the median score for the three becomes the data point used for risk assessment. In some cases, the probes can be administered to a group or class, which is a time saver, but in other cases, a one-on-one format is selected. Probe data are then entered into the AIMSweb software, which produces a graphic illustrating the results of the probe data point referenced against grade-level standard benchmarks for reading progress at each of the three screening time points.

DIBELS, AIMSweb, and iSTEEP

Two of the most widely used software packages offering bench-mark probes, data analysis, and graphics for reading and math are Dynamic Indicators of Basic Early Literacy Skills (DIBELS, accessed at http://dibels.uoregon.edu/) and AIMSweb (accessed at www.aimsweb.com). (A third universal CBM package, iSTEEP, for System to Enhance Educational Performance, is accessed through www.isteep.com.) These systems offer the advantage of providing quick and easy technology-based systems of probes that provide screening and progress-monitoring functions. The term *probe* here means collecting a data point that is related to but not part of the particular curriculum for a subject that is engaged by a student at grade level. Universal CBMs can thus compare students across different published reading or math programs.

Different reading and math programs also have their own software packages with criterion-referenced CBMs germane to the particular program. Since these are usually highly correlated with universal CBMs, the latter are preferable for most purposes.

DIBELS is a product of research at the University of Oregon and as of this writing was the least expensive of the universal CBM systems I looked at (one dollar per student). The software package is frequently updated and provides a wealth of analytical information as it massages a school or school district database. The system can be used to evaluate teaching effectiveness on the basis of pupil progress, and schools can develop their own databases for internal use. Finally, DIBELS provides a large number of alternative probe forms so students receiving level 2 interventions, for example, can be monitored more frequently.

Advantages of Universal CBM Screening for Teachers

In their book, *What Do I Do When. . . The Answer Book on RTI*, Sheila Fernley, Stephen LaRue, and John Norlin list advantages of universal CBM screening for school administrators, central office administrators, and teachers. These are the advantages for teachers:

1. Being able to tell from a glance at a laptop graphic how an entire class is performing on a chunk of a particular curriculum

2. Track progress of identified students (progress monitoring)

3. Have the ability to provide valid and reliable evidence of teaching effectiveness inferred from student progress

4. Have evidence of student progress to show to parents at a glance

5. Be able to identify problems in student performance as they emerge, to address through differentiated instruction

6. Compare individual student as well as whole class progress measured against benchmarks for each grade level identified by the curriculum publishers

Combining Results of Behavioral and Academic Screening Under RTI

The purpose in focusing on the screening function of schoolwide RTI is to enable teachers to identify potential problems in student academic progress before they become severe enough that a student might be held back a grade or be determined to be ineligible to graduate. High school dropout rates and incidences of violent crime have been directly linked to academic failure, and the problem is particularly serious in urban core schools. By screening all students for behavioral risk early in the school year and for academic risk three times per year, teachers gain information that can inform their teaching practice and get needed help to a student in time to prevent a small problem from growing into one that is potentially catastrophic.

The purpose in focusing on the screening function of school-wide RTI is to enable teachers to identify potential problems in student academic progress before those problems become severe enough that a student might be held back a grade or be determined to be ineligible to graduate.

A good schoolwide RTI model enables teachers, administrators, and specialized school professionals to use screening information to:

- Examine the relationship of problem behavior to academic indicators (and vice versa)
- Have a valid and reliable basis to decide whether to engage a team process leading to a level 2 or level 3 intervention
- Have a basis for deciding when students in levels 2 or 3 should be moved to a lower-tier set of interventions
- Have a basis for developing an intervention plan for individual students as well as a group-level basis for structuring lesson plans and
- Have a sound basis for requesting specialized assistance, materials, or personnel from the school administration

RTI Team Processes and Coaches

Matching additional resources and extraordinary interventions to identified needs from screening is beyond the scope of responsibilities of the classroom teacher, particularly if screening results suggest the need for level 2 or 3 interventions for particular students. The solution that has emerged in most schoolwide RTI applications to date is to make modifications to traditional school structural operations by establishing teams and introducing highly specialized personnel called coaches.

RTI and School Teams

The function of teams in schools is quite different from their predecessors, school committees. Committees were usually established to take on particular issues and come up with recommendations for the principal. An example familiar to many veteran teachers would be the school's library committee or the playground committee. Teams are an outgrowth of the more recent conception of distributed leadership and the advent of teacher-leaders. Engaging a school in the complex task of undergoing systems change to implement schoolwide RTI requires many school functions to be guided by personnel in addition to the principal. Teachers and other professionals who are empowered by the principal to assume leadership roles for specific structural functions came together to do so in problem-solving teams—hence, the term *problem-solving RTI*.

How many teams a school should have, with how many members each, and to address which functions are a matter of choice as well as what is a good fit for the culture of the school. Teams are burdensome because they require dedicated time on the part of busy teachers with no extra compensation for their participation. Nevertheless, teachers volunteer for team membership because they recognize the value of the process for their work and for the good of the school and its students.

In our work, we consider two types of teams to be essential to the schoolwide RTI process in schools with any combination of grades from pre-K to 8. First, a school should have a site leadership team (SLT). (These may be called something else, such as school improvement team, reflected in NCLB language, or school advisory team.) The function of this important team is to ensure the full integration and coordination of all school supports, services, and operations. The mantra of the SLT should be "no silos." All pieces of the school puzzle must fit together at the level of the SLT. Representatives of grade-level teams, the second essential type of team, sit on the SLT which is usually chaired by the principal.

How Effective Teams Work

All teams at some early point in their constitution should undergo a team-building experience. Time is precious in schools, and team time cannot afford to be wasted. In our schools, all teams with more than five members who meet throughout the school year undergo a professional development experience where they learn how effective teams work:

- Learn to set and communicate advance agendas
- Have a committed membership that attends all team meetings
- Elect officers (usually chair, vice chair, note taker, and sometimes a timekeeper)
- Avoid sidebar conversations and stay on task with agenda items
- Compile minutes of each meeting reflecting who is to do what by when
- Disseminate the minutes (and solicit agenda items) to the relevant school, families, and community stakeholders of the work of the particular team.

Membership on teams is usually voluntary in consultation with the principal.

For high schools, team structure is somewhat different. Essential high school teams in our view should again include a site leadership team. We recommend that high schools undertaking RTI develop smaller learning communities (SLCs) so that faculty can have closer contact with individual students. An SLC, sometimes called a "house," is a particular grouping of students and teachers within the high school that results in more frequent, personalized contacts between students and school staff. Rather than pursuing particular themes for SLCs (i.e., advanced placement track), we suggest random constitution, that is, SLCs made up of randomly selected students of all types and randomly selected faculty to the extent that all content areas can be represented. A friendly rivalry across SLCs can become a motivating factor in student achievement, attendance, and graduation. SLCs should be represented on the SLT.

A third type of team important to successful high school operations is subject matter teams. Math and literacy teachers in particular need a self-contained discourse community to gain and disseminate new knowledge and focus more closely on particular students.

In addition to essential function teams, many of the schools we work with have a number of special function teams, usually to put a particular innovation or set of modifications needed at the school in place. Schoolwide positive behavior support (SWPBS) is a major component of RTI and is likely to require a positive behavior support team to function at the school until SWPBS becomes business as usual. When that occurs, usually after one or two years of professional and staff development supported by coaches, my recommendation is to fold the functions of that team into the SLT. When special function teams become institutionalized in schools, the danger of silos emerges. RTI requires all parts to work together and everyone to be knowledgeable of the parts.

Examples of other special function problem-solving teams are student study teams, parent outreach teams, and community partnership teams. Of particular concern to us in addressing the issue of what happens after screening identifies some students are at risk, is whether to create an RTI team. In his book *RTI Toolkit: A Practical Guide for Schools* (2007), Jim Wright makes a strong case for creating an RTI team that pursues a problem-solving model to examine data on students identified as at risk, select interventions matched to a student's identified needs, and monitor identified students to ascertain the effectiveness of the resultant intervention plan and convey that information to the teacher. In Wright's view, RTI teams exist to serve the purposes of the level 2 RTI interventions.

Wright's recommended RTI teams are made up of a variety of professional and support staff at the school including general education teachers and also parent representatives. He recommends that teams meet for at least thirty minutes and proceed through the following steps:

1. Take input from teachers on particular students

2. Create an inventory of each student's strengths and talents

3. Review data collected on students to date

4. Select one or two target concerns expressed by the teacher for each student

5. Set intervention goals for each student and a means to monitor the progress toward each goal

6. Design an intervention plan to address each goal in concert with the teacher

7. Designate a staff member to convey the intervention plan to the parent

8. Conduct a final review of the intervention plan and progress-monitoring system to ensure all players are knowledgeable and in agreement before beginning the intervention

Other RTI advocates describe similar teams, for example, effective intervention teams, early intervening services teams, and teacher support teams. Most of the schoolwide RTI advocates suggest similar functions to Wright's model in pursuing RTI teams.

Sunset RTI Teams

Whether a school needs to create a stand-alone RTI team is an issue of deciding what is the best fit with the culture (meaning "community of practice" in this sense) of the particular school. Since schoolwide RTI is likely to be a substantive departure from business as usual at the school, formation of a team to guide the systems change processes, particularly in the early stages, may be a good idea. My recommendation to schools setting up RTI teams to get started is to limit the team to two or three years and ask the team to develop a transition plan in the final year, so that team functions can be subsumed under the SLT and grade-level teams. In other words, when schoolwide RTI becomes enculturated and is therefore business as usual at the school, there is no longer a need for a team to be dedicated to it. Since schools tend to embrace new innovations as these emerge across the country, there is a danger of RTI becoming "siloized" if it continues to be understood by the professional community of the school as a subpart of overall school functioning rather than its core.

My school reform colleagues and I tend to lean more toward involving grade-level teams in RTI intervention planning and progress monitoring rather than creating a separate stand-alone team. We do, however, recommend that grade-level teams include special educators, particularly those who are teaching collaboratively with general education teachers, Title One teachers, English Language Learning (ELL) teachers, teachers of gifted students, or any specialized support teaching staff who are collaboratively engaged with teachers at any grade level. We also suggest that school psychologists, counselors, and social workers be available to grade-level teams for RTI processes on an as-needed basis.

Susan Hall, in her 2008 book, *A Principal's Guide: Implementing Response to Intervention*, nicely sums up our view:

> It is common to hear the term "'data meeting'" around schools that are implementing RTI. What does a data meeting look like? One type typically occurs with a grade-level team, and the purpose is to evaluate the effectiveness of the overall approach to intervention for the students at that grade level. Another is one in which all the staff that serve an individual below-benchmark student meet to analyze the student's data and discuss whether any changes in his or her intervention plan are needed.
>
> RTI offers an opportunity to convert the discussions that occur at grade-level meetings. Too often the discussion is around administrative topics such as staffing for the field trip or deadlines for report cards. Nearly all such details can be handled via e-mail or through staff mailboxes. The grade-level meetings should be dedicated to talking about curriculum and instruction [pp. 90–91].

By making RTI guidance and requisite systems change the responsibility of the SLT and grade-level teams, the process more quickly becomes everybody's responsibility rather than the responsibility of some team. In our view, this setup creates a dynamic tension within the total system that makes it harder for resistant teachers, administrators, and staff to seek refuge from the implications of the changes. Furthermore, it puts RTI discussions into the common discourse of those who know the affected students best: their classroom teachers.

So to return to the question, "What next after screening?" the answer is either referral to the RTI team, if that is the structural element in place, or to the agenda of the grade-level team. Another advantage of using grade-level teams for intervention planning and progress monitoring is that the problem-solving process around each identified student helps teachers tailor more effective interventions in their own classrooms and keeps recommended interventions closer to the ongoing curriculum of the student's class.

One final note on the relationship of team processes to RTI levels is important to this discussion. Several prominent RTI advocates argue in their books for confining the work of grade-level or RTI teams to levels 1 and 2, with level 3 wholly deeded over to special education. In other words, if a student's needs are determined through screening or progress monitoring to be sufficiently great as to exceed what can be accomplished through level 2 interventions, then a disability is presumed (in the absence of further testing and diagnostic work, as required in NCLB) and the student is referred for evaluation under IDEA.

I take a different view. I believe that the specialized skills and knowledge of special educators should engage RTI at all three levels. In our school reform model, SAM, special educators teach collaboratively with general educators when grade level classrooms have one or more students with individualized education programs. This way specialized teaching for hard-to-teach students can benefit not only students with these programs but all of the students in the class. This practice is fully consistent with and allowable by IDEA.

I believe that the specialized skills and knowledge of special educators should engage RTI at all three levels.

Some students will immediately be identified as level 3 students on the basis of obvious or previously established disability. In our view, they should still come under the purview of the grade-level teacher with collaborative support from a special education teacher, and a student's progress, even in a modified curriculum, should be monitored by the grade level team. To do otherwise is to again "siloize" the school. Special education, as with all other categorically funded specialized programs, must be fully integrated into the total school program for RTI to be successful.

Coaches

The second critical structural component in schoolwide RTI is embodied in the concept of the coach. The coaching concept in schools is not new, but the name and current practices are. The basic idea is that of the teacher who has a wide spectrum of knowledge and skills gained through professional development and further courses through higher education, who can be a resource to classroom teachers on an itinerant basis. In California in the 1980s, for example, most schools had resource specialists whose role and function were similar to the coach concept of today but also much broader in scope of support than most coaches today.

The coaching idea gained prominence and visibility under the Reading First agenda of the George W. Bush administration and NCLB. It was felt that teachers would need ongoing assistance in implementing new, sophisticated, technologically assisted reading curricula. A cadre of highly trained reading specialists could be added to schools to support grade-level teams and classrooms on an itinerant basis. Often these personnel were called *literacy coaches*. Next came math coaches. I have worked with school districts that as of this writing were using financial support from private philanthropic sources to fund a math coach and literacy coach at every school in the district.

While I agree that coaching functions are valuable and perhaps essential, particularly for urban core schools, I am not comfortable with the microfocus on particular curriculum content areas for this degree of specialization. My recommendation is to equip schools with coaches at each grouping of grade levels but to broaden the job description to require expertise in both math and literacy and also SWPBS and RTI. My rationale is this. When a teacher completes the screening process and forwards the results to the grade-level team, the referring teacher will probably need ongoing support for accurately carrying out the recommended intervention plan with fidelity. A coach who was involved in the intervention planning process and continues to be involved in progress monitoring is in an ideal position to function as a human bridge between the grade-level team and the classroom teachers.

Obviously such a person should be highly trained and skilled, have a great deal of requisite experience, and have the kind of personal qualities that engender trust on the part of teachers. For RTI coaches, we prefer teachers certified in both general elementary (or secondary) education and special education. Where dually certified teachers are lacking in up-to-date math and literacy curricula, instructional innovation, SWPBs, and RTI, I recommend a program of ongoing highly specialized professional development in the areas determined to be in need of updating. I further recommend that compensation for these highly skilled personnel be commensurate with their levels of responsibility.

To Sum Up

In this chapter I laid out the basis and operations for the first stage in the implementation of schoolwide RTI, universal screening. The function of screening was determined to be the need to detect early on students who may need more interventions than those provided through level 1 teaching practices.

School-based screeners were examined as well as standardized screeners (criteria-referenced instruments). A case was made to use SSBD as the behavioral screener and DIBELS or AIMSweb for academic screening.

Next, teams and their roles in RTI screening processes were discussed. Students identified in the screening process who may be at risk for behavioral or academic problems, or both, that could, in isolation or combination, impair their responsiveness to level 1 instruction would be placed for data review and discussion purposes on the agenda of either a grade-level team or an RTI team. That team would determine if a level 2 or level 3 intervention is required, design an intervention plan if needed, and monitor the progress of the students in question.

Coaching as a further structural element in schoolwide RTI was also discussed. It was recommended that coaches have broader responsibility than reading or math alone and that they also have knowledge, skills, and experience (if possible) in special education, SWPBS, literacy and math, and RTI. These coaches would then help to guide the RTI process at the classroom level.

5

Progress Monitoring to Measure Success

The federal government leverages education policy through the Elementary and Secondary Education Act (ESEA), its statutory authority in providing funds to the states for public schooling. The ESEA affords an opportunity for an incoming president to exert influence on the direction of public education. Under President Bill Clinton, the ESEA was called Goals 2000 and contained a number of ambitious goals, such as "every student will arrive at school prepared to learn," to be realized between 1992 and 2000. Following the election of George W. Bush, ESEA became No Child Left Behind (NCLB) in 2004.

Where Goals 2000 focused on family and child welfare as it bears on education, NCLB shifted the focus to scientifically validated teaching and curriculum innovations. The language of NCLB contains numerous references to "evidence-based practices" and scientific measurement. These sharp differences in philosophy of education exactly mirror the political perspectives of the two presidents. Clinton, a Democrat, was aligned with his party's overarching concern for demand-side policies. Funds under this philosophy are largely directed to specialized services and enhancements for underprivileged children and youth. Bush, a Republican, favored supply-side policy and placed a much greater emphasis on improvements in the school management issues of curriculum and instruction.

Using Scientific Research

Reading First and Early Reading First, as discussed in Chapter Two, were major policy initiatives designed to bring ongoing scientific research into a full-scale attack on the problem of massive failure in acquisition of early literacy skills in many American children, particularly those living in circumstances of poverty. With large doses of federal research and development funding during the early 2000s, a variety of packaged reading curricula, enhanced by technology, have been published, tested, and become operational in schools across the country.

Educational Accountability

When the Individuals with Disabilities Education Act was reauthorized in 2004 as the Individuals with Disabilities Education Improvement Act (IDEIA), it contained extensive new language directed to the greater use of scientifically validated practices in determining who should receive specialized supports and services. A focus was placed on the determination of specific learning disabilities. Where before 2004, this determination could be made largely on the basis of psychological testing, now local educational agencies can take into account a student's responsiveness to scientifically grounded instruction. Furthermore, these agencies were granted authority under the statute to use up to 15 percent of their IDEIA allocation to provide *early intervening services* for students who are not served under special education but have been determined from scientific measurement to require additional behavioral or academic support in order to avoid being referred for special education and to succeed in the grade-level curriculum.

The unifying elements in NCLB and IDEIA responsible for the explosion of interest in RTI are scientifically grounded assessments, curriculum, and instructional practices, coupled with a strong prevention orientation and topped off with accountability provisions stemming from measured annual student academic achievement progress. Where Goals 2000 tracked indicators of children's readiness to learn in school by collecting annual data on the health of children and families, NCLB directly tracked student achievement by requiring annual grade-level standardized state assessments on reading and mathematics. Schools that failed to show annual increases of 5 percent under the adequate yearly progress (AYP) provisions could become subject to punitive consequences, including vouchers for families to be able to transfer their children out of public schools deemed to be "low performing" into other schools, including those in the private sector; replacement of all staff at the school under restructuring provisions; and even state takeover of the schools by the state educational agency. These punitive consequences have been referred to as "high-stakes-assessment" because the standardized annual assessment process uses data from students to drive the resources needed to operate schools.

All of this on the face of it would be very highly regarded if it worked. Who, after all, is not awed by the accomplishments of science, particularly in the physical world? Things in the social world of schools, however, seem not to deliver the same dramatic results that are achievable in rocket, medical, and computer sciences. Very recently, large-scale scientific studies have begun to appear evaluating the impact of the Reading First initiative and comparing student achievement in public schools versus private schools with comparable demographics, including those receiving vouchers. In both cases, the results are disappointing. Children in schools using Reading First curriculum and instruction materials and processes are performing no better at each grade level than those using a standard curriculum and instructional practice. Children receiving vouchers to attend private schools for the most part are achieving at no higher levels than they previously had done in their public schools.

> *Children receiving vouchers to attend private schools for the most part are achieving at no higher levels than they previously had done in their public schools.*

So how can it be that a massive infusion of modern rigorous science into public education, backed up with high-stakes accountability, still cannot achieve significant jumps in grade-level math and reading assessments?

Problems with Accountability

There appear to be two major problems that together probably have the potential to doom the whole enterprise embodied in NCLB. The first has to do with some deep flaws of logic in the statute itself, and the second with a problem in the use of external accountability mechanisms to drive scarce resources.

The Problem of Unrealistic Goals

Stanford professor Linda Darling-Hammond, writing in the winter 2006 edition of *Harvard Educational Review*, summed up the problem:

> The accountability provisions of NCLB have been the subject of much analysis and considerable protest. In particular; the requirement that schools make AYP on test scores toward the goal of having 100 percent of students score at the "proficient" level by the year 2014 was set without an understanding of what this goal would really mean. Recent studies have suggested that most states will fail to achieve this goal . . ., and in diverse

states like California, 99 percent of schools are expected to fail. . . .

One fundamental problem is that the goals are unrealistic. Using a definition of proficiency benchmarked to the National Assessment of Educational Progress (NAEP), one leading measurement expert has calculated that it would take schools more than 160 years to reach such a target in high school mathematics if they continued the fairly brisk rate of progress they were making during the 1990s. [p. 654]

The logic of AYP is similar to that of a track and field coach telling a high school shot-putter that he must increase his put-distance by one foot per month for eight months (to equal the high school world's record) or be thrown off the team. States and school districts have long argued that raising the expected achievement bar while level funding or even scaling back school finance is completely nonsensical.

The Problem of School Culture

The second major problem confronting NCLB has been extensively analyzed by American Institutes for Research member Jennifer O'Day. O'Day's thesis, set out in a 2002 article in *Harvard Educational Review*, is that schools cannot be expected to respond to efforts to impose external accountability without considering professional accountability. Schools are organizational entities, subject to the forces of group and organizational dynamics familiar to sociologists and cultural anthropologists. As organizations, schools cannot be conceived as if they were factories, with a mix of humans and robots turning out automobiles.

Teachers in a school, together with staff and administrators, are a community of practice: they are contributors to, as well as recipients of, the culture of the school. *School culture* in this context means the sum of the values, norms, expectations, and beliefs of members of the community. Researchers of school culture collect data, for example, on school climate. Measures of school climate have been shown in recent studies to be highly positively correlated with positive trends in student achievement. In other words, the more positively that teachers regard their jobs and their schools, the higher the achievement test scores will be from their students. Other research has shown that chronically low-performing schools can be differentiated from higher-performing schools on the basis of measures of school climate.

> *Teachers in a school, together with staff and administrators, are a community of practice: they are contributors to, as well as recipients of, the culture of the school. School culture in this context means the sum of the values, norms, expectations, and beliefs of members of the community.*

O'Day's analysis leads to the conclusion that solutions to problems of failure to learn to read and do math must take into account both the social world of the community of practice and the more physical world of scientifically engineered curriculum and instruction enhancements evaluated with external, standardized accountability processes. RTI as a comprehensive logic model to address school performance affords a way to confront both problems head-on. It nurtures professional practice by distributing leadership through teams and coaching relationships and by fostering discourse among professional staff through problem solving. At the same time, it moves external accountability closer to the day-to-day teaching-learning process through examining student progress with curriculum-based measures (CBMs). Rather than addressing a sole concern with arbitrary percentages of school gains on an annual standardized test, teaching is informed by regular consideration of growth curves of month-to-month student performance within and across subject matter areas. The logic of schoolwide RTI is to guide teaching by using science to match available resources to measured student needs.

Finally, RTI abrogates the need to teach to the test. I have seen schools lose ground in annual standardized assessments because so much pressure was put on students to perform on the test day that they suffered test anxiety and in some cases froze. I watched a nine-year-old girl break into tears when asked by a local TV reporter how she thought she would do on the state test the next day. The girl said that if she did not do well, it might hurt her whole school. Curriculum-based assessments and other short-term measures of pupil performance are predictive of state annual grade-level test results. Given that established fact, surely it makes more sense to focus on day-to-day short-term measures of performance on elements of the sequenced curriculum than to interrupt that process to spend a month, or more in some cases, to prepare students to take the annual test.

Types of Assessment for Progress Monitoring

A wide spectrum of approaches to the evaluation of pupil progress in response to general as well as tailored educational interventions can be found in the RTI literature. Some are applicable primarily to behavioral interventions and others to academic interventions. In this section, I provide a framework for understanding progress monitoring assessments and some examples of specific tools for measuring progress at all three levels of RTI, considering interventions directed to behavior as well as to academics.

Proximal Versus Distal Assessments

When we speak of progress monitoring with schoolwide RTI, we are working in the realm of proximal assessments: those that are scientifically valid and reliable (that is, they have good psychometric properties) and measure near-term changes. A teacher who gives a short math quiz every other week is collecting proximal data but is not engaging in proximal assessment for RTI purposes. A teacher who employs a monthly assessment, say from AIMSweb, that is referenced against state math standards for each grade level and has been properly standardized is engaging in proximal assessment that lends itself to RTI progress monitoring. Distal assessments are measures with good psychometrics that are given no more often than annually. State standardized grade-level assessments are a good example of distal assessment.

Formative Versus Summative Assessments

Another set of terms captures this process: *formative* versus *summative* assessments. Proximal measures are formative in that they capture learning responses to educational interventions as these are accumulating over time. Distal assessments are summative in that they reflect the end process: the sum of what has been gained over the formative process. Proximal assessments are measures of progress under conditions of teaching and learning at a particular grade level. Distal assessments are outcome measures—the result of progress (or lack thereof).

We know from research that proximal measures are preferred for progress monitoring under RTI because they follow a prevention logic and are significant predictors of the results obtained on distal measures. RTI is about detecting problems in the teaching-learning process and intervening to prevent the problems from worsening and to return the student to level 1 expected performance ranges. Prevention by this logic is much more than intervening in problems identified in the first grade, so that a large problem will not show up by the fifth grade. It can also mean intervening in the fourth week of school to head off a problem that might become worse by the tenth week.

Categorical Versus Aggregate Assessments

It is easy to think and react categorically rather than to process information across categories and respond accordingly. But categorical assessments may not always lead to the best problem-solving means toward a selected intervention. An example of a categorical assessment for progress monitoring purposes might be to focus on behavior alone. Suppose our assessments with systematic screening for behavior disorders (SSBD) determined that a level 2 intervention called check/in–check out (CICO) was warranted for Estevan. The intervention was then planned and put into place by the RTI team in conjunction with the classroom teacher and in consultation with Estevan's parents. A decision was made to monitor Estevan's progress with a behavior scale instrument three times each semester. The team was ignoring Estevan's academic performance because it was his behavior that led to the decision for intervention.

Suppose, however, that Estevan was also performing in the range of basic on both math and reading benchmarks. We know from research that behavior and academic achievement are positively correlated. The possibility exists that the behavior problem actually resides in the academic area.

Learning Versus Performance

In thinking about screening and progress monitoring, it is useful to consider the issue of learning versus performance in the genesis of problems. A student determined to be at risk for problem behavior may simply need to be taught a different way to behave (this is then a learning problem) and the problem is solved. Another student determined to be at risk for behavior problems may be reacting to failure in the academic area. This student knows how to behave (he meets the behavioral expectations of the class or school) but is not motivated to display what he knows.

Aggregate assessments are those that engage the problem-solving process by examining data from a variety of sources. If a student has been determined to be at risk in one categorical area but is doing fine in other measured areas of schooling, then the problem is likely one of learning and can be treated independent of extraordinary interventions in any of the subject matter categories. But if the student's performance is low or downward trending in areas other than just the problem identified in screening, a problem of motivation may exist. The result would be a more complex intervention addressed to more than just a particular behavior. Without looking at multiple sources of data, it would be difficult, if not impossible, to reveal that possibility.

Behavioral Progress Monitoring

At level 1 of RTI, the usual way to monitor behavior is through keeping track of office disciplinary referrals (ODRs). I have already pointed out the problems with ODRs as a reliable and valid measure, but at level 1, they do have the potential to enable a teacher or an RTI (or positive behavior support) team to detect a problem that may be emergent or slowly increasing. A student with increasing ODRs who also was listed on the SSBD risk ranking may be a candidate for a level 2 intervention.

ODRs at level 1 can also reveal a pattern of acute problem behavior that may be reflective of changes in a student's life. I once sat in on a middle school SWPBS team meeting where one agenda item had to do with a sixth grader who had no history of ODRs over a three-year period in district schools, but suddenly obtained five referrals in the previous two-week period. After consultation with the teacher, the team recommended a referral for the student to a school counselor, who after three sessions determined that the student had recently become a victim of abuse by a person who had moved into the home over the previous month. A referral for a level 2 intervention was postponed pending a home visit and consultation with the student's mother by the school social worker. That visit resulted in a solution to the problem, and the student obtained no further ODRs.

Level 1 or level 2 progress monitoring of internalizing behavior poses a challenge. Internalizers rarely get ODRs, so referrals are not a useful measure for picking up increased severity in chronic patterns or an acute episode. My recommendation to teachers with students who were in the top six ranked students on the SSBD internalizing list is to informally monitor those students for any changes in pattern in the direction of greater severity and consult with the school counseling staff when such changes are noticed. Counseling psychologists have measurement tools at their disposal to assist in their recommendations for level 2 interventions, but to my knowledge, none of these are suitable for level 1 or level 2 progress monitoring in general.

Level 2 progress monitoring for externalizing problems requires more rigor in our evaluation of success (or lack thereof) resulting from a level 2 intervention. In my work with urban core schools, we recommend that students selected for level 2 interventions be monitored with two types of measures: a general change indicator and a direct change indicator. For general change, I recommend the second edition of the *School Social Behavior Scales* (SSBS). This instrument is a simple questionnaire to be filled out by the classroom teacher monthly for each identified level 2 student where behavior intervention is the primary issue. SSBS has sixty-four Likert-scaled items on two scales: social competence and antisocial behavior. Research using SSBS indicates that the tool is psychometrically sound, lends itself to repeated measures without compromising its integrity, and is significantly correlated with direct measures of problem behavior. In other words, as scores on social competence rise and as antisocial behaviors decline, one can expect to see reductions in episodes of measured problem behavior and increases in measures of prosocial replacement behaviors.

Direct Measures of Problem Behavior

A direct measure of problem behavior is one that a positive behavior support or RTI team designs in consultation with the classroom teacher and a school psychologist. The usual form of a direct measure begins with operationally defining the problem.

Operational definitions are careful specifications that permit observational measurement. "Violent acts toward others" is a conceptual definition. "Ricky physically pushes or strikes another student" is an operational definition since it can be counted as long as it is observed.

Ideally a direct measure would have several days of baseline data prior to the intervention so that the change in the pattern of occurrence of the behavior can be evaluated. Some RTI proponents call for full-blown functional analysis to be performed using single-subject research designs. An example would be five days of baseline on Ricky's aggressive behavior (measured as frequency of occurrence per day) followed by a level 2 intervention (say, a peer mediation conflict resolution) for five days (treatment); followed by withdrawal of treatment for six days (baseline 2); and finally reinstatement of treatment until the problem is well on the way to being solved. Figure 5.1 illustrates such a pattern using hypothetical data. The advantage of classroom functional analyses to monitor progress at level 2 is that a scientific procedure is carried out to evaluate the success of the intervention. The disadvantage, and the reason I do

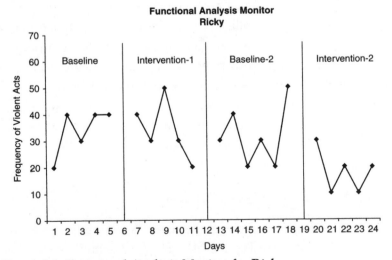

Figure 5.1 Functional Analysis Monitor for Ricky

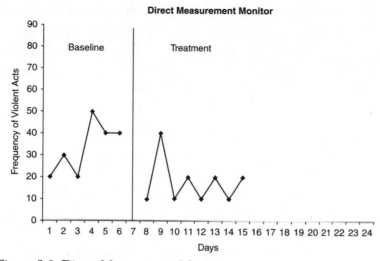

Figure 5.2 Direct Measurement Monitor

not recommend its general use, is that it is too demanding of teacher time to be carried out faithfully in most cases.

A simple baseline treatment evaluation is sufficient to answer the question, "Is the problem solved?" and is not an undue burden on the teacher, particularly if supported by a school team in the process. Figure 5.2 illustrates the simpler baseline treatment monitoring data path, again with hypothetical data.

Alternately, a teacher could measure frequency of acquisition of Ricky's replacement behavior instead of the problem behavior. In my experience, data taken on the problem tend to be more reliable than on its replacement. Also the problem behavior is more likely to capture the attention of the teacher immediately. Finally, some teachers prefer to track both the problem (pushing) and the replacement (request peer mediation), in which case both behaviors can be represented on the same chart. The pattern would show frequency of requests rising as episodes of pushing or hitting declined.

There are no universally suitable tools for monitoring the progress of students undergoing level 2 interventions directed to internalizing problems that are impeding learning for a student.

Tools are available to counseling and school psychologists for estimating and tracking the progress of students undergoing therapeutic interventions at the secondary level of RTI. None of these, however, has been evaluated and published for its general utility in application under a schoolwide RTI model.

Level 3 Progress Monitoring for Behavior

Level 3 progress monitoring tools for externalizing behavior problems are under development and being field-tested under the U.S. Office of Special Education's (OSEP) National Centers on Tertiary Interventions program (www.ed.gov/about/offices/list/osers/osep). Level 3 interventions usually signify that on the basis of progress monitoring data from level 2 interventions, a team has decided that a student requires a more extensive, and perhaps individualized, intervention under level 3. Because level 3 interventions often require broad participation on the part of personnel at the school in addition to the classroom teacher, my recommendation is for a schoolwide RTI system to have a tertiary intervention team responsible for evaluating students referred by the school's RTI team. The team then works with the classroom teacher and grade-level team to conduct a functional behavioral assessment and develop a behavior intervention plan if needed. Typically a tertiary intervention team has a general education teacher, a special education teacher, a school psychologist, and a social worker as members. Others may be added or be available to consult as needed.

Special education is often a significant source of support for students identified for level 3 interventions for reasons of externalizing behavior problems. A tertiary-level team may recommend that a student who has been referred to it be evaluated for an individualized education program. Of course, RTI data at level 2 would become part of the overall evaluation protocol in this case.

Amy McCart, at the University of Kansas, and I partnered recently with Lucille Eber of the Illinois State PBS Network to attract a grant to operate one of the OSEP National Centers on Tertiary Interventions. Through this effort, we have been piloting a comprehensive progress monitoring system for level 3 behavior that Eber developed. This system, systematic information management for educational outcomes (SIMEO), enables an electronic portfolio of information from several measurement tools to be compiled to track a student's progress as he or she moves from grade to grade and, perhaps, to a secondary-level intervention status.

In the past, tertiary-level students were relegated to special classes for severe behavioral disorders, emotional disorders, or emotional and behavioral disabilities. Teachers in these classrooms spent the majority of their time trying, often unsuccessfully, to cope with extreme problem behavior on the part of usually eight or nine students. The burnout rate among teachers with this specialization has been understandably excessive relative to the teaching profession as a whole. In my opinion, special classrooms for students with extensive behavioral support needs is an idea whose time has gone—and none too soon. Neither students nor staff benefit from these arrangements, and in many cases reported in the literature, behavior problems worsen under congregate arrangements.

Until recently, the alternative, inclusion, has been strongly resisted by general educators for obvious reasons. A child with extensive behavior support needs cannot be educated in a grade-level classroom with only an assigned paraprofessional and occasional consultation from a behavior analyst or a special education teacher. Segregated education and inclusion are equally problematic. So what is the solution?

Wraparound and SIMEO

Eber and her Illinois associates chose to pursue a different strategy altogether, and one that is aligned with a response to an intervention problem-solving logic model. Called *wraparound,*

Eber's approach to tertiary intervention is based on the following recognition:

- Even very difficult students who present severe behavioral challenges are learners. Given adequate support and good instruction, they can learn new behaviors that are socially acceptable and can remove impediments to academic achievement.

- Support for these students requires casting a wide net and involving family members as well as community agency personnel in the tertiary intervention plan.

- A wraparound approach, historically grounded in the field of community mental health as well as school mental health, can address the needs of both internalizing students and externalizers.

- The process must be anchored in the systematic collection of formative (proximal) data so that precious resources, human and fiscal, are not wasted in the process.

A tertiary-level intervention plan using the wraparound approach proceeds through four phases. Phase 1, initiated by a tertiary team facilitator, brings the grade-level and special education teacher together with family or other primary caregivers to build a lasting relationship. Family members are empowered under this approach through being asked to tell their stories and contribute important information in structuring an intervention plan.

In phase 2, the tertiary-level team develops the initial wraparound plan. The team is expanded during this phase to add community representatives from resource agencies such as community mental health, police, parks and recreation, and after-school providers as needed. The product of this phase is a written plan that specifies goals, strategies, personnel, time lines, and usually a safety plan that dictates what to do in emergency situations.

In phase 3, the team uses ongoing progress monitoring data to make decisions about plan refinement. Finally, in phase 4, the transition begins from intensive, tertiary–level interventions to less intensive engagement at RTI level 2.

Through the SIMEO data management system, the tertiary team's actions are guided by an electronic portfolio of information collected from a set of time-tested instruments addressed to evaluation of the lifestyle of the student rather than simply focused on a problem behavior. SIMEO begins with a fidelity estimation tool, the wraparound integrity tool. This instrument assesses the extent to which the four phases of the process are faithfully engaged, in appropriate detail. Fidelity estimation is critical to schoolwide RTI because it follows the scientific dictate for external validity. In other words, if you are implementing wraparound as the tertiary-level intervention process, how can you be sure that what has worked well in Eber's northern Illinois schools will work well for you? Estimating the fidelity with which processes and interventions are applied across settings with psychometrically sound instruments helps to ensure replicability (external validity) of the system.

Through the SIMEO data management system, the tertiary team's actions are guided by an electronic portfolio of information collected from a set of time-tested instruments addressed to evaluation of the lifestyle of the student rather than simply focused on a problem behavior.

SIMEO includes a referral and disposition tool to carefully track the history of engagement of the student with wraparound; a home-school community tool to provide a comprehensive picture of how the student functions in a variety of settings; an educational information tool that captures the student's functioning in school environments; a youth satisfaction tool that gets at the perception of the process from the perspective of the student (when possible); a family or other caregiver satisfaction tool for this perspective; and a survey that is used to evaluate the entire process at phase 4, again from the perspective of the family or other caregiver.

The Critical Importance of Fidelity

Fidelity is one of the key scientific elements of the process that helps to ensure teaching occurs at a high quality. Among the types of fidelity measurement, the one that concerns us here is intervention fidelity. Such a measure identifies the extent to which an educational intervention, behavioral or academic, is carried out faithfully in accordance with the procedures that generated the evidence that the intervention worked for the purpose for which it was designed. High scores on a measure of intervention fidelity ensure that there is a reasonable probability that the intervention will succeed.

The wraparound process captures the essence of the behavioral side of RTI at level 3. It recognizes the need to seriously address the problems presented by a student with extensive behavioral support needs. To fail to address them at school age is to condemn a child to a lifetime of segregation and greatly restricted lifestyle. It is transdisciplinary and empowers families. Finally, it employs methods of science and data-based decision making in determining when to add or subtract supports and services.

Progress monitoring at level 3 interventions for students with internalizing behavior that impedes their learning is, as with level 2, still a work in progress. Students who have been determined through psychoeducational assessments to be eligible for special education supports and services on the basis of having an emotional disability such as childhood schizophrenia or bipolar disorder may have intervention plans that include medication and counseling. Behavioral progress monitoring at level 3 with these students may include portfolios of ongoing assessments by counseling and school psychologists. Measures of academic achievement such as CBMs may be particularly sensitive to level 3 interventions, and thus important supplementary progress monitors for level 3 internalizers.

Obviously there are challenges to progress monitoring assessments with level 3 students who have IEPs. (Or, in some cases, section 504 plans. Section 504 of the Rehabilitation Act provides for services directed to students with chronic health care needs such as hepatitis.) Such students may require extensive plans, including wraparound, with significant family and community provider system involvement. If the primary issue is a severe behavior disorder, then direct measurement of positive behavior support plan progress on a behavioral goal is a necessary component. Students with significant physical issues such as cerebral palsy might be monitored for incremental gains in body mechanics and hand-eye motor coordination geared to the grade-level curriculum. Often the special educator becomes the primary determiner of what services and supports are needed, and the grade-level teacher becomes the expert on how to relate the intervention plan to the grade-level curriculum, no matter how remote the connection, in the early stages. In the case of students with extensive needs for services and supports through special education or section 504 primary health care needs, a documented response to intervention under level 2 may not be required to qualify for an IEP or 504 services.

Academic Progress Monitoring

The difference between screening and progress monitoring is the difference between detecting if a problem exists and evaluating whether an intervention is working. Monitoring student performance occurs across all three levels of RTI and examines the effects of both academic and behavioral interventions. Some tools help to conserve teacher time by providing both functions. DIBELS, for example, can be used to establish grade-level benchmarks for a classroom, determine who is at risk for an emerging or persistent reading problem, gather information on the specific locus of the reading problem, and provide alternate assessment templates for progress monitoring. Alternate templates or forms of the test eliminate the problem of learned carryover from test period to test period, which could lead to a false negative, or failure to identify an ongoing problem where one exists.

CBMs are alternate assessment forms to sample the entire grade-level lesson for the term. Most RTI researchers recommend that CBM progress monitoring occur at least three times a year. CBMs differ from end-of-chapter tests in that tests cover only an aspect of the total curriculum unit. A student's performance may vary from unit to unit each week, making it hard to establish a pattern of performance. CBMs function as an ongoing probe of the overall mastery of the subject matter, apart from single chapter content.

Software programs such as DIBELS, AIMSweb, Edformation, and Intervention CBM Probes allow teachers and RTI teams to quickly and easily examine progress relative to benchmarks of the whole class, groupings within the class (such as students with IEPs or those identified for English as a Second Language interventions), and individual student progress. Many of the software options allow generation and display of graphics that convey much useful information at a glance, for example, comparing each student's performance on a CBM probe with the other probes and with the class as a whole.

In their book, *RTI and Behavior: A Guide to Integrating Behavioral and Academic Supports*, Jeff Sprague, Clayton Cook, Diana Browning Wright, and Carol Sadler describe the relationship of behavior and academics through schoolwide RTI:

> The RTI approach to behavior support uses the identical three-tiered logic that has been adopted for literacy, and this ultimately simplifies the work of schools in both realms—academic and behavioral. If students are having a problem with learning, they are, more likely than not (and sooner or later), going to present problems in behavior, and vice versa. So the effort to screen and support early on both fronts becomes mutually serving for students, families, and educators. The mirrored

three-tiered structures allow schools to continually monitor individual progress for behavioral and academic supports in an integrated and efficient fashion. It is close to self-defeating not to make a serious commitment to both. Clearly, integrating the approaches—from assessment to intervention to progress monitoring—makes the most sense [p. 3].

This concept of integration of processes is critical to a successful schoolwide RTI system. In looking at individual student needs at each of the three levels, it is important to consider the real or potential interaction of behavior and academic achievement. With that in mind, I now move into an examination of progress monitoring directed to academics at each of the three levels of RTI intervention. In later chapters, I provide examples of how these compartmentalized sources of information can be brought together to structure interventions from an integrated perspective.

Level 1 Progress Monitoring

Most research to date on progress monitoring for academic achievement has emerged in the area of reading and language literacy. More recently, tools have begun to emerge addressed to mathematics progress monitoring. Some CBMs exist for writing proficiency and other subject matter, but outside the areas of math and reading, there is little guidance in scientifically grounded progress assessment. Since the purpose of progress monitoring in an RTI system is to inform a team-driven decision process responsible for matching resources to identified student needs, reliability and validity of assessment are important considerations.

Since the purpose of progress monitoring in an RTI system is to inform a team-driven decision process responsible for matching resources to identified student needs, reliability and validity of assessment are important considerations.

The National Association of State Directors of Special Education (2006) in its book *Response to Intervention Policy Considerations and Implementations* (pp. 25–26) listed nine characteristics of assessment procedures that should be in place in order to inform a team decision-making process:

- Directly assess the specific skills embodied in state and local academic standards.
- Assess "marker variables" that have been demonstrated to lead to the ultimate instructional target (e.g., reading comprehension).
- Are sensitive to small increments of growth over time.
- Can be administered efficiently over short periods.
- May be administered repeatedly (using multiple forms).
- Are readily summarized in teacher-friendly data displays.
- Can be used to make comparisons across students.
- Can be used to monitor an individual student's progress over time.
- Have direct relevance to the development of instructional strategies that address the area of need.

The best tools for monitoring student progress are proximal measures—those closest to the day-to-day elements of the classroom curriculum. Assessing progress at year's end is too late for ongoing decision making, and weekly textbook tests are too unreliable to inform ongoing progress monitoring. The solution is found in technologically enhanced CBMs. Some of these tools offer the additional advantage of providing scientifically sound data at the level of screening (baseline data) as well as repeated-measures assessments required for progress monitoring.

Here we look specifically at DIBELS, a tool that screens as well as monitors progress for early literacy reading (preschool through first grade) and oral literacy at first through sixth grades, and AIMSweb, which is particularly sensitive to RTI decision-making data requirements and offers specific student management information geared to tracking students within and across RTI levels. AIMSweb provides a set of comparable progress monitoring assessment forms for grade levels paralleling DIBELS and extends to grade 8 for some literacy assessments. (Readers interested in detailed information with examples on uses of DIBELS, AIMSweb, and other CBMs for progress monitoring should consider the excellent books on RTI by Susan Hall written for principals and by Rachel Brown-Chidsey and Mark W. Steege for classroom teachers.)

The timing of progress monitoring assessments is open to debate. Some recommend assessments as frequently as every two weeks. As Hall points out, however, progress monitoring at level 1 falls to an already overburdened teacher. Two assessments per month may be too frequent. Others recommend a frequency of three times per year, which may be too spread out to lead to timely decisions to correct emerging problems. In level 1 universal applications, a percentage of students in a class will make expected benchmark performance without extraordinary attention from the teacher. Those at issue for progress monitoring are the students who were determined to be at potential risk on the basis of the screening assessments. My recommendation is to use flexibility in decisions around level 1 progress monitoring for academics and tailor assessment frequency to perceived degree of risk (for level 2 interventions). Students considered most at risk should be monitored most frequently: at least twice per month.

Level 2 Progress Monitoring

The estimated percentages of students who need level 2 interventions vary as a function of demographics. In my experience, suburban middle-class schools may have as few as 15 percent of students at each grade level who require frequent progress monitoring in one or more subject areas. In urban core schools, the number can exceed 50 percent in the initial stages of RTI implementation.

The purpose of level 2 interventions is to provide additional supports to students who fail to achieve benchmarks (expected achievement levels) through high-quality instruction, including differentiated instruction, using a curriculum grounded in science with progress monitoring for all students in the level 1 grade-level classroom. The question for the teacher at level 1 is, "Can I find a way to motivate [or teach] Susan, who is falling way below benchmark in math, before committing to engaging the resources of the RTI team to begin level 2 interventions?" Research shows that often simply tweaking the level 1 process for behavior, academics, or often both can bring students to benchmark performance in the absence of extraordinary interventions. In classrooms using collaborative teaching models such as Marilyn Friend's *The Power of Two*, the perspective of a highly trained special educator can be particularly useful in solving level 1 problems.

How to deliver level 1 interventions is a matter of choice among several alternatives and is an important target for ongoing RTI research. I will return to the issue of available interventions in later chapters, but for now, the options vary from conceiving of level 2 interventions as additional instructional time (for example, add thirty additional minutes to the level 1 schedule of ninety minutes for a literacy module, using a small group format), to focusing more on creative deployment of personnel and resources within the grade-level classroom and with the use of additional space for small targeted groups of students.

Levels 2 and 3 are always considered to be temporary and supplemental to level 1 instruction. The goal for all students is progress at benchmarks in level 1, although for some students in level 3 supports, usually those with extensive needs for support from special education or section 504 resources, this goal may be unrealizable but valuable nonetheless in guiding interventions. Level 2 is therefore a transitional level and thus in need of frequent progress monitoring. Use of CBMs at two-week assessment periods for level 2 interventions is recommended; however, schools with large numbers of students in need of level 2 supports may find it difficult to assess more frequently than monthly. The rule is, the more the better. However, there is a caveat: frequent assessment is valuable only if the teacher and the RTI team have been trained in data management and data-based decision making. Some of my most depressing moments in schools have come while gazing at "data walls" and looking at quantities of DIBELS progress results that have not led to any program adjustments other than to be displayed.

These guidelines should be kept in mind while progress monitoring at level 2:

- Until research clearly validates CBMs beyond math and reading, stick with these assessments for decisions about interventions and movement across levels.

- Consider data from multiple sources in making decisions. CBMs are the primary source of evidence for progress, but criterion-referenced tests, classroom textbook quizzes, parental reports, and data from after-school tutoring programs, among others, are important supplemental sources. (Teachers interested in developing their own progress-monitoring tools for supplemental information may wish to check out www.informationcentral.org for resources and ideas.)

- Integrate findings from behavioral as well as academic sources to form a basis for decision making. More than a few times, I have seen students return to benchmark performance in reading following a simple functional behavioral assessment and a shift in differentiated instruction strategies when all along, it was assumed that the student's problems were in the mechanics of reading.

- Keep in mind the distinction between learning and performance. Sometimes falling below benchmark is a problem of motivation leading to a decrement in performance rather than a failure to understand and thus to learn.

- Scheduling is a major issue in achieving a well-run schoolwide RTI program. Space must be identified for small group breakout sessions, personnel identified for supplementing level 2 instruction, and consideration given to the makeup of groups (for example, cross-grade or ability level). Special education should not be the sole support provider in all cases.

- Consider the power of peer-mediated instruction in level 2 interventions. Peer problem solving can lead to breakthroughs for struggling students. Research increasingly supports the finding that children sometimes learn as much or more from their classmates who have achieved mastery than they do from adults. Peer-mediated instruction should be a factor in determining the makeup of level 2 intervention groups.

Level 3 Progress Monitoring

Schoolwide RTI has essentially developed from the base of the pyramid upward. The process started in earnest with NCLB and its focus on school accountability measured by distal estimators of student achievement. The Reading First initiative laid much of the groundwork for level 1 screening, progress monitoring, and classroom-based interventions. Level 2 components are in the stage of emerging development, with active research projects, many funded by the Institute of Education Science. Level 3 is in its infancy, particularly on the academic side.

To complicate the issue, there are differing schools of thought on processes for determining who should be provided level 3 supports and which services and support systems should be engaged. Some would argue that special education should be the sole provider of services and interventions at level 3. In other words, any student being considered for level 3 engagement should undergo a full evaluation for special education services.

A different viewpoint on level 3 is offered by Susan Hall in her book, directed to principals. She writes, "In most schools, Tier III is not special education but is more intensive intervention to try to improve the progress and avoid the necessity of placement in special education" (p. 68). This version of level 3 is also reflected in *RTI and Behavior*, by Sprague, Cook, Browning Wright, and Sadler. I side with this perspective largely because of my orientation toward collaborative teaching at grade level between general and special educators. Ownership of level 3 tends to reinforce the separateness of special education and could, under RTI, perpetuate the conception of the service system as a place for high-intensity needs students rather than a service with expertise that can be brought to bear in problem solving at all three levels.

> *Ownership of level 3 tends to reinforce the separateness of special education and could, under RTI, perpetuate the conception of the service system as a place for high-intensity needs students, rather than a service with expertise that can be brought to bear in problem solving at all three levels.*

Susan Hall seems to me to get it right when she defines *intensity* as the way that a concept is taught. Instructional staff under this idea create scaffolding for a student that consists of the sum of extraordinary supports and services that are required to enable the student to progress toward benchmarks in level 2. She writes, "Providing more repetition cycles and more corrective feedback can intensify instruction. Increasing the amount and types of cues and prompts also helps. The teacher will gradually remove scaffolding until the student can demonstrate mastery" (p. 69). What Hall is describing here is simply individualized, differentiated instruction in a context of supplementary supports. General educators can and should engage this kind of level 3 intervention rather than deciding it is the purview of special education. Best is when the two professionals collaborate and with input from the tertiary team formulate the scaffolding in a level 3 plan.

Level 3 progress monitoring for academics needs to be multifaceted, unique to each child to a degree, and frequent. Those who advocate for additional minutes of instruction for level 2 interventions similarly advocate for more additional minutes, typically sixty to ninety, for students receiving level 3 supports. My view is that additional instructional time may well be needed, but a more important consideration may be the nature of the intervention and supplementary supports. For our purposes here, a key component of level 3 academic interventions needs to be frequent progress monitoring.

The following important questions must be addressed by a tertiary team:

- Is the student falling drastically behind benchmark levels in a single subject area, or is the problem manifest across the board?

- Have level 2 interventions been determined on the basis of data to be failing to correct the downward slide?

- Are there social and behavioral issues identified from screening or levels 1 or 2 assessments that need to be monitored in addition to the academic problem?

- Does the sum of existing assessments and progress monitoring point to a need for full evaluation for special education if the student does not have an IEP in place?

- Have all sources of available information, including consultation with the family and contacts with external community agencies, been exhausted?

- Have issues of familial culture, community living circumstances, and native language been taken into full consideration?

Schoolwide RTI models vary greatly on their conceptions of interventions and assessments at level 3. For some models, level 3 is a continuation of level 2 with simply additional minutes of instruction in deficit areas. For other models, it is automatic referral for special education placement. In the absence of research-based decision rules with which to guide decisions about movements across levels, levels-of-engagement decisions should grow out of the discourse of duly constituted teams made up of professionals, including parents where possible, who bring a variety of training histories, knowledge, skills, and perspectives to bear on the problem.

Moving to Level 3

Admission to level 3 should be a big deal. Level 3 implies a concentration of services and supports and lots of individualization of educational processes, and it is likely to be costly and time-consuming. It should come into play when it is clear from data that neither grade-level classroom instruction (level 1) nor supplementary supports in a context of small group instruction (level 2) can provide the student with the ability to reverse course and make progress toward benchmark levels. A decision to move to level 3 engagement under schoolwide RTI should originate in a grade-level team discussion, follow a written recommendation from the school's RTI team, and undergo a written plan developed by a tertiary-level interventions team. Progress monitoring should be geared directly to the objectives listed in the tertiary intervention (level 3) plan.

Progress monitoring using CBMs should continue at level 3, with frequency of assessment occurring at least once every two weeks. If the intervention plan calls for multiple small group sessions including those occurring in after-school programs, fidelity of intervention needs to be assessed. In level 3 engagement, everyone needs to be working together so that the student experiences consistency in the teaching-learning process. Specific individualized assessments to supplement CBM results will be helpful to the tertiary interventions team in evaluating the ongoing success, or lack thereof, of the intervention plan. Finally, if the tertiary intervention plan specifies interventions for both behavior and academics, a wraparound plan may be warranted. If so, comprehensive data management systems such as SIMEO may be expanded to include CBM and individualized data sets reflecting academic interventions.

Table 5.1 summarizes behavioral and academic progress monitoring data sources at each RTI level of engagement.

RTI and the Organization of Services and Supports

The role of special education in newer schoolwide RTI models is becoming more complex. Early RTI applications essentially deeded over level 3 to special education. Under these models, special education was for the most part not a presence at levels 1 and 2 (academic or behavioral), and general education was not to be seen at level 3. Under these models, special education was as much a place as a comprehensive set of services and supports, since many students with IEPs were either pulled out into special-purpose rooms for much of the education day or were served in separate special education classrooms.

In my opinion, special education is an essential component of schoolwide RTI at all three levels. Collaborative teaching involving general and special educators is an essential component of RTI at all three levels. If special educators are in modular units in the parking lot or in basement classrooms they are unavailable

Table 5.1   Progress Monitoring Sources at Each Level of RTI

Behavioral	Academics
SSBD screening assessments	DIBELS screening assessments
Level 1	Level 1
Office disciplinary referrals	Benchmark assessments from grade-level curricula
	Infrequent curriculum-based measure assessments using DIBELS or AIMSweb
Level 2	Level 2
Social Sciences Behavior Scales (SSBS)	Frequent curriculum-based measures
Direct observational measures	Direct measures from specific interventions
Level 3	Level 3
Comprehensive, multisource assessment inventories (SIMEO)	Very frequent curriculum-based measure (CBM) assessments
	Direct measures from specific interventions
	Sources of data from families and community-based agencies

to large numbers of other students who could benefit from their highly specialized expertise while they work with the grade-level teacher to address the support needs of students with IEPs in the general education classroom. For that reason, plus a glaring lack of scientific evidence in support of positive academic or social gains from separate classroom instruction, I recommend operating school-wide RTI models without having any separate special education classrooms.

That said, appropriate educational delivery for students who require extensive services and supports from the day they arrive at school becomes an important consideration for RTI team planning. Students with severe disabilities are almost always served in special classes in traditionally operated schools. General education teachers argue appropriately that they have not been trained to work at grade level with such students, and special educators often argue, again appropriately, that they do not know the general education curriculum.

Under schoolwide RTI, there is an opportunity for categorical teachers to learn from each other and impart an improved educational delivery to all students. This process can be difficult and time-consuming in its early phases but with a significant payoff after the transition is complete. I know of no teachers, out of hundreds at this point, who would agree to go back to special classroom instruction after having become proficient in a coteaching arrangement. Issues of providing appropriate educational services, support, and instruction to students with extensive special needs become focused on deployment of personnel and efficient use of school space. Such students may spend some time in the general education classroom, some time in smaller groups for special-purpose instruction outside the grade-level classroom, and perhaps some time off-site in community-based instruction such as learning to use public transportation or to make purchases from a store.

To Sum Up

This chapter has examined progress monitoring as a key feature of schoolwide RTI. Using scientifically established measurement tools to evaluate effects of teaching interventions on student performance is a logical outgrowth of the emphasis on school accountability that has been a key feature of NCLB and IDEIA. The nature of RTI-related assessment tools and processes was examined, along the lines of several dimensions: proximal (near term), distal (far term), formative (interventions), and summative (student outcomes); and categorical (single source) and aggregate (multiple sources). Types of progress monitoring data from integrated protocols (behavior and academics) were discussed as curriculum-based measures; norm-referenced measures and individualized sources of data.

The behavioral side of RTI at level 1 is typically progress monitored with frequency of office disciplinary referrals. At level 2 in schools we work with, SSBS is used with direct measures of behavior change resulting from a planned behavioral intervention. Level 3 progress monitoring requires comprehensive assessments spanning a wide variety of sources and interventions. We use the SIMEO system from Illinois.

Progress monitoring for academic interventions uses ongoing benchmark assessments for all students at level 1 together with infrequent CBMs. We use DIBELS and AIMSweb. At level 2, academic monitoring is done with more frequent CBM assessments supplemented with individualized assessments related to specific interventions. At level 3, very frequent CBM assessments are used with additional sources of data from specific interventions and possibly from parent and community-based sources of information.

6

Sustaining RTI Through
School Reform

Amerian education is an amazingly unstable system, nearly always in a state of flux, besieged by critics on all sides. Nowhere is this instability more apparent than in urban schools. Big city superintendents are tracked like college graduates in the NBA draft. If one lasts on the job more than five years, it is considered a minor miracle.

Furthermore, urban school boards are highly political, often consisting of elected or appointed representatives of a variety of demographically determined special interest groups. Often ethnic politics are at issue, with community tensions reflected in school board decisions pitting the perceived interests of one ethnic group over another.

All of this tension contributes to instability. When a new superintendent comes in, the former programs of his or her predecessor are often out the door, and teachers as well as building administrators must come to grips with a new reality. New programs are put in place, and the cycle moves on, through stages of initial anger, followed by resignation to the inevitable, followed in turn by hopeful regeneration of energy and commitment, and ultimately, in most cases, concluding with disappointment when the new third- or fourth-year annual grade-level assessments fail to show change in the right direction.

Since for the past two decades I have spent virtually all of my research, training, and technical assistance hours in urban core schools, I have become intimately familiar with the reasons that schools fail. Some will say it is because poor African American or Latino/a children cannot learn at the level of benchmarks set for more affluent Caucasian students. In fact, this racial disparity hypothesis has been disproved repeatedly in cities around the country. Showcase schools with low-income, primarily Latino/a, students exist in South Central Los Angeles where the annual assessment scores at grade level are far above the California state average and well ahead of mostly Caucasian affluent schools in West Los Angeles.

Consider Unified School District 500, Kansas City, Kansas Public Schools, for example. Kansas City, Kansas (KCK) is the heart of Wyandotte County, Kansas, a former free-slave port for blacks fortunate enough to escape the slave block at Westport, Missouri, before the Civil War. Wyandotte County is one of the lowest per capita income counties in the United States. Yet White Church Elementary School in KCK, a multicultural school with 80 percent eligibility for free and reduced-lunch participation, became the highest-performing public elementary school in Kansas in 2005 and was recognized by President Bush as one of the top two hundred or so schools in the nation. Students of all colors and including students with individualized education programs were approaching 100 percent at or above proficient in math and literacy in that year. White Church Elementary has since undergone changes in administration, including its lead academic coach and principal. The students' test results have, however, bounced back to close to the results obtained in 2005, a fact that suggests that the "magic" at White Church has sustainability. It is engrained in the culture of the school. I will say more about this "magic" a bit further on in the chapter when I describe the Schoolwide Applications Model (SAM).

> *White Church Elementary School in Kansas City, Kansas, a multicultural school with 80 percent eligibility for free and reduced-lunch participation, became the highest-performing public elementary school in 2005.*

With the rapidly changing demography of most American communities, these more traditional woes of urban schools are now becoming endemic to American schools in general. The point is that the failure of urban education cannot be blamed on the students. Neither can it be blamed on poverty, although poverty greatly complicates the process. Given a level playing field, African Americans, Latino/as, Pacific Islanders, Native Americans, and any other ethnic group can demonstrate that they can learn as well as anyone else given certain circumstances. Those circumstances are what concern us now in contemplating a systems change engagement to move to schoolwide RTI.

Challenges Confronting Schoolwide RTI

Two substantive challenges must be overcome in any plan to put a full-blown schoolwide RTI model in place in any school. The first is the silo. Desiloization (my term for fully integrating general, special, and second-language teaching) is no simple matter. In our school reform model, SAM, we are finding that the process takes three to five years, even with full district-level support.

The second major challenge is what I describe as stable human capital. To achieve sustainability of a major systems change agenda requires that some key players and stakeholders be involved from the planning stages to full-scale implementation. Turnover in key leadership positions at the school, as well as the district levels, can doom the enterprise before it can come to fruition.

Silos Revisited

The two sturdiest silos in any traditionally organized school are general and special education. General education is a large silo, say metaphorically about ninety feet tall. Special education is much shorter, usually about ten feet, but much thicker, making the task of taking it down much harder. In my view, this has to do with the separateness with which teacher training programs prepare new teachers at the preservice level.

At many large universities, special educators are prepared in a separate department within the college or school of education. In fact, general and special educators at the preservice level take very few, if any, of each other's courses. Not only that, but when I interview newly graduated grade-level teachers, I learn that they were specifically taught that when a child falls behind benchmark performance, the solutions are to refer to special education and seek an alternative placement. Conversely, special education master's students are often taught that their students can best be educated in self-contained classrooms. The fact is that higher education institutions have been very slow to come around to any pressures to blend programs at the departmental level. Smaller teacher training programs are able to adapt more quickly since they rarely have enough student enrollment to justify the expensive overhead of a wholly separate departmental structure.

Sustainability of schoolwide RTI depends on a successful transition away from siloized teachers, programs, and, in my view, classrooms. The preservice silo training problem will eventually resolve itself but probably not until fully integrated systems are in place at a critical mass in the nation's schools. So resolution of this challenge will necessarily lie, in the short term, with in-service personnel preparation, now generally called *professional development*. (The term *staff development* is increasingly applied to in-service training for nonteaching school resource personnel.)

University Structures for Teacher Education

Large university schools of education often reflect a paradox: much of their research output is directed to advancing a more fully integrated service delivery system in the school, while at the same time, their teacher training programs are directed to maintaining separate structures. The reasons for this paradox are largely economic. Research dollars flow mainly from government and philanthropic sources whose policies are focused on solving problems through innovation and systems change. Student enrollment dollars, however, are significant contributions to funding faculty positions and teacher training courses. Schools of education dole these dollars out to departments based largely on their student enrollments. In other words, the health of a department of special education will be largely determined by how many students it can attract to take its courses, and the more courses, the better. The prospect of blending training programs at the preservice level can look to a department faculty as a certain financial loser with some threatening implications for job security among teaching faculty.

Human Capital

The second substantive challenge to sustainability has to do with the fact that teachers and other building staff bring a wide range of attitudes, experiences, knowledge, and psychology to bear on any systems change effort. The term "human capital" emerged during the Ronald Reagan era at the start of our country's fascination with corporations and workings of big time capitalism. Just as money ("venture capital") greases the machinery to get a large scale renovation underway in a market enterprise, so do human qualities of the workers involved come to the fore as an investment opportunity. Failure to pay attention to the well-being, competence, and dedication of the workforce can doom an enterprise. Whether a massive systems change effort such as schoolwide RTI comes about or melts down may well depend on the investments made at the level of human capital.

Professional Development

Professional and staff development opportunities are essential elements of systems change and transformation to a schoolwide RTI program. In my view, sustainability of RTI (or any other systems-level transformation) will be strongly dependent on the quality and durability of professional and staff development.

Planning is essential to ensuring quality and durability. The worst kind of professional development is, unfortunately, the one with which we are all familiar. Many teachers converge, usually on a summer day or a Saturday and listen to a motivational speaker, often one who relies on humor to warm up the audience. Teachers then move into breakout sessions, discuss key topics among themselves, nominate someone to represent the group's discussion later, and break for lunch. Lunch is often accompanied by another speaker with high name recognition. More small group discussions follow in the afternoon, which concludes with a panel session where breakout group representatives share the findings from their respective groups. The day concludes with a summary presentation with questions and answers from the audience. Participants then depart, often with a special bag commemorating the occasion, a notebook, and a CD with instructions on how to proceed following the training.

The problem with this kind of activity is that it lacks quality and durability. The notebooks usually sit on shelves in classrooms and the CDs in desk drawers. When busy teachers finally find a moment to review the materials, too much time has gone by, and recapturing the mechanics of the process becomes too tedious, particularly if technology is involved.

The preferred alternative to this kind of training is longitudinal, mentored professional engagement. Teachers like to get together and have fun, so there is nothing inherently wrong in large group sessions, but there needs to be more. Coaches who have already been trained in the innovative process guide the problem-solving discussion in the breakout sessions, which produce action plans for phase-by-phase implementation of the innovation. Following the general session, coaches mentor teachers in putting together the steps of their school's action plan. This multiphase process ensures durability, a major contributor to sustainability of practice.

To come back to the problem of deconstructing professional silos, the premise begins with a dedication to undertake the difficult, expensive, and time-consuming process of systems change by taking steps to ensure against meltdown. We all, I'm sure, have witnessed seemingly good ideas gain a start within a school, only to get sidetracked when something newer surfaced. But schoolwide RTI is far too comprehensive a systems change endeavor and holds far too much potential to make a meaningful difference in the lives of teachers and students to be allowed to fail to reach fruition because of poor planning. Professional and staff development must be at the heart of the planning process.

> *To come back to the problem of deconstructing professional silos, the premise begins with a dedication to undertake the difficult, expensive, and time-consuming process of systems change by taking steps to ensure against meltdown.*

Every school has its own unique culture, so one-size-fits-all systems change models are doomed to fail in any effort to institute them in all schools in the district. These efforts are always up against the human quality of buy-in: the motivation that any member of a school organization brings to the initial planning and implementation processes. If a critical mass of teachers in a school do not buy in to the systems change effort proposed by the principal or, more likely, the district central office, the plan will not proceed in a desirable direction. Buy-in is often an artifact of empowerment. If my department chair tells me that I need to use more technology in my teaching and directs me to a professional development activity on teaching-technology enhancements, I may or may not buy in. But if my opinions are solicited on ways to improve university instruction and one or two of my ideas find their way into a teaching-enhancement proposal, my motivation to buy in to the proposed process is quite likely to increase. At least I have some ownership of and vested interest in the success of the endeavor if I contributed to the planning process.

One implication for professional development of school culture and professional buy-in is the need to build flexibility into the training process. School districts always have priorities for what teachers need to know and do. The vehicle for imparting these priorities is district-directed professional development. Schools, however, by virtue of their unique cultures, also have their priorities. This necessitates another kind of training activity: school-directed professional development.

Consider the case of a school district that decides at the top of the administrative ladder, with the blessing of the state education agency and the local school board, to take schoolwide RTI to scale in the district. If there are, say, one hundred schools, the level of systems change is massive. Out of the one hundred, some subset of the school's personnel will caucus with their principals and with enthusiasm ask, "Can we go first?" A large block in the middle will take a passive wait-and-see posture, and another subset will quietly say, "This too shall pass. Count me out."

School-directed professional development will play an important role in generating buy-in at the level of the school. Different schools have different priorities depending on the knowledge and competency base of their personnel. If there are ten major components to the systems change agenda, five or six of those can belong to district-level planning initiatives. The remaining four or five, however, should result from school-level planning. The district wanting to take schoolwide RTI to scale in a hundred schools will be wise to generate discussion at the school and community levels and then solicit volunteer participation from schools to begin the process in cohorts. Let the schools prioritize their training needs through their action planning process and gain access to school-level professional development sessions, as well as have their staff participate in the district-level sessions. Adequate time should be planned for the process (plan on years) and budgeting considerations built into the long-range plan. Finally, opportunities should be created for cohorts of schools to come together in retreats to engage in information sharing and joint problem solving. Sustainability will rest in part on maintaining the enthusiasm and dedication of the teaching staff.

School Reform as a Context for RTI

School reform is a catchall term that encompasses all policy-driven efforts to make schools perform better as measured by student standardized achievement scores in math, science, and literacy. Today's school reform policy originated in Congress following the 1983 publication of *A Nation at Risk* by the National Commission on Excellence in Education, which encompassed numerous tables and charts reflecting downward trends on the part of American students compared to other developed nations, particularly in math and science. This report of extensive Carnegie-funded research had the net effect of raising a long-term specter of the United States falling into third-world status due to an inability to compete in the global marketplace. Under this scenario, a failure of public education would lead to a sacrifice of our traditional competitive edge.

In the mid-1980s, public education was a high priority for government social policy, and large-scale school reform efforts were launched to begin to correct the problem. Now, two and a half decades later, the competitive edge theory has faded, largely due to the emergence of private and quasi-private charter schools and their substantial enrollment of former urban public school students of more affluent means. Since urban and even suburban public schools increasingly are demographically more multicultural and private schools are largely Caucasian middle and upper class, the policy driver has begun to shift back to the earlier civil rights agenda following *Brown* v. *Board of Education of Topeka* in the 1950s.

Comprehensive School Reform Demonstration Project

The most ambitious of the various waves of school reform efforts stemming from the federal government came during the Clinton administration in the 1990s. Called the Comprehensive School Reform Demonstration Program, this large-scale effort invested millions of dollars in mostly urban schools, naming a few prominent school reformers, such as Robert Slavin of Johns Hopkins and Henry Levin of Columbia University, in a kind of "menu" framework in which school districts could receive large grants if the chosen developer would agree to commit to a multiyear effort through partnering with the district. In most cases, large local foundations provided a match for the federal funds, creating a sizable source of additional revenue directed to reform efforts. Because most of the prominent school reformers of the period pretty much agreed on the same core components (for example, instituting smaller learning communities within large schools), it almost did not matter which developer worked with which district, as long as he or she was on the approved list.

From 1996 to 2006, approximately six thousand schools serving millions of students used federal funds, sometimes matched by private sources, to create more than five hundred different comprehensive school reform (CSR) models. But by 2006, it was becoming clear that the movement was not succeeding in terms of achieving scientifically acceptable student outcomes. Today, several of the more innovative practices growing out of the CSR era have become standard practice in many schools, such as grade-level teams, smaller learning communities at the secondary level, and family partnership programs.

In my view, the CSR approach in general had two serious flaws in the manner in which the federal grants required models to be implemented by districts. First was a lack of attention to nonschool factors that have a direct impact on the teaching-learning process. These factors include health issues and issues of social development such as those that affect children who grow up in poverty. Children must arrive at school ready to learn. Schools alone cannot be the sole target of reform efforts if they are to have a chance of succeeding. Home and community are key players in the education process. Some CSR models call for parent outreach efforts, but sharing information with parents is not the same as parent empowerment: engaging with parents in an interactive way to enhance the education of the child. Only the community school movement (www.communityschools.org) grasped the importance of community and family engagement, but to my knowledge, it was never one of the CSR options.

The second factor that may have brought about the end of the CSR movement (at least the federal support for it) is that in implementation, it was imposed on schools by the district as a top-down mandate. Schools are busy organizations with their own unique structures and cultures. A top-down mandate might achieve results with schools that believe in the process and whose professional communities buy in to the process from the outset. The schools for which the reform model resonates get the best results as a model becomes enculturated at the site. Unfortunately, positive results from a subset of schools in a large district will not be sufficient to approach a standard of scientific acceptability.

A Universal Design for Learning

In 2008, the question that abounded at educational conferences was, "What's next?" The school restructuring movement of the 1980s produced little by way of reversing the declining progress of urban schools. The CSR movement is winding down with only a glimmering of success with one or two models. One answer to the question may be in moving to a universal design for learning (UDL) approach. UDL approaches systems change and curriculum development with the intent of ensuring that all students, representing a wide spectrum of learning strengths and challenges, successfully engage the general curriculum beginning at each student's point of contact with that curriculum. Differentiated instruction is a key UDL concept and includes a multiple means of teaching (referred to as multimodal), multiple means of expression (such as oral and written tests), and multiple means of student engagement (including finding motivational enticements for students to tackle difficult material).

> *The school restructuring movement of the 1980s produced little by way of reversing the declining progress of urban schools. The CSR movement is winding down with only a glimmering of success with one or two models.*

Schoolwide RTI, then, becomes a process of building in scientifically acceptable measures and decision rules for linking resources to measured student needs in order to fully activate the UDL framework to guide teaching and learning. There is no one-size-fits-all top-down mandate, but rather a set of guiding principles and critical features that can be enculturated through discourse (team processes) and new knowledge (professional and staff development). The result is a scaffold of structural elements directed to boost student achievement through resources within the school, as well as within the surrounding community, and certainly including family or other primary caregivers.

So I would answer the "What's next?" question by calling for public policy initiatives directed to assisting schools to engage family and community partnerships and to fully integrate all of their resources, including special education and English Language Learner programs, into a universal design for learning that will enable all students to benefit academically and socially.

The Schoolwide Applications Model

My colleague, Blair Roger, and I began in 2003 to assist the Ravenswood City School District in East Palo Alto, California, to implement the Schoolwide Applications Model (SAM), a model of this type. Ravenswood is now at scale with the process in all eleven district schools and has enculturated the system. Whether SAM helps to produce the level of student progress required to meet scientifically acceptable standards is a matter to be decided by the editorial review boards of scientific journals, a process that is in the works as this book is being written.

SAM is a comprehensive, schoolwide RTI model that encompasses the principles of UDL. It offers schools a set of processes to enable them to accomplish the systems change transformation at their own pace. Schools proceed by setting their own priorities for which critical features to engage at the outset and which ones to tackle later.

Portions of the background research that led to the SAM framework arose from a series of experiments by University of Kansas researchers in partnership with USD 500, Kansas City, Kansas, public schools. Much of this work was done at White Church Elementary School, mentioned earlier in the chapter. Schoolwide positive behavior support was a key element in previously low-performing schools. This ten-year program of research on schoolwide positive behavior support (SWPBS), inclusive educational practices, data-based decision processes, and literacy enhancement provided a solid basis in research with which to begin to construct a fully integrated universal design application that might be replicable in schools elsewhere in the country.

Meanwhile, Blair Roger had been working as an educational consultant to southern California school districts seeking to increase inclusive educational practices with students requiring extra supports and services under IDEA. This led to a series of discussions about combining her insights from working with low-performing, high-poverty schools with our findings from a decade of ongoing research in similar schools into a comprehensive school reform model. This model, which became SAM, differs from its predecessors by adopting insights from educational anthropology in addition to behavioral psychology and focuses on school culture as a critical variable in accomplishing systems change. Much of this initial series of discussions was strongly influenced by the writings of Michael Fullan, a University of Toronto professor.

Fidelity of Implementation

It is one thing to come up with a complex, organized set of operations that make up a school reform package, and another thing to see these operations carried out in practice by implementing schools. I walked into a high school recently in a southern city and saw a prominent banner hanging in the school's front office proclaiming that it was a school that followed a particular CSR model. When I asked the principal, who was about to show me around the school, what the banner signified, he replied, "Beats me! It was hanging there when I took this job two years ago, and I never got around to taking it down."

> *When I asked the principal, who was about to show me around the school, what the banner signified, he replied, "Beats me! It was hanging there when I took this job two years ago, and I never got around to taking it down."*

In anthropological terms, the banner is an artifact representing a past cultural influence that is no longer in place. I have had the same experience in schools that in previous years had undergone extensive professional and staff development in schoolwide positive behavior support. The schools still had the "Be Safe, Be Responsible, and Be Respectful" signs on the walls, but no one, including the students, could remember their purpose and implications for teaching and learning.

Sustainability is a matter of enculturation of a set of practices. An organized set of operations that works must be implemented with fidelity if replication elsewhere is to occur and have a chance to succeed. Failure of fidelity of implementation will inevitably lead to that oft-repeated maxim of public education: "Oh, yeah. We tried that once. It didn't work."

SAM Fidelity Assessment Tool

With this cautionary note firmly in mind, Blair and I started the SAM process with a fidelity-of-implementation instrument called the Schoolwide Applications Model analysis tool (SAMAN). We knew that schools would undertake the total systems change package uniquely, with each setting different priorities as to how to progress toward total implementation. With literally hundreds of possible indicators to track, we decided to pick a manageable number, fifteen in this case, that we felt would sample the most challenging and difficult aspects of the transformation. We constructed the tool such that trained assessors could spend a full day in a school and, through interviews with key informants, records searches, observations of practices, and participation in team meetings, would rate each of fifteen critical feature statements on a Likert scale from 0 to 3. A score of 0 would indicate the school had yet to undertake that element of the transformation. A score of 3 would indicate full implementation of that process. The list that follows presents the fifteen SAMAN critical features. Each of these features is an indicator of overall SAM progress and each comes with an operational definition (i.e., what to look for to arrive at a score) and sources of information to pursue to score the item (i.e., principal interview).

Schoolwide Applications Model (SAM) Critical Features

1. School serves all students.
2. All students at school are considered general education students.
3. General education teachers assume responsibility for all students at the school.
4. School is inclusive of all students for all classroom and school functions.
5. School is organized to provide all specialized supports, adaptations and accommodations to students in such a way as to maximize the number of students who will benefit.
6. All students are taught in accordance with the general curriculum.
7. The school has an active, schoolwide Positive Behavior Support (SWPBS) program operating at all 3 levels.
8. The school is a data-driven, collaborative decision-making, learning organization with all major functions guided by team process.
9. School effectively utilizes general education students in instruction of students in need of supports in all instructional environments.
10. All personnel at the school participate in the teaching/learning processes and are valued for their respective contributions to pupil academic and social outcomes.
11. School personnel use a uniform, non-categorical lexicon to describe both personnel and teaching/learning functions.

12. School has established a Site Leadership Team (SLT) empowered by the school and the district to implement SAM at the school.

13. School has working partnership with families of students who attend the school.

14. School has working partnership with its community businesses and service providers.

15. SAM implementation at the school site is fully recognized and supported by the district.

These assessments under the SAM process occur once each semester and, averaged across the fifteen critical features, produce a total scale score that can be tracked over three to five years to show each school's progress toward full implementation. The pattern of scores across features following each assessment helps the site leadership team at the school prioritize its SAM action plan objectives for the next semester.

Intervention Fidelity Versus Implementation Fidelity

Fidelity of implementation is a core component of schoolwide RTI. Chapter Five examined one type of fidelity estimation: that directed to interventions. Whereas intervention fidelity estimates the faithfulness with which specific educational interventions are carried out by teachers, implementation fidelity estimates the integrity with which an entire systems change process is implemented.

SAMAN is a fidelity estimator for implementation processes in accomplishing a full-blown RTI school reform agenda. Read 180, by contrast, is a level 2 academic intervention to enhance language and literacy that has a built-in intervention fidelity tool. For it to succeed, reading interventionists must stick to the procedures that are grounded in scientific research in order to give the intervention a fair test. Skipping operations or differing from protocol compromises the research grounding of the intervention and may fail to produce expected results. The Read 180 fidelity estimation tool helps to ensure the process is carried out according to specifications.

To estimate the fidelity of SAM processes, we elected to sample indicators associated with the most difficult (and most tempting to defer or skip) operations: (1) dismantling silos, particularly special education; (2) integrating all supports and resources; (3) improving scope and quality of instruction; (4) using progress monitoring data to make intervention decisions; (5) forging strong educational linkages with families and other caregivers and with community agencies and businesses; and (6) interacting effectively with the district through team processes to ensure adequate supports and services are in place.

The last indicator, critical feature 15 (see preceding list), takes the unusual step of holding SAM schools accountable for getting the district on board with SAM requirements. We did this in recognition that the correct unit of analysis for school reform is the individual school. Schools can undergo systems change more rapidly and efficiently than can districts. Districts are much more likely to respond to a critical mass of schools nudging them toward a reenculturation to embrace the full implications of a schoolwide RTI school reform system than they are likely to respond to advice (and cajoling) from outside technical assistants. Districts, as it turns out, also have their unique cultures. Replicability of a successful school reform model depends to a large degree on its becoming part of the district's business as usual.

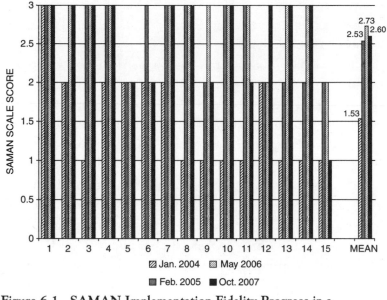

Figure 6.1   SAMAN Implementation Fidelity Progress in a Ravenswood School

Figure 6.1 reflects the progress on fidelity of implementing of one of the schools in the Ravenswood City School District. Each of the clusters of bar graphs represents a SAMAN assessment at that school on each of the fifteen critical features and, on the right side of the chart, the average of the fifteen for each assessment. The SAMAN tool has good psychometrics thus far, meaning that trained assessors can independently assess a school and come up with at least 80 percent agreement on the score for each feature and the total (average) score. Psychometrics of a tool consists in part of at least two scientific criteria. The first estimates the reliability with which the tool measures indicators of critical features of the overall concept (or theory of change). Interrater agreement, whereby two independent assessors score the same phenomenon the same, is one way to ascertain reliability of measurement. This tells us the extent to which we can have confidence that the instrument is faithfully estimating progress of implementation. A standard cutoff point for scientific acceptability is 80 percent. SAMAN thus far averages above 90 percent interrater agreement on data collected when new assessors have been trained.

The second key component of psychometrics is concerned with the validity of the measurement. This component is directed to the question, "How do we know that the tool measures what it is supposed to measure?" SAMAN is, for example, supposed to estimate progress in implementation of SAM, an RTI school reform model. Thus far, we have chosen to estimate validity by examining the relationship of SAMAN assessments with measured estimates of progress on SWPBS. Since SWPBS has a tool (the Schoolwide Evaluation Tool, or SET, for tier 1) with scientifically grounded psychometrics and since SAM includes the behavioral side of RTI using SWPBS as the core process, we would expect that the strong partial correlation between SAMAN progress scores and SET scores would lend credence to the validity of SAMAN as an estimator of overall progress on schoolwide RTI. Thus far, correlations of SAMAN and SET average above .80, a reasonable criterion for scientific acceptability. We are broadening our validity study by correlating SAMAN assessments with Individual Student Schoolwide Evaluation Tool (ISSET) assessments, which measure tiers 2 and 3 SWPBS processes in RTI schools.

Scaling Up School Reform

SAM schools use SAMAN data to reflect on their progress toward full implementation of the model following each assessment. The school assessed in Figure 6.1 adjusted its action plans during meetings of the site leadership team following examination of the pattern of progress on each critical feature. Critical feature 7, for example, measures progress on implementing all three RTI tiers of SWPBS. If the scores on this feature slip over repeated assessments or fail to progress toward the ceiling score of 3, the leadership team might elect to request a professional development or technical assistance intervention to move to the next level on that feature.

Schools implementing SAM can evaluate their overall progress toward enculturation of the systems change process by analyzing their progress on the total score pattern over repeated assessments. Progress on SAM implementation typically goes through three distinct phases. The first phase, when a school is getting started with the process, is called the phase of *initiation*. SAMAN total scale scores in this phase average below 1.5 for those assessments. Scores between 1.5 and 2.5 on the total score scale signify that the school has moved into phase 2, *implementation*. Whereas scores reflecting initiation mean the school is getting started with figuring out how the school reform process works, scores reflecting implementation signify that the school has mastered the overall systems change agenda and is beginning to fine-tune overall implementation through the action planning process. Finally, total scale scores that fall between 2.5 and 3.0 signify that the school has reached the phase of *enculturation*, meaning that the full-blown RTI model has become business-as-usual at the school.

Moving Schoolwide RTI to Scale in a District

When two consecutive assessments of SAMAN at a school produce scores in the range of enculturation, the ongoing technical assistance provided by SAM technicians is phased out as the school is felt to be self-sustaining in its implementation. This process typically takes three to four years for each school, although we are finding that later cohorts of schools within a district implementing SAM reach sustainability sooner than schools that begin earlier.

Figure 6.2 reflects the overall scale-up pattern of eleven schools making up the Ravenswood City School District. The figure shows that repeated assessments of cohort 1 schools (schools A, B, C,

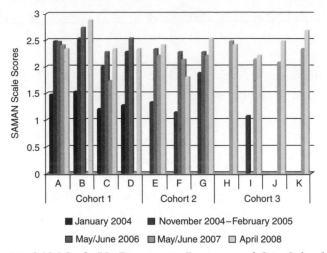

Figure 6.2 SAM Scale-Up Progress in Ravenswood City Schools

and D) between 2003 and 2007 are taking between three and four years to cross the 2.5 enculturation line, whereas schools E, F, and G (cohort 2), which began a year later (2004), are proceeding more quickly than cohort 1. Finally, cohort 3 schools, which began in 2005, are rapidly moving toward or have reached enculturation in only two years.

These accelerated cohort scale-up data provide good estimates of the extent to which the systems change process has become enculturated at the level of the district. When SAM processes have essentially become the language of the district in its interactions with its principals and through its ongoing professional and staff development activities, the process becomes less reliant (for later schools) on the external technical assistance provided by Blair Roger and me and more reflective of the internal capacity of the district to move the agenda forward. For this reason, those of us associated with SAM train district-level personnel in the RTI systems change processes, so that particularly large districts with many schools can scale up the RTI process on their own resources in a reasonable period of time.

Action Planning in Schoolwide RTI

Establishing a schoolwide RTI model in any school is a significant systems change agenda that should not be underestimated. The possibilities for different elements in a school organization to work at cross-purposes and for negative feelings to come to the fore can occur daily. Careful, manageable planning is needed, often facilitated by sources external to the district.

In choosing to anchor schoolwide RTI in a comprehensive school reform approach, we gave ourselves the advantage of having a fidelity estimation tool (SAMAN) that could serve as a driver for the ongoing action planning process. Although the fifteen indicators sample only a few of the requisite elements of RTI systems change, focusing on these criteria enables the discourse within the SLT to encompass many additional issues and set objectives that go far beyond what is needed to advance the fifteen. In other words, each of the fifteen critical feature indicators taps into a much wider pool of activities needed to transform a school. The SAM action planning process represents one way to enable schools to move the systems change agenda in accordance with the unique culture of each and within the assets and constraints each school undertaking the journey faces.

Program Evaluation

The SAM action planning mechanism, called school-centered planning, is a variant of empowerment program evaluation, a participant evaluation approach developed by Stanford professor David Fetterman and his associates. Most forms of program evaluation are impact evaluations and rely on objective assessments conducted by evaluators from outside the activity being evaluated. Formative assessments report the extent to which a project is putting into place the components of the process as proposed, and summative assessments estimate the degree to which the project is succeeding in terms of its promised results. Finally, an estimate of the extent to which funds are expended as proposed comprises the third element in an impact evaluation. This problem with impact evaluation is that it requires sticking exactly to what was proposed. There is very little wiggle room if things do not go as expected.

> *This problem with impact evaluation is that it requires sticking exactly to what was proposed. There is very little wiggle room if things do not go as expected.*

Fetterman, a medical anthropologist, conceived empowerment evaluation as a way to enable the implementers of a project to respond to new information as it arises during implementation. In other words, as a form of participant evaluation, empowerment evaluation empowers implementers to make adjustments to the process of implementation of a project if they see that some things are working well but some things not so well. Since SAM is an anthropologically oriented approach to RTI school reform, Fetterman's system provides an opportunity for each school to select its own route and change that route from time to time as it moves along.

School-centered planning begins with a full-day retreat at the start of each semester by the site leadership team. If a school also has a separate RTI team or an SWPBS team, the members of both teams come together for the retreat. A SAM technical assistant facilitates the process, which typically is a blend of intense brainstorming activity and fun stuff to keep the process interesting. At the end of the day, the product of the effort is a site action plan that subsequently is sent to all school staff electronically or in newsletter form. This document will list up to seven or eight specific objectives with activities for each. The activities list who is responsible for implementation, on what date the process will begin, the expected date of completion, and how evidence of the change will be estimated and provided.

Once the action plan is developed, the site leadership team then meets at a minimum of every two weeks for ninety minutes to evaluate progress on implementation of the plan as well as other RTI agenda items, and revises the plan as needed. At the beginning of the next semester, the process is repeated with new and continuing (if needed) objectives for the new term. This guiding process continues until SAMAN assessments reflect that the transformation is complete and SAM has become enculturated at the school. Schools may then elect to continue the action planning process with facilitation provided by district personnel trained by SAM technical assistants.

If all of this seems like overkill, there is, we think, at least a method in our madness. My colleagues and I over the years have seen too many educational innovations discarded before their power could be translated into student achievement outcomes. SWPBS is a recent case in point. It has been around for at least eight years as a fully developed system with at least a fidelity estimator (SET) for level 1 implementation in schools. Scientific research has contributed a substantial and growing body of evidence that SWPBS significantly enhances school climate, increases the number of hours students are in instruction by reducing office disciplinary referrals, and through these processes has improved measured student achievement. Yet in many urban schools that once had SWPBS in place, the process was interrupted and something else substituted as a "school discipline" package before it could become enculturated.

Schoolwide RTI has enormous potential to have a positive effect on academic achievement in urban schools. The research to back up that statement is only now getting underway in response to federal government initiatives on RTI research, development, and personnel preparation. My optimism comes from the fact that many of the components that make up RTI have solid research grounding. Schoolwide RTI simply combines these ingredients into a fully coordinated system. Driving schoolwide RTI through a comprehensive school reform model such as SAM buttresses the process by setting up an interactive capacity-building process between implementing schools and their districts. Most educational innovations never make it to scale in large urban districts because newer, ostensibly better innovations surface before the process is complete, and so it recycles.

Schoolwide RTI is not like that. It is foundational rather than episodic. It enables schools, through data-based decision processes, to introduce episodic (frequently occurring upgrades) innovation without altering the ongoing organizational processes of the school. So in our work, we go to great lengths to assist schools and their districts to proceed at their own pace and according to their own priorities, while always keeping their eyes on the prize. My colleagues and I are betting that through these interactive processes, driven by school reform, the foundational elements of schoolwide RTI will become sustained over time at both the school and district levels because they will have become enculturated.

> *My colleagues and I are betting that through these interactive processes, driven by school reform, the foundational elements of schoolwide RTI will become sustained over time at both the school and district levels because they will have become enculturated.*

Structural Elements of SAM

Here is how the interactive process is structured under SAM. Each school that is selected to begin implementation as the first cohort of schools is chosen on the basis of volunteering to go first. My SAM colleagues and I begin the process by explaining SAM (and RTI) to a meeting of principals convened by the district. Principals then caucus with their schools and try to get answers to the teachers about what the process entails. We provide additional information through our Web site (www.samschools.org). Schools that signal an interest in going forward are then brought into a cluster for purposes of receiving technical assistance, training, assessments, and data processing services from us. A cluster is defined as a single comprehensive high school, one elementary and two middle schools, three middle schools, or four elementary schools. Other possible combinations are cost-estimated based on that formula. With urban districts, we typically set a limit of four clusters of schools per cohort and one new cohort per year so that our resources and the district's do not get spread too thin.

A Model for Technical Assistance

My colleagues and I deliver technical assistance services by providing two-person teams for each cluster that meet with each school in the cluster four times per academic year. The makeup of technical assistance teams can vary from visit to visit depending on the particular expertise needed at each site, as determined from the previous visit. SAM teams made up of experts from around the country have expertise across all behavioral and academic RTI components. A team may work with a school during one visit on implementing a Reading First program at each grade with tier 1 and 2 interventions, and on another visit, with a different SAM faculty member, assist a school in implementing tier 3 interventions under SWPBS. We provide training to districts through three- or four-day summer and/or winter institutes that bring together all of the SAM schools' teachers and administrators for specific professional development activities. Those trainings are followed up with mentoring from coaches and assistance from schools' RTI teams. Finally, SAM data processing services are provided electronically from our data lab in Kansas. Schools receive updated graphics on all assessments and statistical analyses for level of impact when requested.

As an example of how the structural elements of SAM work, consider our newest partner: Washington, D.C., schools. We began in spring 2008 by presenting to school administrators who elected to attend the presentation after learning of the model from district sources. To engage SAM, each district partner must name a SAM coordinator from within the district administration. This person is typically a general education administrator with experience in and knowledge of student support programs such as special education and English Language Learners. In Washington, D.C., schools, SAM coordinator Dr. Linda Rohrbaugh followed up after the presentation by identifying two clusters of volunteer schools to begin, as SAM cohort 1, to implement the process during the 2008–2009 academic year.

The district sent a team of administrators to East Palo Alto to view the processes in the Ravenswood District. We then sent a team of assessors to the District of Columbia to gather the baseline assessment data for each school on SAMAN and SET, which site leadership teams at each school then used to begin their action planning process.

Our technical assistance teams met with a subset of the schools in spring 2008 to initiate the action planning process (school-centered planning) and distribute a SAM self-assessment survey tool to be filled out by all professionals, administrators, and staff at each school. The purpose of the tool, which mirrors SAMAN for the most part, is to get everyone at the school thinking about the implications of each of the fifteen critical features as a way to get started. We have created data chart portfolios for each school and transmitted those electronically to the schools and the district so that they can begin to track their progress. Finally, a summer training institute was conducted in July 2008 that began with training of the RTI coaches at the cohort 1 schools. University of Kansas research professor Jim Knight, a national expert on educational coaching, provided that training. Coaches joined the professional staffs of the schools for extensive initial training on behavioral and academic components of RTI during the remainder of the summer institute.

District and Site Leadership Teams

In addition to the SAM coordinator and RTI coaches provided by the district, two additional structural features are required of partner districts to engage the SAM process: a district leadership team and a district resource team. The district leadership team is made up of the superintendent and members of his or her top administrative unit for district functions. The purpose of this team is to undertake discussions concerning rearrangement of resources at SAM schools as these arise in the implementation process. Since some of these issues will have budgetary considerations, the top-level discourse must be available. In the District of Columbia schools, chancellor Michelle Rhee or her designate, SAM coordinator Dr. Linda Rohrbaugh, assistant chancellor for special education Dr. Richard Nyankori, and others make up the district leadership team for the 2008–2009 academic year.

The district resource team is not a standing team but rather one that is convened to undertake specific requests originating from school site leadership teams. For example, in Ravenswood, one school's site leadership team decided that because of its earlier service model for special education, there were too many paraprofessionals at the site and not enough special education teachers. Its members drafted a memorandum to the assistant superintendent for curriculum and instruction, the position that typically chairs district resource team meetings, to request a personnel trade. The chair constituted a team made up of potential stakeholders to the implications of the request—in this case, other principals and the director for special education. The request was discussed, a potential solution considered, and a favorable recommendation transmitted in writing to the district leadership team for approval. A copy was sent to the site team that originated the request. The district team put the recommendation on the agenda for its next meeting, where the request was approved. It then notified the district resource and site leadership teams of the approval, and the plan was put into motion.

This process results in transparency in the resource allocation process, a feature we consider important in building trust within and across schools (some of which will not be implementing SAM as yet) and between schools and their district. We have learned from experience that schools seeking to implement a difficult systems change agenda can react with suspicion and negativity if the district administration seems not to be committed to the process. Putting interactive discourse communities (the teams at both levels) in place and creating an archive of the communication processes and decisions helps to reassure schools that the district is on board with the agenda and doing what it can reasonably do to facilitate the process.

> We have learned from experience that schools seeking to implement a difficult systems change agenda can react with suspicion and negativity if the district administration seems not to be committed to the process.

To Sum Up

In this chapter, I provided a survey of some of the issues that affect whether a new approach to education such as RTI can sustain itself over time. Sustainability is a function of enculturation and district support. Urban school politics were examined as a reoccurring issue. Urban schools typically leap from one new set of practices to another, with insufficient time for enculturation of any of these to occur.

New innovations in education often fade away before they can reflect accomplishments verified by research due to siloization and inattention to human capital. Stakeholders in innovative practice must buy in and be provided with new knowledge and sources of evidence.

Professional development is a critical issue for sustainability. Preservice personnel preparation often lags behind innovation, and so in-service training takes on new importance. The importance of longitudinal, mentored professional development followed up by coaching was discussed. The distinction between school-generated and district-generated professional development was discussed, with a recommendation for greater emphasis on school priorities. The culture of the school is a paramount issue.

SAM was presented as a comprehensive school reform context that offers a pathway to RTI sustainability. SAM uses a universal design for the learning framework, as well as a rigorous fidelity estimation tool to assist research on its efficacy. It also offers a possibility for sustaining schoolwide RTI since it is an anthropological model guided by empowerment strategies, including its school action planning process.

Anchoring schoolwide RTI in school reform has potential for sustainability of innovation but should be phased in with cohorts of schools over time. Finally, interactive processes among schools implementing school reform and the district need to be built into the ongoing scale-up process.

Part III

Seeing RTI in Action

7

How RTI Looks at the Schoolwide Level

RTI is about applied science, in this case, science applied to pre-K through grade 12 education. But is science enough? There is certainly artistry in teaching, and there are organizational phenomena that can seem like magic to the uninitiated. Just as the African proverb says, "It takes a village to raise a child," it takes a school to educate a child. The whole, where it comes to schools, is much greater than the sum of its parts.

Critical Features of Schoolwide RTI

Schoolwide RTI consists of scientifically validated components of which the following are critical features of any model in application (examples are given in parentheses):

Universal Screening

- Behavior (internalizing and externalizing)
- Academics (literacy and math)

Evidence-Based Interventions at Three Levels

- Level 1: Universal application
  - Behavior (teach expectations)
  - Academics (differentiated instruction)
- Level 2: Increased intensity for some
  - Behavior (check in/check out)
  - Academics (reading enhancement strategies)
    - Smaller group applications
    - Additional time in content instruction
- Level 3: Maximum intensity for a few
  - Behavior (functional behavioral assessment and positive behavior support plan)
  - Academics (individual tutoring)
    - Increased time in content instruction
    - Family and community engagement (after-school programs)

Progress Monitoring at Three Levels

- Level 1
  - Behavior (systematic screening for behavior disorders-SSBD)
  - Academics (DIBELS)
- Level 2
  - Behavior (office disciplinary referrals, SSBD; specific behavioral data)
  - Academics (Read 180; curriculum-based measures)
- Level 3
  - Behavior (changes in frequency; positive behavior support plan data; Information Management for Educational Outcomes)
  - Academics (Read 180; curriculum-based measures)

Fidelity of Application

- Of implementation of schoolwide RTI
- Of educational interventions

Data-Based Decision Making

- Teams
- Coaches

Each of these critical features has evidence from research to suggest its efficacy. Some of the features have a strong basis, such as level 1 schoolwide positive behavior support, while others, such as level 2 progress monitoring for behavior, have an emerging basis from ongoing research.

RTI and the Achievement Gap

Taken as a whole, schoolwide RTI has the potential to significantly ratchet up American public education. But is it enough to close the achievement gap between white students and children of color? Can it significantly improve the performance of all students? Probably not. There is a social chemistry in good schooling that must be factored into the mix to achieve the kinds of results enjoyed by Elizabeth Street School in South Central Los Angeles and White Church Elementary School in Kansas City, Kansas. Scientifically grounded practices must be introduced into a social context that enhances quality teaching and is guided by effective leadership to close the gap and raise the output of all students.

Science is a rational-technical enterprise. When dramatic new findings from brain research inform educators about where to look for key points of breakdown in reading competence, such as fluency and comprehension, an RTI model in application is enhanced in much the same way that a carpenter's ability to create cabinets is enhanced by new tools that employ laser technology: the level of precision in application goes up. But will these interventions alone quickly help Jamal to become a skillful reader? The teaching-learning process is complex, and there is much that occurs in the social-constructivism domain.

Our faith in rational-technical solutions is perhaps higher than it has ever been. No Child Left Behind (NCLB) stands as a monument to the belief that science coupled with accountability can bring our public educational systems to glory. As Tom Skrtic observes in his book, *Disability and Democracy* (1995), when this promise is observed to fail, we see the same proponents of rational-technical solutions to school failure reacting to that failure with exclusionary tactics. The national infatuation with charter schools and vouchers is really a set of policies that facilitates the exclusion of students who, for whatever reason, are not responding to the rational-technical enterprise. The data from large-scale evaluation studies of NCLB tend to show that it works only for students who are not provided an exclusionary pathway out of the system and into private or quasi-private alternatives where the structures of NCLB are not required.

The Problem with Reinforcers

Alfie Kohn, in his book *Punishment with Rewards: The Trouble with Gold Stars, Incentive Plans, A's, Praise, and Other Bribes*, notes a shortcoming of an exclusive reliance on rational-technical applications. Guiding a student's learning process with external reinforcers results in students who approach new learning in a passive manner: waiting for the expert to guide the way. Applications of behaviorism in education certainly have their place, particularly in special education, but as an overarching, guiding construct for education, it is woefully insufficient.

One way to look at the problem is to ask, "What does the child bring to the teaching-learning process?" Science has given us a great deal in recent years addressed to the teaching side of the equation, but the interaction of teaching and learning is still poorly understood. On the teaching side of the equation, differentiated instruction (level 1 intervention) and content enhancement strategies (level 2 intervention) are evidence-based practices that improve the overall quality of instruction. But although quality of teaching is the single most powerful predictor of increases in student academic achievement, research shows it is not enough to raise academic performance in low-performing schools.

Student Motivation

We know from research that externally provided rewards for staying in school, such as cash payments and tokens exchangeable for after-school rewards that are given for increased test scores, are insufficient to overcome more systemic barriers to learning and performance such as boring curricular material, punitive school experiences such as bullying, and negative peer pressure for "being a good student." The inspirational element in teaching and learning is directly addressed to the question of what the child brings to the process.

Teaching and learning may be viewed as a process of cultural exchange. Most of my work takes place in urban core schools such as Ravenswood, where most of the students are Latino/a, and Washington, D.C., where many of the students are African American. The curriculum, however, in almost every case, is "white." Textbooks show a mix of ethnic characteristics on their covers, but inside there is usually little of direct relevance to the day-to-day cultural experiences of children of color living in the urban core.

A Case for Ebonics in the Classroom

About a decade ago in Oakland, California, public schools in African American neighborhoods, a proposal was floated by the board of education to permit some schools to teach in "Ebonics." The theory behind the proposal was that the pattern of English spoken by most, if not all, of the students in some inner-core schools constituted a distinct dialect or pidgin (for example, "You is what you is"), which could be reliably identified and translated into "ordinary American English." Since the students communicated with each other and across their communities in Ebonics, perhaps a learning bridge, or cultural exchange, could be established between the teacher and students if teaching were conducted in Ebonics.

The proposal was greeted with outrage not only in the Bay Area but across the nation when the proposal was picked up on news services and broadcast media. Imagine, the argument went, teaching in improper English! Research, however, has consistently shown that learning is enhanced by examining the negative case (Ebonics) in contrast with the desired, or positive case, "proper English." I have observed teachers in classrooms in the Deep South and have witnessed in these environments a linguistic cultural transmission that is fully acceptable but not standard English (for example, "Y'all hand in y'all's papers now"). And in the Midwest, there are similar examples (for example, "Where's Sarah? She's went up to the library"). Studies in Hawaii, where a distinct pidgin is in place, indicate that students are motivated to learn English when taught in their dialect and then asked to translate back and forth from pidgin to English. So perhaps the outrage against the Ebonics proposal, which was subsequently withdrawn as a result of the brouhaha, was motivated by factors other than a real concern with proper English.

Teaching-learning as a cultural exchange may lead to one way to increase student motivation (there is little research on the topic), but a perhaps more powerful predictor is the curriculum. Studies of the performance of African American students on curriculum-based social studies measures using "Afrocentric" versus "Eurocentric" modules favored the former over the latter. Black students were more motivated in their studies to learn material that reflected their own cultural perspective than material reflective of the white European perspective. None of this is particularly new, but if we are serious about turning around low-performing schools, student motivation needs to be revisited, and certainly more research on the topic is needed.

During the years of the Clinton administration when the Elementary and Secondary Education Act was called "Goals 2000," a number of important experiments were conducted around the country on urban partnerships between universities and the inner city. The question was whether universities that are increasingly becoming surrounded by poverty-stricken, nonwhite neighborhoods, such as the University of Southern California, University of Chicago, and Yale, can increase campus safety and develop better relationships with their communities by forming interdisciplinary academic units such as faculty task forces representing several departments.

One well-known experiment in the 1990s was undertaken by a group of professors and their graduate students at the University of Pennsylvania with residents of a very poor inner-city Philadelphia neighborhood. The high school in the community had poor attendance and an equally poor graduation rate when the experiment started. Faculty represented such diverse departments as theater arts, education, and history. The faculty group met with groups of students to address the question, "What could we do that would make the high school experience worthwhile?" Out of that discourse came a joint project in which high school students conducted research on the history of Black Bottom, their community.

Groups of students took on different aspects of the historical research, conducting library searches and oral histories in the community, examining old photos, watching archived films, sketching examples of architecture, and so forth. Attendance at school skyrocketed, and books flew out of the library. Students became inspired to learn, a rare event in the recent history of the high school. Finally, based on the mountain of material processed by these students and guided by the Penn theater arts faculty and students, the students wrote a play and presented it to the community in the high school auditorium. It was sold out. Multiple engagements had to be scheduled and a bigger theater located. Grades went up and graduation rates increased as aspects of the experiment became incorporated into the high school curriculum. Cultural relevance, including linguistic factors in cultural exchange in the teaching-learning process, is clearly important for student motivation and for capitalizing on what the student brings to the educational process.

> *Cultural relevance, including linguistic factors in cultural exchange in the teaching-learning process, is clearly important for student motivation and for capitalizing on what the student brings to the educational process.*

School-Based Video

A recent manifestation of some of these culturally relevant school experiences can be found in the rapidly emerging school-based educational video movement. Most education videos are produced by companies that specialize in preparation of supporting materials for professional development. The Indiana Forum on Education, headed by Leonard Burrello, now at the University of South Florida, offers a good example (www.forumoneducation.org). The forum's video production unit, Elephant Rock Productions, has produced a number of useful DVDs on topics such as RTI, positive behavior support (PBS), coteaching, the Schoolwide Applications Model (SAM), and high-school reform. These kinds of professional quality videos are indispensable to the goals and outcomes of professional development as well as preservice training activities.

School-based DVDs differ from this genre only in that they are produced by the students in the schools, with technical assistance from the faculty. There is a value-added component to school-based video production accruing to the enhanced motivation of the students and the positive climate of the school accelerated by the opportunity for students and teachers to work together on a common project. An example of a school-based educational video, which can be accessed at www.samschools.org, was produced by the faculty and students of Cesar Chavez School in Ravenswood for the purpose of acquainting prospective and ongoing family members of Chavez students with the critical features of the SAM school reform process, including schoolwide positive behavior support.

Hand-held video cameras are now ubiquitous and affordable, and young people are technologically savvy. The advent of school-based video may afford a breakthrough in efforts to motivate students through cultural enhancement (a number of languages are spoken in the Chavez video). If students can take on a long-term project with multiple learning components, which creates the opportunity to work in partnership with their teachers and results in a product in which they take pride and is indispensable to informing parents and training teachers, a potential breakthrough is at hand.

Leadership and Structure of the RTI School

Thus far, I have argued that schoolwide RTI offers an opportunity to rethink schools, particularly those, often located in the urban core, that are described as chronically low performing. By focusing on prevention and matching evidence-based interventions to, and focusing all school resources on, measured student need with varying levels of intensity, we are putting science to work in the service of education. But the rational-technical innovations of science are not enough. The cultural identities and traditions of the students, teachers, and the community, as well as the culture of the school as a community of practice, are essential elements as well. They are, however, much less well understood.

Distributed Leadership

A school that seeks to undertake and succeed with the complex systems change agenda of schoolwide RTI requires extraordinary leadership. We know from research that the concept of leadership embodies more than a single building leader. Distributed leadership is a key element in the implementation of schoolwide RTI. There are far more responsibilities involved in such a complex transformation as RTI than can possibly be handled by a principal.

The effective distribution of leadership is tricky business, with issues of equity, fairness, and competence to consider. Schools, as with all other busy organizational environments, have their internal dynamics. One of the reasons schools have become siloized has to do with maintaining organizational stability by subdividing functions into smaller organizational units such as special education, safety and security, and designated services (for example, speech therapy). Under RTI, desiloization must occur so the buffer provided by subdivided specialized units against destabilization of the organization can be replaced with a more efficient and effective mechanism. Distributed leadership has emerged as a key to better school organization.

Every organization has its power relationships. The principal is the top-level authority in the school, and so most of the power and responsibility rest with him or her (although some would argue that it actually resides with the school secretary). Some principals find it hard to relinquish authority to others, even for specifically delineated responsibilities. Authoritarian principals communicate a lack of trust to the professional community, which breeds mistrust among professional and line staff. Other principals delegate nearly everything, creating the impression of a leadership vacuum and reducing any perception of a need for personal accountability.

Research indicates that neither leadership style is well suited for schools, and particularly RTI schools. Effective leadership begins with a principal who has earned the mantle of authority through achieving the respect of his or her community of practice. The principal who is comfortable with the authority and responsibility that comes with the job and is democratically inclined will have little trouble distributing leadership functions. The trick will be in the emergence and/or selection of who else assumes leadership functions.

Leadership Teams

The process begins with pulling together a leadership team. Membership on the team might consist of a mix of members of the professional community of the school and nominees from existing teams, particularly grade-level teams. However it is accomplished, the goal is to assemble a cadre of function leaders who can effectively guide the systems change process of RTI while maintaining the trust and support of the total community of practice to carry out leadership tasks. When this aspect of leadership is carried out skillfully, the culture of the school is enhanced and can be reflected in measures of "school climate."

Chronically low-performing schools that have accomplished the transition to high-performing status consistently have four qualities:

- Effective distributed leadership
- High-quality instruction
- Evidence-based interventions and a high-quality curriculum
- A positive school culture

The key variables that characterize effective leadership teams are creativity, experience, respect, and ability to reach out to others in the community of practice and to communicate effectively.

Constructing a leadership team on the basis of job titles, seniority, and gender or ethnic balance is unlikely to produce an engaged school. Effective leadership needs to be a balance of recognition by an astute principal of who has the qualities to carry out leadership functions for particular domains or tasks and the sensitivity to respond to impulses from within the community of practice for certain individuals to emerge as school leaders.

White Church Elementary School in Kansas City, Kansas, went from a chronically low-performing school to the top elementary school in the state through effective leadership, which has been documented in the video *Creating a Unified System: Integrating General and Special Education for the Benefit of All Students* (www.forumoneducation.org). Principal Nedia Riley and instructional coach Susan Keetle assembled a leadership team that quickly and efficiently put most of the cultural features of schoolwide RTI together while enjoying the respect and cooperation of the rest of the community of the school. Parents were nurtured and brought along each step of the way, and all members of the school community, including custodians and secretaries, felt themselves to be contributors to the success of the students. Consistent measures of school climate over a five-year period showed steady increases in the emergence of a positive school culture. The children at White Church responded to these events by scoring in the highest ranges of the state annual grade-level assessments and earning the distinction of becoming the top-performing public elementary school in the State of Kansas in 2005, and remaining at high levels of performance through 2008 despite changes in site leadership.

The organizational structure and the leadership of an RTI school are essential elements in guiding the systems change process that will result in strong academic and social achievement on the part of the students. Schoolwide RTI remains largely a work in progress—a bit like building an airplane as you fly it. There are still few schools where all of the critical features are in place at any one time. The whole transformational effort is still new as of 2009. There are, however, some advanced examples, and we next look at one of them.

Madison Elementary School

Madison Elementary School is a K–4 school of some 350 students in the Gardner-Edgerton School District in northeast Kansas. A suburban Kansas City area school, Madison has only 17 percent of students on free and reduced-price lunch, and about 2 percent of the students are of color. The school is quite new: it opened in fall 2005. Principal Christie Whitter and her staff feel they have benefited from district support in developing their school as a site representative of Multi-Tiered Systems of Support (MTSS), the Kansas state RTI initiative.

The Gardner-Edgerton area, formerly two small agricultural communities, is undergoing a boom in subdivisions as it becomes part of the suburban sprawl of the metropolitan Kansas City area. With rapid expansion in the housing industry come Latino families as Mexican, Mexican American, and Latin American immigrants find new jobs in construction. The district operates an English Language Learners Center, a school with a high proportion of Latino/a students, so Madison attracts some Latino/a students but fewer than would be expected from the population demographics of the community.

Madison elected to begin its RTI program in 2005 by focusing on reading as a pilot site in conjunction with a state initiative. The model focuses on interventions associated with specific literacy components such as phonetic awareness, alphabetic principle, vocabulary, comprehension, and fluency. As Whitter puts it, "We are a work in progress. We elected to begin with reading and are adding new features each year to the RTI framework." In 2008, Madison's model was still focused on academics, but a plan was underway to begin to introduce schoolwide positive behavior support (SWPBS) in 2009 and is underway as this is written.

Screening at Madison

Students at Madison are assessed with DIBELS three times per year. DIBELS also is used for progress monitoring, and so students determined to be falling below grade level are assessed more frequently. Additional screening tools include Fountas and Pinnell, and Quick Phonics, particularly when teachers feel more information is needed to pinpoint early reading problems. As of 2009, Madison had yet to introduce screeners for math and other content areas as well as for social development and behavior.

Madison takes a somewhat unique approach to schoolwide RTI by including all students in both level 1 and tier 2 interventions. Level 2 interventions are usually reserved for students determined to be at risk for falling well below grade level on benchmark assessments; nevertheless, the leadership team at Madison chose to develop intervention plans for all students below measured benchmarks and enrichment plans for all students at or above benchmarks. Madison thus views tier 2 as added support for both remediation and acceleration.

Students below benchmark assessments are placed in smaller groups focused on reading enhancement interventions. These students' progress is monitored with frequent DIBELS assessments to see if they are moving to grade level. Those who are "floating" or showing further discrepancies are deemed eligible for tier 3 interventions. Tier 3 at Madison is defined as an additional thirty minutes of instruction beyond the tier 2 "dosage" each day, provided by a special educator or the building reading specialist. Efforts are made at tier 3 to individualize instruction so that it is tailored to each student's identified and prioritized need.

The basic RTI model at Madison provides cross-grade instruction in reading and an additional 30 minutes of reading instruction associated with the tier 2 groupings (120 minutes total for tiers 1 and 2). Students for whom tier 3 interventions are determined to be appropriate by the RTI team, the school improvement committee, are taught in small groups by the reading specialist. Tier 3 students with an individualized education program (IEP) are taught by the special education teacher in a resource room. Special education staff, including paraprofessionals, assist the tier 2 interventions. Tier 2 interventions are also assisted by reading paraprofessionals funded by the district general budget.

Building-Level Versus State-Level Assessments

Madison presents an interesting case study in the relationship of state grade-level annual assessments, which are often high stakes, that is, linked to punitive consequences for schools that consistently fail to make adequate yearly progress, to progress monitoring assessments, such as DIBELS and AIMSweb, that are independent of specific reading curricula such as Reading First–supported curricula, or to specific state standards. The issue cuts to the heart of the teach-to-the-test controversy that swirls around NCLB.

The issue is this. The Kansas State Reading Assessment and its published standards are largely grounded in the Reading First indicators, particularly Open Court Reading, a heavily phonics-based program. The Gardner-Edgerton District provides a specific reading curriculum for its schools with benchmark specifications for each grade, geared directly to the state standards. Indicators of progress at each grade level are assessed quarterly and reported to the district. The district provides Open Court Reading to its schools to augment the curriculum.

Madison fulfills the district requirement but does not use Open Court. Guided Reading is used consistent with the school's philosophy that any one-size-fits-all curriculum will leave many children behind (a philosophy that is a good fit with RTI). As a result,

Table 7.1   Madison Elementary's Results on the Kansas State Reading Assessment

Madison Elementary Kansas State Reading	Academic Warning	Approaches Standard	Meets Standard	Exceeds Standard	Exemplary	Meeting Standard
2006: All students	0	4	19.5	36.5	39.8	95.9
2007: Third grade	0	0	13.3	25.3	60	100
2007: Fourth grade	0	0	1.8	19.3	78.9	100
2007: All students	0	0	8.3	22.6	67.7	100

students at Madison do very well on the Kansas State Reading Assessment (see Table 7.1).

In Table 7.1 all numbers are expressed in percentages. The last column on the right reflects total percentage of assessed students at grade levels meeting or exceeding the state standard. 100 percent means no students scored in the ranges below "meets standard." Madison students also do well on the DIBELS assessments, but do not show the steep progress reflected for performance on the district assessments. A question of interest is whether students would become more proficient readers if they were freed from a curriculum required by the district and taught in accordance with the site-based expertise of the literacy specialists consistent with a RTI model. With the rapid advent of schoolwide RTI, this issue is likely to surface in many areas of the country as schools implementing RTI seek more authority to match interventions to measured student needs rather than adhere to a one-size-fits-all curriculum. The issue becomes even more important in the face of large-scale research studies that are calling into question the overall efficacy of Reading First curricula.

In my view, districts should give RTI schools plenty of rein, particularly in the early stages of implementation. Schools are cultural entities and need to apply the expertise of their professional communities of practice in a spirit of mutual engagement and building momentum. NCLB ushered in the age of accountability, a heavily rational-technical endeavor with its adequate yearly progress yardstick for assessing school progress according to its performance standards. Is this the best way to get students excited enough about reading to become proficient? I vote no. However, when the stakes for the school are high and encompass vouchers and state takeovers, and the yardstick's metric is state annual grade-level assessments in math and reading, who can blame districts and schools for putting structure and processes in place to try to ensure that students do as well as possible on the state assessments?

Reading Interventions

Under its developing schoolwide RTI model, Madison Elementary pursues an intervention strategy with a broad scope. Students receive explicit instruction and then are provided opportunities to apply and practice their new skills. The focus is on teaching students early on how to read so that they can move on to reading to learn and for inspiration (a word that has all but disappeared in the age of accountability).

The reading program integrates activities through reading, writing, discussion, and exploration activities with increasing levels of complexity. Curriculum integration is enhanced through technology in application to real-life projects that require students to integrate learning from reading, math, and other content areas. Students are provided access to Student Anthologies from the Open Court series, the extensive Guided Reading library (1,076 fiction and nonfiction titles), and the Reading A-Z site (with 2,400 books).

Madison embeds reading content enhancement strategies in its literacy instruction. For example, students are taught to:

- Search for and find main ideas from text
- Recall facts and details
- Understand the sequence of events
- Look for and recognize cause-and-effect relationships
- Compare and contrast ideas and themes
- Predict outcomes
- Achieve the meaning of words from context
- Draw conclusions based on inferences
- Distinguish between facts and opinions
- Identify the author's purpose
- Interpret figurative language
- Distinguish between reality and fantasy

Students at each grade level are read to from selections that are slightly above their instructional reading level, followed by class discussion. They engage in reflective opportunities such as writing in journals and participating in projects and discussion groups. Students are taught a consistent writing process with specifications at each grade level. Each student creates a portfolio of writing that teachers use to guide further direction.

Each week grade-level teams meet to review progress monitoring data and revise intervention plans for individual students. The school sets up a homework policy that requires two nights of language arts work at each grade level every week. Teachers routinely reach out to parents to implement reading logs so that both parents and teachers can gauge the amount of time that students are reading at home.

Two of the fifteen critical features of our SAM school reform model are school-family partnerships and school-community partnerships. Our research is consistently showing strong correlations between measured school progress on implementing these features and increases on academic achievement scores on the part of the students assessed from curriculum-based measures.

Madison Elementary's schoolwide RTI model also incorporates these processes. Having parents keep a reading log at home and sharing data with grade-level teachers is an excellent way to build trusting relationships with families, who often respond by taking on greater responsibilities in their children's education. Madison has also worked to build a partnership with its community in ways designed to facilitate student achievement. Parents and community leaders, for example, serve as guest readers and listening volunteers each year. The Gardner National Bank, in conjunction with the parent-teacher organization, sponsors a "Book in a Bag" program where each student in the school gets to select a free book. Local businesses contribute certificates and other prizes for the school to give to students when they achieve benchmarks and other goals. The Johnson County Library works collaboratively with Madison by offering a summer reading program at the school and shares progress information with the school so that it can recognize the students.

> *Having parents keep a reading log at home and sharing data with grade-level teachers is an excellent way to build trusting relationships with families, who often respond by taking on greater responsibilities in their children's education.*

Fidelity of Intervention

Reading First scientists would have a bone to pick with Madison Elementary: neither Open Court Reading nor Guided Reading is implemented with fidelity. This, however, is not unusual. RTI schools differ on a dimension that moves from culture, based at one end, to science, based at the other. RTI is a science-driven structural approach to education, so leaving out many parameters of data collection would be a serious violation of its basis. Madison Elementary is clearly defined by its leadership as a culture-based model. It seeks the flexibility required to adapt "canned" curricula to meet student needs as dictated by its content experts through team processes. Although the school is clearly using data-based decision making with rigorous and appropriate measures, fidelity of intervention is left out by design.

Professional Development

Madison Elementary and the Gardner-Edgerton School District have worked out a mix of school-based and district-based professional development time slots. Six and a half days of professional development are available for the staff of the school. Of these, one and a half days are district driven, and five days are allocated to Madison to pursue its own priorities. For district-driven slots, grade-level staff from all schools come together, for example, to be trained in fluency and comprehension interventions. In an example of school-based professional development, technology integration specialists meet with grade-level teams on enhancing the data-based decision process at grade-level team meetings. The school plans to allocate professional development slots to SWPBS training. Since there are costs associated with school-based professional development, the district allocates ten thousand dollars annually to the school for that purpose.

Scheduling

Personnel associated with development and implementation of schoolwide RTI say that scheduling is one of the most difficult tasks in the endeavor, and perhaps the most difficult one. The more fully integrated the model, the more complex scheduling becomes. Educational software developers have tackled the problem, and

Table 7.2   Madison Daily Schedule, Grades 1 to 4

	First Grade	Second Grade	Third Grade	Fourth Grade
8:15	Arrival	Arrival	Arrival	Arrival
8:30	Reading	Reading	Content	Tier 2 math
9:00	Reading	Reading	Content	Math
9:30	Reading	Reading	Tier 2 math	Math
10:00	Reading	Recess	Math	Specials
10:30	Recess	Tier 2 reading	Math	Specials
11:00	Tier 2 reading	Content	Specials	Lunch
11:30	Math	Lunch	Specials	Recess
12:00	Tier 2 math	Recess	Lunch	Reading
12:30	Lunch	Specials	Recess	Reading
1:00	Recess	Specials	Tier 2 reading	Reading
1:30	Specials	Content	Reading	Recess
2:00	Specials	Math	Reading	Tier 2 reading
2:30	Content	Tier 2 math	Recess	Content
3:00	Content	Math	Reading	Content

schedule generators are available, but I have yet to come across one that I could recommend.

Table 7.2 shows Madison's daily schedule for grades 1 to 4. (The schedule for kindergarten is separate and set up for a half-day program.) Note that first graders begin the day with ninety minutes of reading at tier 1 followed by recess. Grades 2 to 4 receive sixty minutes of reading in tier 1 instruction daily. An additional thirty minutes of reading is scheduled daily for tier 2 for each grade level. The tier 2 reading schedule is staggered across grade levels to accommodate the reading specialist's schedule. Tier 3 reading interventions are on a pull-out basis and therefore not shown on the schedule.

The pattern for math is similar, with half an hour of instruction at tier 1 for the first grade and sixty minutes for grades 2 to 4. All students get tier 2 math for an additional thirty minutes of instruction with a math specialist. Lunch is staggered by grade level between 11:00 A.M. and 1:00 P.M. "Content" refers to other content-area instruction (all tier 1). "Specials" refers to physical education, music, computer instruction, and library use. Finally, all personnel other than grade-level teachers, such as special educators and music teachers, have their own personal daily schedules. The school maintains backup schedules to enable it to adjust to staff absences.

Reflections on Madison Elementary School's RTI

The example provided by Madison Elementary clearly reflects schoolwide RTI in progress and at a developmental midpoint in its evolution. Next steps are planned to be the addition of a three-level SWPBS component with requisite measures and data-based decision rules, and a more fully integrated system of supports to include a coteaching approach (with special education) at tier 1. Coaching is not yet an issue in the Madison evolution. The school is, in my view, doing a remarkable job of charting a course for RTI that reflects its philosophy of culture building and autonomy, on one hand, and navigating the more top-down, prescriptive require-ments of the state's MTSS model for RTI and the district's required curriculum and benchmarks, on the other.

The discrepancy between progress on district and state assess-ments versus DIBELS is worthy of some reflection. The usual case is for measured improvement on DIBELS assessments, coupled with progress on benchmark assessment measures, serving as a powerful predictor of increased achievement scores on state annual grade-level assessments. At Madison the students score very well on the state assessments but tend to remain stable on DIBELS. I suspect the culprit in this case is the required district-level curriculum with its associated benchmarks geared to the state assessments. My recommendation is to let RTI schools organize educational inter-ventions on the basis of their DIBELS and perhaps other CBM data rather than hold such schools accountable for the same curriculum specifications as non-RTI schools. My prediction is that RTI schools will reflect even greater grade-level gains on the state assessments.

> *My recommendation is to let RTI schools organize educational interventions on the basis of their DIBELS and perhaps other CBM data rather than hold such schools accountable for the same curriculum specifications as non-RTI schools.*

Coaching and Collaborative Teaching

Two enhancements to schoolwide RTI programs are coaching and collaborative teaching.

Coaching

The responsibilities of an educational coach, according to Jim Knight in *Instructional Coaching,* are to be a professional developer on site who partners and identifies with grade-level teachers and assists the teachers in implementing research-based interventions in the classroom.

April Stout and Lena Van Haren are instructional coaches in the Ravenswood City School District in East Palo Alto, California. As this is written, Stout is assigned to Green Oaks Academy, an elementary-middle school, and Van Haren to Cesar Chavez Academy, a middle school. Both are working within the SAM RTI model and are in transition from being strictly literacy coaches to becoming RTI coaches with broader responsibilities. They recently described their coaching responsibilities:

- Support their school in the use of a data-based, collaborative team decision model
  - Facilitate grade-level team meetings.
  - Assist teams to analyze current classroom and schoolwide data.

- Create protocols and organizers for teachers, administration, and support staff to keep track of data.

- Meet regularly with all members of the staff on an individual and small group basis during the inquiry cycle (monthly school-level and districtwide grade-level meetings to view child progress data) at the school and district levels.

- Share strategies that teachers used in areas where their students showed greater mastery.

- Implement the RTI process

  - Assist teachers schoolwide in the assessment cycle of individual children and in small groups of students for tier 2 interventions.

  - Serve students in tier 2 interventions as a reading recovery teacher.

  - Assist teachers to implement Guided Reading and provide professional development or coaching in program implementation.

  - Assist teachers in interpreting assessment data to determine student-guided reading levels, student decoding and comprehension, and where breakdowns occur.

- Assist teams to proceed to sustainability of evidence-based practice

  - Serve on the school's site leadership team and the PBS team, both of which meet bimonthly.

  - Provide professional development to the entire school staff on evidence-based teaching practices such as differentiated instruction and collaborative teaching and interventions at each of the three levels of RTI.

  - Work with all school personnel to plan events and opportunities to partner with the community and with families of the school—for example, field trips and Read Across America Week.

- Facilitate continuity between and among grade levels and classrooms by action planning, and share plans with new teachers.

- Facilitate the involvement of parents in the school's decision-making teams and in after-school programs.

Instructional coaching is not for everyone. It should never become the next rung on the organizational ladder of upward mobility. RTI coaches must have an important mix of knowledge and competencies across many areas. At a minimum, they need to be grounded in all three levels of RTI, including SWPBS; in literacy instruction and enhancement for the grade levels of schools they will serve; and in math instruction and enhancement at appropriate grade levels. New coaches may need to add to their skills through ongoing coach training as they become established in their schools.

Knight points out in *Instructional Coaching* that knowledge and competence in teaching and curriculum are not the only prerequisites for becoming an effective coach. Personal attributes are also an essential element. Coaches must be skilled collaborators in addition to being skilled technicians. Knight sums up coaching features in this way:

- Coaching is about building relationships with teachers as much as it is about instruction. The heart of relationships is emotional connection.

- To get around barriers to change, coaches often start by working one-to-one with teachers.

- ICs [instructional coaches] adopt a partnership philosophy, which at its core means that they have an authentic respect for teachers' professionalism.

- The partnership philosophy is realized in collaborative work between the coach and the collaborating teacher. Together, coach and teacher discover answers to the challenges present in the classroom.

- ICs model in the classroom so that teachers can see what correct implementation of an intervention looks like.

- ICs model in the classroom so that teachers can see what research-based interventions look like when they reflect a teacher's personality.

- To be truly effective, coaches must work in partnership with their principals. [p. 33]

Collaborative Teaching

A second additional enhancement to schoolwide RTI implementation can be found in collaborative teaching. Pat Parrott of the University of Richmond describes it as "an educational approach in which general and special educators work in a co-active and coordinated fashion to jointly teach academically and behaviorally heterogeneous groups of students in educationally integrated settings" (i.e., regular classroom)(p. 18).

The first step in moving to collaborative teaching in conjunction with schoolwide RTI is to integrate special education students into grade-level classrooms and tier 2 integrated intervention settings. When special educators are locked up in their special classroom silos, all other students are deprived of the highly specialized knowledge and repertoire of skills they bring to the teaching-learning process, and children with IEPs are deprived of the benefit of general education.

In Ravenswood Schools, in conjunction with the SAM RTI model, special and general educators collaborate on grade-level action planning, lesson plan development, interpretation of classroom tier 1 data, interpretation of small group tier 2 data, and tier 3 individual intervention and support data. General education teachers, in my experience, are quick to spot strengths that can be capitalized on with individual students. Special educators can be equally quick to spot remedial strategies for use with struggling students.

> General education teachers, in my experience, are quick to spot strengths that can be capitalized on with individual students. Special educators can be equally quick to spot remedial strategies for use with struggling students.

Collaborative teaching can take different forms depending on the partnership formed between the professionals involved. When I go into Ravenswood classrooms, I am likely to see arrangements where two teachers, one grade level and one special education support teacher, teach a reading section together, effectively playing off one another and creating an enjoyable atmosphere with which to tackle difficult material.

In other classrooms, I see a special educator teaching the whole class while the general education teacher is freed to move around the room and provide targeted instruction to groups of students in work stations. Or I might see a general education teacher teaching the whole class while a special educator is working with a small group of students, two of whom have IEPs.

The essence of collaborative teaching is that special education teachers know and can teach the general education curriculum. It is also the case that general education teachers know and can teach requirements of written IEPs for special education students. Collaborative teaching is "one for all and all for one." For RTI models, it is beginning to look like a clear winner. Research will continue to verify or cast doubt on that statement.

To Sum Up

In this chapter I considered the application of schoolwide RTI from the perspective of the elementary or middle school. I reviewed the key features of RTI with attention to the scientific requirements for careful measurement. I pointed out, however, that applications of pure science to the teaching-learning process are insufficient. Busy organizations such as schools are rational-technical enterprises, but they are also cultural entities. School cultures reflect a community of practice where integration of function and mutual respect is paramount. School cultural health can be assessed by measures of school climate that reflect indicators of the school as a learning community.

I discussed the importance of school leadership and examined forms of leadership that will be required to develop and sustain RTI schools. I examined structural issues of leadership such as forms of distributed leadership and qualities of members of leadership teams. I presented a case study of a school in northeast Kansas that is undergoing transformation to a schoolwide RTI model that is a good fit for the Kansas State RTI initiative called Multi-Tiered Systems of Support (MTSS). Madison Elementary School in the Gardner-Edgerton School District of Johnson County, Kansas, provided a look at how specific schoolwide RTI processes are moving into sustainable practice in one school.

Finally I discussed two additional emerging components of exemplary schoolwide RTI practice that are in place in some RTI schools but not yet in others. The first is instructional coaching, an important enhancement that bridges the time between professional development and technical assistance activities and day-to-day practice in schools implementing RTI. The second emerging practice discussed in the chapter is collaborative teaching, an instructional enhancement that brings grade-level teachers into teaching and planning partnerships with special educators and English Language Learner teachers.

8

How RTI Looks at the Districtwide Level

S ome of the weakest efforts to implement schoolwide RTI that I have encountered around the country have been in districts that have tried to "sneak it in" piecemeal. The pieces of the puzzle seem to actively resist fitting together one piece at a time. The silo problem looms large. Teachers begin to feel they are victims of a conspiracy to add to their workloads. Turf battles over who pays for what erupt early in the process. Moving RTI to scale by pursuing a strategy of implementing one critical feature such as universal screening at a time across the board in all schools is, in my opinion, likely to fail.

The strategy pursued in the Knox County School District in eastern Tennessee, which John McCook described in *The RTI Guide*, has a much better chance of taking root and growing over a reasonable period of time. The Knox County District planners began with a mission of using RTI to reduce the number of referrals for special education, about 20 percent of fifty-three thousand students when they began, down to about 13 percent under scaled-up RTI.

The Knox Country RTI model, different from the schoolwide problem-solving model represented in this book, is really a mix of standard protocol RTI, to put eligibility determination for learning disabilities on a scientific basis, and problem-solving RTI. The planning process for scale-up, however, is directly relevant.

Scaling Up in the District

Taking a Process to Scale

Taking a process to scale means beginning with a subset of the units making up an entity and adding units over time until all units exhibit the key elements of the process. Scaling up in the school district can be a challenging process. Decisions about how many and which schools to start with can be crucial. Deciding how long a period of time to allow for completion can also be crucial, as can budgeting time to allow for completion. Budgetary constraints are often a key factor in making decisions about scale-up.

Knox County went about the process in phases. In the first year, around 2003, six schools were selected, most of which had the highest rates of special education referrals in the district. At the end of that year, the six principals reported the results of the process to the remaining elementary school principals, after which an additional thirty principals asked to join the effort. To scale up in a manageable fashion, the district added fourteen schools in year 2 and, by the end of the fourth year had twenty-six schools in full implementation at tiers 1 and 2 of RTI, with multiple components of the process in place at all schools. Knox County thus scaled up in cohorts of schools, which phased in a full-scale RTI model by starting with the earlier grades and moving up the grade ladder. By phasing in a planned model over a period of years, the district was able to maintain a strong positive motivation for later schools to join; proceed to scale in a manageable fashion given district and school-level resources; and benefit from lessons learned at each step in the process with respect to interactive processes between structural elements of the district and corresponding elements within the schools.

Creating Some Fanfare

Schoolwide RTI is a substantive departure from traditional siloized education. As any school reformer will tell you, one of the biggest obstacles to effecting systems change is lack of adequate communication to and across all stakeholders in a complicated process. Any systems change, particularly in schools, requires energy, enthusiasm, and a critical mass of people who buy in to the proposed changes. Effective communication (preferably two-way) and empowerment through participation in planning are key to building momentum.

One way to get communication started in the district is to create a special event to launch the process. When my own children were students in the Berkeley (California) Unified School District, the administration launched a major school improvement program. A one-day community retreat was held in the Berkeley High School auditorium. Attendance, which was surprisingly large, was generated from mailings to families of district students; all teachers, staff, and administrators of the district; and the heads of all community agencies that had worked with Berkeley schools in the past.

The superintendent welcomed the participants and introduced a keynote speaker who laid out the key features of the proposed systems change. A series of critical issues was presented, and all participants were invited to sign up for problem-solving, breakout meetings to produce recommendations addressed to the issue. After the break, participants went to designated rooms to tackle their issue of interest in a format that was facilitated by a district administrator. In the afternoon session, representatives from each breakout session presented the recommendations of their group to the participants as a whole. Volunteers who would join teams at individual schools to help advance the recommendations were recruited through this process. As participants, my wife and I felt that our voices were heard and that we were contributing to a process of improving education in our town that could ultimately benefit our own children.

The district created a newsletter that went out to all participants as well as others who requested to be added to the list later. Volunteers from each issue group and from each school contributed progress information for each edition of the newsletter. The net effect of this event and the subsequent communication system was to create a buzz in the community and the schools, which served to go a long way toward generating buy-in and creating momentum to start the process.

RTI can look at first glance to parents as a way to save money by withholding services and supports under special education. It can similarly look to teachers like a plot to add to their workload through added assessments without explaining why the data processes matter. As every urban district administrator knows, it is particularly important to include special education child and family advocacy organizations in the initial planning and communication stages, so that they can assist families in understanding the implications of the proposed changes.

> *RTI can look at first glance to parents as a way to save money by withholding services and supports under special education. It can similarly look to teachers like a plot to add to their workload through added assessments without explaining why the data processes matter.*

Policy Analysis

Schoolwide RTI has numerous implications for interpreting and, importantly, assessing compliance with federal, state, and local statutes, regulations, and educational codes. Planning for launching an RTI initiative at the district level requires careful attention to all policy implications. In some cases, existing policy interpretations may need to be revisited and updated.

When Ravenswood City School District began implementing the Schoolwide Applications Model (SAM), one of the first major systems change endeavors was to close special education classes, a process that required numerous individualized education program (IEP) conferences, professional development activities, parent information meetings, and more. The California special education classification system categorizes students by the type of placement that the level of severity of the disability would seem to require. Students with extensive needs for special services and supports are often classified as special day class (SDC).

Since Ravenswood had students labeled SDC but was phasing out the separate classrooms, a compliance team from the California Department of Education questioned the grade-level classroom placement of these students. Loss of the SDC classification would have resulted in a loss of funds needed to adequately support the students. Ravenswood sought and obtained a policy interpretation from the state director of special education that interpreted SDC to mean level of support rather than a physical space in which to be served. Since Ravenswood as of 2009 is the only school district in California that serves all students with IEPs in fully integrated environments, the policy language became an issue for the compliance process.

Both No Child Left Behind (NCLB) and the Individuals with Disabilities Education Improvement Act of 2004s (IDEIA) have language that facilitates and supports movement by districts toward standard protocol applications of RTI. The relevant language is less clear in its implications in both statutes for schoolwide, problem-solving RTI, since the latter goes far beyond the issue of eligibility determination for special education. NCLB comes closest in its language emphasizing accountability and evidence-based interventions. Emphasis on the Reading First initiative, for example, is a good fit with schoolwide RTI. Reading First and Early Reading

First (the early childhood version) are grounded in a three-tier prevention logic model that in part mirrors schoolwide RTI.

IDEIA similarly contains language emphasizing evidence-based interventions for reading in particular and for data-based decision making, at least in application to a determination of whether a child has a learning disability. Interestingly, the focus on evidence-based interventions in IDEIA is placed exclusively on reading, and no other components of the overall curriculum. This probably reflects a vote of no confidence by Department of Education officials in the Bush administration on the strength of the research in support of math, science, biology, and other published programs.

Policy language tied to eligibility for designated funds can be particularly important in RTI planning. Any systems change initiative at the district level requires creative use of existing funding streams as well as sources of new funds to get started. Title I of NCLB, for example, presents both an opportunity and a challenge.

Title I exists to provide additional supports to students who are struggling in math or reading or who can be shown to be at risk for academic failure due to adverse economic circumstances. Schools that have some students who meet the risk criteria are eligible to receive funds under the Title I targeted assistance program. Schools with large numbers (at least 40 percent) of students affected by poverty may be eligible for funding as a Title I Schoolwide school. Regulations under the targeted assistance program are somewhat restrictive and may confine teachers funded under Title I to the provision of levels 2 and 3 interventions.

Since urban school districts often have schools in high-poverty areas, the less restrictive Schoolwide Title I program, where it applies, can afford greater flexibility in the operation of a schoolwide RTI program. In other words, under Schoolwide Title I support, funds can be directed to support of schoolwide RTI.

IDEIA also provides sources of supplementary funding that districts can use to start schoolwide RTI. The early intervening services provision of IDEIA Title 6, Part B allows up to 15 percent of earmarked funds under the title to be directed to prevention of special education determination by providing additional academic or behavioral support to struggling students in kindergarten through grade 12.

Other areas of educational policy can be accessed creatively to help fund schoolwide RTI initiatives. They include Section 504 of the Rehabilitation Act, addressed to children with special health care needs; funds in both NCLB and IDEIA earmarked for professional development; funds to implement new models of school reform (Title V); transferability funds to facilitate pooling resources; and school improvement grants.

Finally, local philanthropy should not be overlooked as sources of funding for RTI. In the 1990s, when United School District 500 in Kansas City, Kansas, sought to link integrated school services and supports within the district to community-based supports and services in a coordinated plan, the Kauffman Foundation, a metropolitan Kansas City philanthropy stepped in. It funded School-Linked Services, a new agency set up to facilitate linkages and to broker connections between the schools and community agencies. As a result, the schools worked with the community to put beneficial after-school programs in place. Community philanthropies often have funding priorities directed to school and neighborhood improvement projects.

Engaging the Board of Education

Urban school district superintendents earn their keep when they successfully manage and gain buy-in from their boards of education. Urban boards are often very political, with members who are elected from areas of the city that have particular demographics. Board members want the best for their schools and also see themselves as representing the segment of the city that elected them. This special interest, if it is largely composed of ethnic concerns, can bring a dynamic to the work of the board that can quickly become counterproductive to the needs of the schools. When resources are scarce and pressures to show results are high, mistrust can surface, often with racial overtones. The urban superintendent must successfully navigate these troubled waters and build trust among the various special interests represented on the board.

Urban school district superintendents earn their keep when they successfully manage and gain buy-in from their boards of education. Urban boards are often very political, with members who are elected from areas of the city that have particular demographics.

Schoolwide RTI brings new challenges to this already complicated process. Board members are usually not experts in education. They bring family and community perspectives to the process. They may see value from a lay perspective in traditional silos. A board member who has a child in need of specialized supports and services may value separate class placement for such students. Furthermore, she may suspect that the desiloization process is an effort to redirect support from children who need it to the whole population of the school. In some cities, African American families (and board members) have come to view referral for special education as a way to get extra educational supports for their children, a viewpoint that has contributed to the problem of overrepresentation of African American boys in high-incidence disability categories in special education. RTI over time reduces the number of referrals to special education, as tiered interventions geared to ongoing analysis of curriculum-based measure (CBM) data solve problems early that formerly would have resulted in referral for special education assessment and subsequent placement.

RTI over time reduces the number of referrals to special education, as tiered interventions geared to ongoing analysis of curriculum-based measure (CBM) data solve problems

early that formerly would have resulted in referral for special
education assessment and subsequent placement.

All of this and more presents new challenges for the urban
superintendent seeking to move a district into schoolwide RTI. Historically, school boards respond to information that shows evidence
of gains in communities with similar demographics. Involving board
members in planning work groups and bringing featured speakers
to board meetings who can share results from successful applications of RTI in other cities should prove to be helpful tactics in
ensuring the support of the board in early stages of implementation.

Managing Publicity

The mass media have discovered RTI, and numerous print media
sources including the Associated Press, the *Wall Street Journal*,
and *U.S. News and World Report* have run articles on the subject. Some of these have been both informed and informing, a
useful community service. Others have reflected a negative bias,
misrepresenting the intent as well as the product of the effort. Print
media can be an important ally to comprehensive school reform,
but it is also important to try to help them get the information
right.

Urban core school districts are all too familiar with the consequences of the insidious process of real estate sales. My wife and
I have had the experience several times when our children were
school age of being driven around by real estate agents to be shown
prospective houses in neighborhoods "where the schools are excellent." We soon came to know that the descriptor primarily referred
to schools where the students were, for the most part, of the same
ethnicity (Caucasian) as ourselves.

Real estate agencies, perhaps unintentionally, contribute to
white (and Asian, more recently) flight by passing along opinions

of schools and school districts to prospective buyers with school-aged children. Since many in the community, including real estate agencies, get their opinions concerning schools from the local newspapers and their Web outlets, the process of gaining support for RTI as comprehensive school reform through informing the media takes on new importance. Issuing press releases from a district-level community outreach office can stimulate interest on the part of reporters assigned to cover educational issues. Favorable press reports can counteract over time the negative image of schools and districts held by the greater community and by the real estate industry.

The Ravenswood City School District in East Palo Alto, California, serves as a case in point. For years leading up to 2006, the *San Jose Mercury News*, the primary print media source for the South Bay Area, ran scathing articles about Ravenswood. The district in 2006 had no Caucasian students, and few Caucasian families lived in East Palo Alto. The City of Palo Alto, on the other side of the main traffic artery linking San Jose to San Francisco, is the opposite: a fabulously wealthy Caucasian enclave, for the most part, with schools highly touted by local real estate agents and with few residents of color.

Press coverage of Ravenswood by local print media started to change in 2006 as reporters began to notice that positive educational results were surfacing in that beleaguered district. Coupled with the astronomically high cost of housing in Palo Alto relative to East Palo Alto, some rare good news about schools served as a starting catalyst to lure whites, as well as businesses and industry, back into East Palo Alto, where housing is a relative bargain for the area and affordable to many. Recognition by a major national educational association for the district's RTI program (the Schoolwide Applications Model—SAM), which was widely publicized by the local media, has served to build community pride in Ravenswood's schools and to attract new students.

Getting Started in the District: Selecting Schools

I am a proponent of "worst first." Schools "on restructuring" in NCLB terms, because of chronic failure to even progress toward, let alone make, adequate yearly progress, are good candidates with which to get started early. Chances are these schools want to change as much as the district, the state, and the families of their students want them to. Often these schools are located in neighborhoods blighted by extreme poverty, so moving up can be as important to the neighborhood and community as it is to the schools.

If there are lots of schools in this category, as is the case in many cities, then offering some incentives to schools that volunteer to go first might be a good way to form the first cohort. I strongly recommend that school districts scale up slowly with systems change of this magnitude. Schoolwide RTI is at risk of melting down early if it is insufficiently nurtured in its initial phases.

> *Schoolwide RTI is at risk of melting down early if it is insufficiently nurtured in its initial phases.*

Clusters and Cohorts

In our school reform process, SAM, we contract with districts to provide training and technical assistance to clusters of schools in phased-in cohorts. We limit the number of schools in a cluster, the number of clusters, and the number of cohorts that we work with in any one year so as to concentrate our resources and help the district develop the capacity over time to sustain the process and then move its schools to scale on schoolwide RTI.

This process enables subsets of schools to be in a position to show other schools interested in RTI, but not yet ready to jump in, how the process is going and, importantly, what results are beginning to be achieved. Bringing schools together to exchange stories is an important part of the SAM process and helpful to establishing buy-in across the district. Signs that things are beginning to turn around in the lowest-performing schools after one or two years of engaging schoolwide RTI can serve as an important catalyst to generating interest on the part of other schools to volunteer to comprise the second cohort.

Leadership Qualities

Robert Marzano, Timothy Waters, and Brian McNulty published in 2005 the results of a major investigation into the qualities of school leadership that research confirms have a direct relationship to greater academic achievement on the part of students at all grade levels. They used an approach called meta analysis that examines the strength of correlations across various scientific investigations to see if a common set of conclusions can be reached on the basis of evidence. Their book, *School Leadership That Works: From Research to Results*, accomplishes that task nicely and offers a reasonably coherent theory of school leadership that is compatible with the evidence-based requirements of schoolwide RTI.

The authors organized their findings into a plan of action that sets out standards for principals to articulate a vision for the school and five key steps to realize the vision:

1. Organize a strong site leadership team.
2. Distribute leadership responsibilities across some members of the team, as well as the team as a whole.
3. Select the action steps to be undertaken by the team for which evidence exists that higher academic achievement will result.
4. Identify the order of magnitude of the work: prioritize among an array of actions some of which will lead to first-order change (that is, extend further along an existing pathway) and some to second-order change (creating a new pathway and abandoning an existing one).

5. Match the management style to the magnitude of the systems change initiative.

A site leadership team that examines a school's education code to see what practices are outdated and should be excised and what new practices should be put into place is engaging in first-order change. A principal who seeks ways to improve the professional community of the school to extend to the limits of their competence is engaging in second-order change.

Moving a school into a full-blown, operational schoolwide RTI system requires strong, effective leadership. It should be noted, however, that the term *leadership* here does not reflect the older "great man" theory. Rather, leadership is concentrated at the level of a team of professionals (and may include a parent or a member of the nonprofessional staff) with guidance and support from the team leader, the principal. Marzano, Waters, and McNulty's book does a good job of fitting the key elements of the process into a conceptual framework, with each of the twenty-one identified elements having been grounded in scientific research.

Having the massive process of sweeping systems change guided from within is greatly preferable to being imposed from without. When schoolwide RTI is the desired change sought by the district, qualities of site leadership should be a key determining factor in selecting schools for the first cohort to undergo the process. Success in the first cohort will make the subsequent scale-up efforts with the next cohorts easier. Because schools have their unique communities of practice, the activities undertaken by the leadership team to get started, such as the mix of first-order and second-order change events, may be expected to vary by school. The district can put forward a vision for change and the standards for realizing when it has occurred, but the schools need to set their own action plans for how to proceed. Leadership will be paramount in getting this process underway. Districts can facilitate the process by ensuring that strong, effective principals are assigned to early-cohort schools and that the principals are knowledgeable about and trained in the practices of distributed leadership.

Having the massive process of sweeping systems change guided from within is greatly preferable to being imposed from without.

Manageable Cohorts

The success with which a school district scales up a significant systems change will likely be tied to how carefully it plans a reasonable trajectory for the process within a reasonable time frame. We know from research on the failed Comprehensive School Reform Demonstration Program that a top-down mandate to all schools to begin implementing a predetermined blueprint for change will likely be doomed to fail. Some schools will resonate with the plan and make the district proud. Others will plod along or flounder, and still others will resist and ultimately defeat the process. How to scale up in a planned, orderly manner is tied to a large extent to the size of the district. Scaling up in the Los Angeles Unified School District will require a very different plan from scaling up in the Santa Monica Unified School District.

When we planned with the Ravenswood City School District in East Palo Alto, California, to take SAM to scale, we set up a cohort system. Ravenswood is a small school district with only eleven schools and no high school. Our plan called for four schools to begin the process as cohort 1. While we provided technical assistance and training to the cohort 1 schools and the district, we used meetings of the district's principals to facilitate communication over the process by cohort 1 principals to the other principals. Out of this discourse came a decision to begin a second cohort (after two years) of three schools. A final cohort of the remaining four schools, cohort 3, started up the year following the start-up of cohort 2 schools.

Scale-Up Planning in a Small to Medium District

The Shawnee Mission School District in northeast Kansas, a suburban Kansas City district, is illustrative of a process of reasoned planning for scale-up of schoolwide RTI in a small to medium school district. With around fifty schools, including five high schools, Shawnee Mission is defining cohorts as feeder school complexes according to innovative projects facilitator Dawn Miller. With thirty-five elementary schools and middle schools, feeder school cohorts can plan to accomplish systems change with one new cohort each year for five or six years. Since schoolwide RTI processes are more fully delineated for elementary schools than for middle schools, and certainly for high schools, the district is choosing to begin with three elementary schools in a feeder complex in its first year of implementation. The remainder of the cohort will begin planning for year 1 implementation in the second year.

Districts the size of New York, Chicago, and Los Angeles would do well to regionalize the process and begin cohorts of schools within administratively manageable units of analysis as defined by clusters of schools within regions or feeder school complexes within regions. Currently too little is known about high school RTI to extend to that population of schools with anything more systematic than local innovative and well-documented experiments. Numerous high school reform initiatives are underway, and eventually some subset of these will begin to form a pattern for schoolwide RTI at the high school level. For now, we lack rigorous instruments for screening progress monitoring and fidelity estimation, essential tools with which to get started.

Professional Development

Just to recap a bit, two forms of professional development (PD) are essential to implementing schoolwide RTI. District-based PD delivers in-service education to subsets or the totality of schools in the district, and school-based PD is specific to the needs of a particular school.

The purpose of district-based PD is to provide the knowledge base and increase the competence of professional staff across the district to engage the planning process for implementing schoolwide RTI. District administrators select the PD priorities and content of district-based PD. Examples of district-based PD are introduction to RTI, early intervention, evidence-based practices, positive behavior support, reading and math curricula, technology supports, and data-based decision making. The point of district PD initiatives is to get everyone in agreement with respect to the vision of the district in beginning the RTI systems change process.

School-based PD reflects the perceived needs of each school's leadership team in meeting the priorities of the action plan set by the team. The needs for new knowledge and competence in getting started with implementation are likely to be different from school to school. Examples of school-based PD include familiarity with and use of specific screening assessments; getting started with benchmark assessments; collecting, analyzing, and selecting interventions with curriculum-based measures; and coteaching configurations involving general education, special education, and other support teachers.

It is important for the district administrator to work with principals around support for PD scheduling of activities so that district-based PD offerings do not eclipse or conflict with school-based plans. One district that I have worked with fell victim to just such a conflict around PD. The district had a long list of new competencies associated with its RTI initiative that it assumed it should take responsibility for and required attendance from all of the schools. The problem was that some of the schools had communities of practice where those competencies had already been mastered.

In addition, the district put its PD plan into effect piecemeal; that is, it notified schools of upcoming PD sessions during the course of the academic year. Some schools getting started with RTI had prioritized elements of their action plans and had scheduled school-based PD activities to meet the requirements of their plan. Since Wednesday afternoons were the designated times allotted to PD, the schools would find their scheduled PD activities trumped by the district with little advance notice. In some cases, schools in early cohorts of implementation were forced to cancel their scheduled school-based PD events to attend a district-based PD on a topic that those schools did not need. The result was demoralization by the schools' leadership teams and a loss of enthusiasm, buy-in, and momentum in getting the process underway. Scheduling of professional and staff development activities should, without question, be sensitive to individual school culture. Enthusiasm and buy-in by the professional community of the school in systems change has been repeatedly shown through research to be significant in implementing practices with fidelity and gaining increases in student achievement.

> *Scheduling of professional and staff development activities should, without question, be sensitive to individual school culture. Enthusiasm and buy-in by the professional community of the school in systems change has been repeatedly shown through research to be significant in implementing practices with fidelity and gaining increases in student achievement.*

Capacity Building

Districts launching RTI initiatives should not approach the task with the assumption that they will need to provide all the expertise required to take each school to full implementation. Our own work in urban school districts has taught us that district initiatives can be realized with only catalytic interventions provided in timely fashion. A catalytic intervention is one that is used to start a process within schools that will be completed by schools' own problem-solving mechanisms. The district's input is, "Here is our goal and what it will look like when realized." The school then figures out which steps to take, and in what sequence, to realize the goal.

When districts pursue catalytic interventions, they are building capacity within schools to achieve their own ends through problem solving, a core ingredient of RTI. Coupled with a reasonable mix of school-based to district-based professional development, the process of catalytic interventions over time can strengthen the confidence of the school's site leadership team that great things can be accomplished even under the most adverse circumstances.

Another way to view this problem is to contrast bureaucratic approaches to systems change with what I call "adhocratic" approaches to the same end. An example of a bureaucratic approach would be for a district, perhaps in partnership with an area university, to lay out an entire schoolwide RTI model from A to Z without involving schools or their parent communities. The district would then schedule an extensive series of professional development events to get schools up to speed on the overall plan in a sequence determined by the district. To top it off, the district would exert bureaucratic accountability processes by sending teams of assessors, armed with checklists, to each school to evaluate how it is progressing in meeting the district's plan. How do you think schools' communities of practice will respond to such a top-down approach to a complex systems-change agenda? In one such district, I was told, "The goon squad's coming tomorrow to do their semiquarterly march-through to see what they can ding us on."

Adhocracy refers to self-organizing through problem solving. An adhocratic approach to launching an RTI initiative would be to engage schools and their communities in planning the initiative; selecting schools in cohorts to get started by soliciting volunteers; ensuring that a mix of carefully preplanned district-based professional development activities do not conflict with developing school-based professional development activities; providing adequate support for initial cohorts of schools' professional development activities; and providing catalytic interventions, thus empowering schools to achieve their own as well as district goals through successful problem-solving efforts. This approach to district-initiated RTI is likely to build capacity within the schools to be able to take the initiative to scale in a reasonable time. The bureaucratic approach is not.

RTI in the Louisiana Recovery School District, New Orleans

When Hurricane Katrina struck New Orleans in the summer of 2005, it spelled the end of a seriously troubled school district and the beginning of a radically new educational agenda. Today, four years after Katrina, schools are more or less back in business, but it is not business as usual. Schools that were under restructuring before Katrina became reorganized under a state takeover, as a separate state-operated school district called the Louisiana Recovery School District (RSD). Some schools were too damaged to be reopened, and some new schools were constructed. Students and their families have been slowly finding their way back to New Orleans after the post-Katrina diaspora. Some are RSD charter schools. Other charters are operated by the original New Orleans School District and still others by private charter companies. The state has signaled an intent for all New Orleans public schools eventually to be charter schools.

For our purposes, RSD is of interest. When Paul Vallas was hired to be RSD superintendent by Paul Pastorek, state superintendent of education, significant new initiatives were launched in the district, one of which was schoolwide RTI. Vallas had an impressive history of school reform prior to arriving in New Orleans. He had been CEO of Chicago Public Schools, where he introduced major reforms in troubled, low-performing schools. Later he became superintendent of Philadelphia Public Schools and reversed a significant decline in that city's troubled district before Pastorek hired him.

Vallas appointed Diana Jones as the RTI coordinator, and it is the district model of largely her design that I describe here. This RSD's RTI model is one of the more elegant and complete district-level systems to emerge to date. When I interviewed Jones in 2008, she was quick to point out that the model is very much a work in progress and that the current framework is likely to change as implementation gets underway in the 2008–2009 academic year.

RSD in its manual, *Response to Intervention (RTI) in the Recovery School District 2007-2008*, defines the process as follows:

> Response to Intervention (RTI) is a process that provides high-quality research based instructional and interventions that are matched to a student's academic and behavioral needs. RTI in Louisiana follows a three-tiered process. Tier I is identified as the level in which students are achieving benchmark success. Tier II is the level for students who need strategic support to achieve benchmark success and Tier III is recognized as a level at which students need intensive support to achieve benchmark success.
>
> The RTI process incorporates data to examine the student's learning rate over time to make appropriate instructional decisions. In the RTI process, students with academic or behavior challenges are provided scientific research-based interventions. In the Recovery School District (RSD), these interventions are provided district-wide according to the needs of the student. The student's academic progress is monitored frequently to see if the interventions are sufficient to help the

student reach the instructional level of his or her grade. If collected data indicate that the student has not shown adequate progress despite implemented research-based interventions, consideration for special education may be warranted [p. 4].

This definition differs from the one advanced in this book only by the statement concerning special education. In my view, special education needs to be involved at all intervention levels rather than coming in only after data indicate a lack of progress following all other interventions.

RTI Team

Each school in the district is expected to constitute an RTI team whose primary responsibility is "to accommodate the needs of all students in the general education setting." Team functions include universal schoolwide screening for academic risk; providing teachers with support and materials to implement evidence-based interventions; facilitating the intervention process; assisting teachers to monitor the progress of students; assisting with analyzing progress monitoring data; and participating in data-based decision making across the three levels of intervention. Each team is to include at least the principal (or designated administrator), a reading interventionist, literacy and math coaches, a general education teacher, a counselor, a nurse, a speech therapist, a social worker, and a school psychologist. Others may be invited to join the team to assist with students who have unique or challenging needs.

RSD provides universal screening for academic risk three times each year (fall, winter, spring) for kindergarten through twelfth grade. Screening for children from kindergarten through third grade is provided through DIBELS for literacy, with grades 4–12 screened through the Scholastic Reading Inventory with the Read 180 intervention program. FASTT Math serves as the risk assessment screener for math at all grade levels.

Progress Monitoring

RSD monitors student progress at each of the three levels of intervention. The RTI team, together with grade-level teams, uses progress monitoring data as the basis for decisions on which interventions are made.

The RSD/RTI Manual describes the progress monitoring approach as follows:

> Progress monitoring differs from traditional classroom assessment because it does not rely on mastery measurement. With mastery measurement, teachers test for mastery of single skills in sequence. Therefore, different skills are assessed at different times of the year. This is an unfeasible method to measure rates of progress and maintenance of skills. Instead, curriculum-based assessment used as part of progress monitoring measures rate of progress as well as acquisition of skills [p. 16].

Progress monitoring for behavior at the time of this writing was still unsystematic and a work in progress. The manual refers to an index consisting of number of office visits, reports of classroom disruptions, tardiness frequencies, absenteeism, and suspensions. Although RSD provided numerous professional development activities on schoolwide positive behavior support, it did not, as of this writing, employ the SWIS (University of Oregon) data tracking system for office disciplinary referrals. Progress monitoring for behavior remains a fruitful area for research and instrumentation, but there is no reliable and efficient system that is as yet economically viable for most urban school districts.

For monitoring progress in academic achievement, the district sets benchmark goals from evidence-based reading and math interventions. The benchmark standards reflect the levels at which students are expected to perform in order to be considered successful in their grade as well as prepared to move on to the next grade.

The RTI manual specifies that assessment tools are "sensitive to changes over short periods of time, produce unbiased results, demonstrate proven technical adequacy (i.e., valid and reliable) are quantifiable, relevant to the curriculum, and practical to administer within reasonable cost and time parameters" (p. 14). The assessment tools listed for use by RSD include DIBELS, Voyager Assessments (built into the curriculum), SRI Assessments (Read 180), and Benchmark Assessments, all for literacy. Skill inventories for assessing math include FASTT Math.

Tier 1 Interventions

Based on screening results, increased instruction and student progress monitoring are applied to students falling below the classroom median. Interventions at this level are geared to curriculum benchmarks and provided in groups or to the class as a whole. The RTI manual lists the following procedures to be followed by teachers with support from the RTI team at tier 1:

- Review the universal screening data.
- Review the information provided in the Reading and/or Math Framework according to the appropriate grade.
- If student falls below instructional benchmark as indicated in the framework, work with support personnel from RTI team to determine appropriate intervention application.
- If several students fall below instructional benchmark, work with support personnel to implement instructional strategies and provide interventions through the core curriculum.
- Monitor, chart and review the progress of students.

- Provide incentives to students to determine if the deficit is due to skill limitations or lack of motivation.

- Organize and analyze results.

- Make data-based decisions.

- Change the Intervention or increase or decrease the intensity of the intervention as needed. Use the Reading/Math framework and the rate of progress to determine if a different intervention strategy is warranted.

- Monthly, review progress monitoring data for all students involved in RTI at the school to consider overall growth and areas for systemic improvement of the process. [p. 10]

Tier 2 Interventions

For students whose progress monitoring data indicate that they are continuing to have problems, evidence-based interventions at a higher level of intensity are provided. For literacy, the manual lists the following procedures:

- Refer to the Short Reading and Math Framework or the Reading Framework by grade level for interventions at the Tier II level.

- Students in grades Kindergarten through 3rd grade use Voyagers as the primary Tier II Reading intervention and FASTT Math as the primary math intervention. Implementation will follow district policy and training. Voyager and FASTT Math assessments identify the skill level of each student, and the student receives the intervention appropriate for his or her skill level. The assessments provide data about the student's progress to make decisions about whether to change, increase, decrease or modify the intervention.

- Students in grades 4 through 12 use Read 180 as their primary Tier II intervention. Implementation will follow district policy and training. Read 180 assessments identify the skill level of each student and adapt the intervention to that skill level. Progress monitoring is provided through the Read 180 assessment process.

- Notify the parent to keep them informed when a review of the data indicates that the student should receive support at home for an intervention specified at the Tier II level.

- The intervention schedule is specified by the intervention format. It should be noted that when the intervention schedule is disrupted, and the intervention protocol is not followed, the fidelity of the intervention process is compromised and the maximum results may not be achieved.

- The intervention provides targeted instruction in skills and concepts. Data is collected and progress monitoring occurs weekly to provide the basis for data-driven decisions. Generally, *three data points* below the student's calculated goal line signal a need to change the intervention. Implementation of this process allows for early identification of students who are at risk and provides justification for more intensive interventions [pp. 10–11].

Note that RSD's RTI process calls for parent notification at level 2 if the intervention plan calls for parent support in home-based activities. Note also that attention is drawn to the need for program intervention fidelity to be strictly adhered to in order to maximize the probability that the results predicted on the basis of evidence from research will occur in application. Finally, note the specifications with which to guide data-based decision making (three data points below students' predicted goal attainment path). This rigorous adherence to evidence-based practices is a strength in the initial developmental stages of RSD's RTI model.

The manual also includes language intended to draw teacher attention to the need to consider behavior in a context of measured academic skill deficit—for example, "Many acting out behaviors may diminish to the extent they are a product of a student's response to academic skill deficits." Teachers are asked to consider SWPBS interventions if a likely interaction of the two deficits is occurring. This too, in my opinion, is a strength of this district-driven model.

Tier 3 Interventions

The manual specifies the following procedures for tier 3:

- Incorporate increasing intensities of interventions or change the interventions based on individual needs. Intensity relates to changes for a relative set of variables, such as time, task or duration. The team needs to specify the intervention schedule by occasions per week or per day and their length, including the progress monitoring schedule and the infrastructure of the intervention (e.g., planning, materials and consultation).

- If prescribed changes in the Voyagers or Read 180 interventions are unsuccessful, or if it becomes evident that the student does not have the reading skills necessary to access Voyagers or Read 180,

Corrective Reading through Direct Instruction is provided by the district as a Tier III intervention. In addition, Fast ForWord is an intensive intervention that will be available for students who have severe language deficits and have demonstrated difficulty in acquiring language skills. Interventions should be implemented according to the research design; however, the district and the principal ultimately determine the schedule.

- The math intervention at the Tier III level is FASTT Math. This intervention focuses on number and operations at the primary grade levels and moves to strengthen math facts and fluency at the middle grade levels.

- Tier III interventions are generally provided for 60 minutes a day in addition to the time for core instruction and are usually applied over a longer period of time (application of total intervention time should be several weeks; research recommends at least 10 to 20 weeks depending upon individual student responsiveness and intervention design).

- For students with behavioral issues, PBS Tier III strategies include intensive behavioral supports determined through a review of the data by the RTI team. These are Tertiary interventions that include social work services, counseling and in school intervention services when needed. *Students who have been hospitalized with severe emotional concerns or have a medical history of emotional issues and their work in school is impacted by these behaviors may be referred for an immediate evaluation at the discretion of the RTI team* [p. 12].

The Role of Special Education

RSD's RTI manual refers to the appropriateness of referral for special education evaluation at each of the three tiers. Since the model stresses the importance of addressing the needs of most students in the general education settings, the involvement of special education at each level through collaborative teaching arrangements becomes a possibility. This sets the RSD model apart from many emerging district-directed RTI approaches that confine special education referral to tier 3. The RSD, however, does retain the option of serving some students in separate special education classrooms under tier 3 if a student is shown to continue to need "curriculum and instruction that is significantly different from that of peers or an identified standard."

Table 8.1 illustrates the three-tier intervention process as it is applied to kindergarten reading interventions. Note that in addition to the three tiers of RTI, RSD also adds a fourth tier, called *Advanced*. This, in my view, reflects a value-added dimension of the RSD approach. Since RTI is a risk-prevention model, it tends to overlook gifted students and those who regularly exceed academic benchmarks. By adding the Advanced level, interventions can be applied and progress can be monitored, designed to accelerate the achievement of advanced students.

> *Since RTI is a risk-prevention model, it tends to overlook gifted students and those who regularly exceed academic benchmarks. By adding the Advanced level, interventions can be applied and progress can be monitored, designed to accelerate the achievement of advanced students.*

Reflections on the Recovery School District

The Louisiana RSD approach to schoolwide RTI is a work in progress. Some might argue that it is too prescriptive and usurps the

Table 8.1 Kindergarten Reading Intervention Process in Louisiana Recovery School District, New Orleans

SCREENING	DIBELS			
Criteria	Scores on ISF >0-3 Scores on LNF>0-1	Scores on ISF 4-7 Scores on LNF 2-7	Scores on ISF 8+ Scores on LNF 8+	Scores on ISF 9+ Scores on LNF 9+
FOCUS	**Tier III Intensive**	**Tier II Strategic**	**Tier I Benchmark**	**Advanced**
	Instructional emphasis on oral language development, phonemic awareness (Initial Sound Fluency) and phonics (Letter Naming Fluency)/ decoding incorporating specially designed instruction to meet the needs of students	Instructional emphasis on continued oral language development, phonemic awareness (ISF), phonics (LNF), fluency, vocabulary and comprehension incorporating specially designed instruction to meet the needs of students	Instructional emphasis on phonemic awareness, phonics, fluency, vocabulary, comprehension and grade level expectations (GLEs).	Instructional emphasis on phonemic awareness, phonics, fluency, vocabulary, comprehension and GLEs through advanced-level activities and higher-grade-level materials
Intervention Program	• Harcourt Interventions • Voyager	• Harcourt Interventions • Voyager	• Harcourt • Empowering Writers	• Harcourt • Empowering Writers
Delivery	Additional 30 minutes oral langague development Ratio 1:3 8-10 weeks—may be repeated once.	(30 minutes within core) oral language development Ratio 1:5 6-8 weeks	Whole class and small group instruction 160 minutes	Whole class and group accelerated instruction in higher grade-level materials. Activities and projects. 160 minutes
Progress Monitoring	• DIBELS • Voyager • Benchmark Assess	• DIBELS • Voyager • Benchmark Assess	• DIBELS	• DIBELS
Certify Progress	Evidence of Benchmark Performance			

flexibility individual schools need to design RTI processes reflective of their own unique cultures. Ordinarily I would agree with such a criticism. As I argue throughout this book, students' achievement is a function of the quality of instruction and as such requires the school, not the district or the classroom, to be the unit of analysis. However, New Orleans presents a unique set of circumstances. Many, if not most, of the students in the RSD are poor and African American, and as such victims of a long history of racism and blatant discrimination; moreover, most are still suffering from various forms of posttraumatic stress. Conditions in the city and its educational system are such that extraordinary interventions are required at every level of government, and, in this case, the district.

Paul Vallas, to his credit, has made strong gains in a remarkably short time. Diana Jones, to hers, has produced a highly prescriptive but creative and efficient RTI model to get the schools on a path to quality education grounded in a risk-prevention RTI model. As time passes and the model continues to be refined, I would hope that the manual becomes a regularly updated set of district guidelines for schoolwide RTI, which individual schools can then adopt to fit their unique configurations and cultures.

To Sum Up

In this chapter I examined issues concerning school district RTI initiatives. The process begins with planning for scale-up, including steps to engage community support and interest. Special events hosted by the district are recommended, with invited participation by families, community service providers, and special education and disability advocacy agencies.

A second issue is the importance of careful policy analysis at the early stages, including examination of the implications of educational statutes such as NCLB and IDEIA. State and local statutes and education codes, as well as established school district board policies, union contracts, and so forth, need careful study before unveiling a plan to take to scale. Informing the board of education and relevant educational associations will be important. Finally, managing publicity concerning the plan can help build community support.

Factors affecting initial site selection were discussed. Schools most in need should be in the early cohorts. The value of scaling up slowly with clusters of schools in cohorts was examined. The importance of site leadership qualities was examined in the context of early cohort identification. Professional development issues critical to any RTI initiative were reviewed, as well as the need to identify processes with which to build capacity and ensure sustainability.

The chapter concluded with an examination of the New Orleans Louisiana Recovery School District's developing schoolwide RTI model as a case example. The school rebuilding effort after the devastation of Hurricane Katrina affords an excellent laboratory with which to examine RTI systems in a context of total school reform.

9

How RTI Looks at the Statewide Level

One hot July afternoon, Daryl Mellard, a University of Kansas colleague, and I had lunch in Milton's Café on Massachusetts Street, Lawrence's main drag. The topic was RTI. I had been closely following the research output of Daryl's group at the university and that of the Vanderbilt team headed up by Doug and Lynn Fuchs. Brick by brick, these meticulous social scientists were developing and researching instruments in reading and math progress assessment and laying a foundation for using evidence-based practices in determining who would require identification for special education services, particularly under the learning disability label.

Daryl's RTI book was soon to appear, and I wanted his reaction to the framework I had outlined for this book. His response came in a word: "Whoa!" For the rigorous social scientist, the cart was getting too far in front of the horse.

The problem for me, Daryl, and many others is that in education as a field, ideas with strong potential are put into play well in advance of the published studies that verify their efficacy (or lack thereof). Much of education in America is in crisis, and significant reform measures are urgently needed. RTI is without question a runaway train. It is also an idea whose time has finally come. The small basis that exists from research as of 2009 is promising. The need to match interventions to measured need at various levels of intensity is immediate. Should RTI be confined to one of the determiners of a diagnosis of learning disabilities? Perhaps. But it is not going to happen. The sheer number of books, Web-based materials, DVDs, and other publications that have appeared on the topic in just four years puts paid to any constraint suggested by scientific conservatism. The question now is not how to stop the train but how to keep it on track and moving in a productive direction. The last words any of us ever want to hear are, "We tried RTI; it didn't work."

What I think sets this book apart from the others that have appeared to date is the notion that RTI can become the basis for structural reform in education by enabling a redesign of the combined pedagogies of general and special education, and perhaps the other siloized systems of specialized practice such as English Language Learners and Title I. RTI offers a pathway to fully integrated supports and services that students need and the possibility of collaborative teaching with a focus on multidisciplinary perspectives, knowledge, and competence on learning problems that affect all children.

> *What I think sets this book apart from the others that have appeared to date is the notion that RTI can become the basis for structural reform in education by enabling a redesign of the combined pedagogies of general and special education, and perhaps the other siloized systems of specialized practice such as English Language Learners and Title I.*

Federal Policy and RTI

The RTI train got underway in earnest with several policy initiatives that began in 2004. (My colleagues and I have published a comprehensive review of the history of RTI in *Handbook of Positive Behavior Support.*)

Much of the substance of the congressional hearings around the reauthorization of the special education statute, Individuals with Disabilities Education Act, until finally reauthorized as the

Individuals with Disabilities Education Improvement Act (IDEIA) in 2004, was concentrated on the issue of eligibility determination for classification as a student with learning disabilities (LD). The Office of Special Education Programs (OSEP) held the LD Initiative, a summit conference on the topic around that time. The results of the LD Initiative were summarized in a publication by Rene Bradley and her OSEP colleagues and contained the operational definition of RTI that I quoted in part in Chapter One of this book. So RTI as a policy initiative had its origins in IDEIA and special education practice, which was summarized in 2006 in the landmark publication, *Response to Intervention: Policy Considerations and Implementation*, by the National Association of State Directors of Special Education.

No Child Left Behind (NCLB) does not specifically address RTI, but its emphasis on evidence-based practices, and particularly the Early Reading First and Reading First sections, made the logical case for a quick jump from special education to general education. The first book for general educators to appear was *Response to Intervention: Principles and Strategies for Effective Practice* published in 2005 by school psychologists Rachel Brown-Chidsey and Mark Steege. With the jump to general education came the shift in emphasis from standard protocol RTI to problem-solving and, ultimately, schoolwide RTI.

Interestingly, schoolwide positive behavior support (PBS), a product of research in special education, made the jump with the three-tiered reading intervention to general education. Schoolwide PBS was not new to general education, having been put in place in schools within a number of states by 2005. Then in 2007, the State Improvement Grant (SIG) and State Personnel Development Grant (SPDG) funding initiatives of the federal Office of Special Education put out the first call for proposals from state education agencies to compete for funds that could be used to establish RTI initiatives at the state level, called "multitiered levels of support." This language avoided the term *response to intervention* (RTI) in an effort to keep RTI identified with LD determination. Together with an OSEP-funded National Center on Response to Intervention (NCRTI: www.rti4success.org), successful state grantees and even some unsuccessful states moved to put statewide RTI initiatives into place. States with grants used IDEIA Part D funds for personnel development to offer training and technical assistance, as well as cash grants in some cases, for districts willing to comply with state RTI requirements. The net effect of this policy initiative was to launch large numbers of districts within a handful of states into schoolwide RTI.

The next piece of the policy puzzle was put into place by the NCRTI. Since most of the policy initiatives up to 2007 were funded through special education at the federal level, state superintendents of instruction were only dimly aware of the relevance of these funding initiatives for state general education planning and personnel preparation. On December 6 and 7, 2007, NCRTI held a summit conference for state schools chiefs on schoolwide RTI and thus brought the state general education policy system into the policy initiative process.

Collectively, these measures served to swiftly accelerate the RTI train down the track. For our purposes here, it is of interest to see how these newly oriented state policy initiatives mirror findings from research, how closely they resemble each other, and the extent to which they offer the potential to fully integrate general and special education practices. For purposes of getting a small sample of representative state efforts, I describe three from the list of SIG and SPDG grantees.

Kansas Multi-Tiered System of Support

Alexa Posny, commissioner of education in Kansas as of 2009, was formerly the director of OSEP, the nation's chief special education officer. As a result, Kansas was well positioned to make the jump from special education innovation to state-level general and special education policy.

The state Multi-Tiered System of Support (MTSS) initiative was launched following receipt of a SIG in 2007–2008 and expanded following Posny's attendance at the NCRTI conference. The state initiative was officially launched in May 2008 with publication of its overall framework on www.kansasmtss.org. MTSS was framed as a discretionary model in Kansas rather than a mandate. The Kansas Department of Education (KSDE) provides personnel development and technical assistance services to districts that volunteer to implement the features of the initiative, funded through the IDEIA, Part D funds for professional development. Consequently, in Kansas, MTSS is directed by Colleen Riley, the state's director for special education (student support services).

The Kansas Special Education Network

Grant funds from the SIG and other sources are used in Kansas to support the Kansas Statewide Technical Assistance Resource System (KSTARS), a special education network of technical assistance providers. Within the KSTARS network, eight technical assistance groups provide interventions to schools and districts on ten priority areas of state educational policy, of which RTI is one. KSTARS interventions are designed to "build the capacity of local districts, support evidence-based research practices and create self-sustaining efforts at the district and building levels for support to students with disabilities and their families." In addition to the SIG grant, technical assistance by KSTARS is funded from IDEIA Title VI-B set aside and preschool set aside, and IDEIA Part C funds for early childhood, which in Kansas is under the Kansas Department of Health and Environment.

The Kansas system has done a good job of documenting the research base in support of each of its MTSS components.

The MTSS Web site provides two downloadable documents. "Innovations Configuration Matrix" lists each critical feature of the model, components of each feature, and sets of descriptive indicators that districts can use to assess whether they are implementing, in progress, or not implementing. "The Research Base" provides a list of research publications in support of each key feature.

The features of MTSS are Leadership and Empowerment; Assessment; Curriculum; Instruction; Data-Based Decision Making; and Integration and Sustainability. Components of Leadership are district leadership, building leadership, and creating an empowering culture. Indicators for earning a check mark under implementing are making changes to the curriculum, instruction, and environment; leadership and school staff engaged in data-based decision making; leadership and school staff have a consensus on implementing MTSS; all professional development and coaching functions are directed to MTSS priorities; student learning is customized to be relevant and enabling; and data on student learning are openly shared and discussed at all levels.

The three tiers of Kansas MTSS are called general instruction (tier 1), supplemental instruction (tier 2), and intense instruction (tier 3). For purposes of illustration, Table 9.1 shows components 1, 2, 3 and 4 of the critical feature Instruction.

Note that component 3, "Schedule allows for protected instruction time," asks districts to work with schools to increase the amount of time students are in "protected" instruction such as reading, meaning that no other school activities can interfere with the allotted time for reading at each RTI level of intervention. Note also that the flexible grouping component asks schools to hold more intensive interventions to smaller groupings of students.

Component 3 is as prescriptive as the state MTSS guidelines get. For the most part, the MTSS guidelines are suggestive, allowing districts flexibility in prioritizing components to implement and selecting from available evidence-based interventions, screening and progress monitoring tools, and other materials.

Table 9.1   Kansas MTSS Innovation Matrix

Component 1: All Instructional Practices Are Evidence Based			
Implementing	In Progress		Not Implementing
The staff has formally evaluated and documented the adequacy of all the academic and behavioral instructional practices used across all tiers.	The staff has participated in discussions about the evidence base of specific academic and behavioral instructional practices for different tiers.	General information about evidence-based academic and behavioral instructional practices is disseminated to staff.	There is an insufficient or unknown evidence base for academic and behavioral instructional practices across tiers. All staff is expected to read information about evidence-based instructional practices.

Component 2: Instructional Practices Are Implemented with Fidelity			
Implementing	In Progress		Not Implementing
All staff is specifically trained in the use of targeted evidence-based instructional practices/ strategies for academics and behavior. All staff under-stands the critical features and application in all settings. Ongoing support and	Some staff is trained in the use of evidence-based instructional practices/strategies for academics and behavior and "take the information back" to their colleagues via Professional Learning Communities, etc.	Selected staff (e.g., reading coach, special education staff, title teacher, counselor, etc.) receives training in use of evidence-based instructional practices/ strategies.	The learning instructional practices/ strategies are left up to individual staff.

(Continued)

Table 9.1   (Continued)

coaching is provided as staff implements the instructional practices/ strategies.			
The staff selects evidence-based instructional practices/ strategies that are an appropriate match for the needs of the learner, academically and behaviorally.	The staff selects instructional practices/ strategies that are an appropriate match for the needs of the learner, academically and behaviorally.	The administration selects a set of behavioral and academic instructional practices/ strategies for use with all learners in all settings regardless of individual need.	The staff uses the same behavioral and academic instructional practices/ strategies for all learners in all settings regardless of individual need.
A process is in place to check the fidelity of instructional practices/ strategies for behavior and academics across all settings with feedback and coaching to staff provided throughout the year.	The fidelity of instructional practices/ strategies for behavior and academics is specifically reviewed through observation of the staff during personnel evaluation, and feedback is	The fidelity of instructional practices/ strategies for academics is checked by having staff note example instructional practices on sample lesson plans turned into their supervisor. A plan is being developed to check for fidelity	It is assumed that all staff are implementing instructional practices/ strategies with fidelity. Practices/ strategies related to social/ behavioral needs are not a concern.

provided at that time.	of implementation of practices related to social/behavioral needs of learners.	

Component 3: Schedule Allows for Protected Instruction Time

Implementing	In Progress	Not Implementing
The schedule provides sufficient time for core, supplemental, and intensive instruction and is protected from all controllable interruptions and monitored to insure that planned time is actualized.	The schedule provides sufficient time for supplemental, core, and intensive instruction and it's left up to individual staff to insure that planned time is actualized.	The schedule does not include specific time for core, supplemental, and intensive instruction.

Component 4: Flexible Grouping Allows for Appropriate Instruction

Implementing	In Progress	Not Implementing
Supplemental and intensive group size is based on the premise that as intensity of instruction increases, group size decreases, and instruction is delivered by highly trained staff.	Some attempts are made to lower group size for supplemental and/or intensive instruction and may or may not be delivered by highly trained staff.	Supplemental and intensive instruction is provided in group sizes based upon staffing availability.

Source: Kansas Multi-Tier System of Supports Innovation Configuration Matrix (ICM), February, 2009, version 2.0 (pp. 10–12). Can be found at www.kansasmtss.org

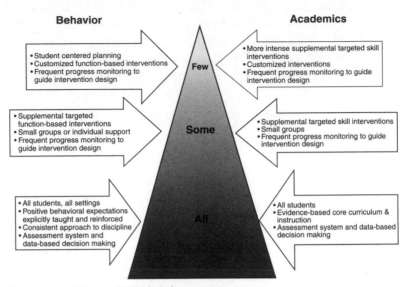

Figure 9.1 Kansas MTSS Schematic

Source: www.ksde.org/Default.aspx?tabid=2004

*For the most part, the MTSS guidelines are suggestive, allow-
ing districts flexibility in prioritizing components to implement
and selecting from available evidence-based interventions,
screening and progress monitoring tools, and other materials.*

Figure 9.1 presents the Kansas MTSS schematic. Figures 9.2 and
9.3 are the schematics prepared by the Shawnee Mission School District (SMSD) in Kansas to show how that district is implementing
MTSS. The graphics show behavioral interventions separately from
academic interventions to conserve space, but the intent is to show
how that district puts teeth into the general guidelines presented
by the state initiative.

Finally, Figure 9.4 reflects outcome data on the part of grades
K–2 from DIBELS progress monitoring assessments in the first
cohort of schools (cohort A) to implement MTSS in the Shawnee
Mission School District. Slight progress was reflected after one year
of implementation (winter and spring assessments) and strong

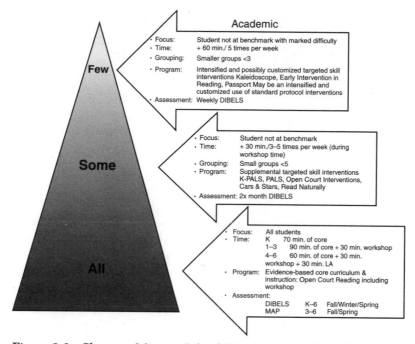

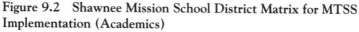

Figure 9.2   Shawnee Mission School District Matrix for MTSS Implementation (Academics)

Source: www.smsd.org

progress by winter of the second year of implementation. These data are typical of findings from around the country, indicating that it typically takes two to three years of progressive implementation of significant systems change before child outcome data at grade level begin to show positive results. Implementers of solid schoolwide RTI models should not get discouraged if they do not achieve dramatic gains within the first two years. If there are no solid upward trends at each grade level by the end of year 3, there may be problems with either the model or, more likely, the fidelity of its implementation.

The Kansas MTSS model has some obvious strengths. It is nonprescriptive for the most part and yoked to a technical assistance network that can assist school districts in getting started. It integrates behavior and academics and provides a solid basis in scientific

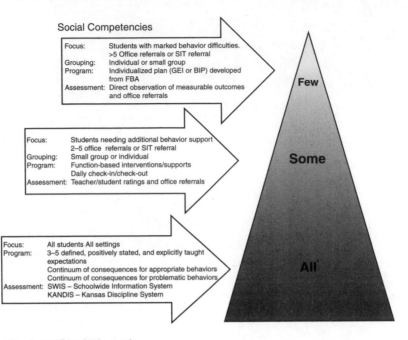

Social Competencies

Focus: Students with marked behavior difficulties.
            >5 Office referrals or SIT referral
Grouping: Individual or small group
Program: Individualized plan (GEI or BIP) developed
            from FBA
Assessment: Direct observation of measurable outcomes
            and office referrals

Few

Focus: Students needing additional behavior support
            2–5 office referrals or SIT referral
Grouping: Small group or individual
Program: Function-based interventions/supports
            Daily check-in/check-out
Assessment: Teacher/student ratings and office referrals

Some

Focus: All students All settings
Program: 3–5 defined, positively stated, and explicitly taught
            expectations
            Continuum of consequences for appropriate behaviors
            Continuum of consequences for problematic behaviors
Assessment: SWIS – Schoolwide Information System
            KANDIS – Kansas Discipline System

All

GEI — General Education Intervention
BIP — Behavior Intervention Plan

Figure 9.3   Shawnee Mission School District Matrix for MTSS Implementation (Social/Behavioral)

Source: www.smsd.org

evidence for its critical features and components. It provides a descriptive tool, the matrix, to enable districts to self-assess on their paths to implementation.

A problem for Kansas MTSS is that it is wholly housed in special education, which provides its funding and administration at the state level. The perception by some Kansas school districts that MTSS is solely for special education somewhat hampers its progress in starting toward scale within the state.

A problem for Kansas MTSS is that it is wholly housed in special education, which provides its funding and administration at the state level. The perception by some Kansas school districts that MTSS is solely for special education somewhat hampers its progress in starting toward scale within the state.

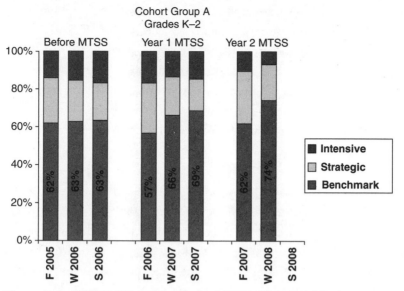

Figure 9.4   DIBELS Progress Under MTSS, Shawnee Mission School District: Cohort A, Grades K–2

Note: F = fall, W = winter, S = spring.

Source: www.smsd.org

Colorado Multi-Tiered Model of Intervention and Instruction

To better understand the rapid evolution of RTI from its origins in special education to its schoolwide application, it is useful to examine the definitions RTI Colorado planners began with in 2004 and its 2008 definition.

In 2004 Colorado began with a definition from the Learning Disabilities Roundtable:

> A Response to Scientific, Research-based Intervention Process ... is a problem-solving framework that may be used to detect student academic and behavioral difficulties and guide the use of scientifically, research-based interventions to provide intense,

individualized, student-centered instruction. Individual student response to general education and intensive specialized instruction are measured periodically and compared to age, grade, or classmate performance. The resulting data of response to intervention measures may be used to inform instruction and, as part of the comprehensive evaluation described in IDEIA [www.cde.state .co.us].

In 2008 the state definition of RTI was, "Response to Intervention is a multi-tiered, problem-solving approach that addresses academic and behavioral difficulties of ALL students. It is an integrated school improvement model that is standards-driven, proactive and incorporates both prevention and intervention. *RTI is effective at ALL levels (early childhood through high school)*" (www.cde .stat.co.us).

Although the claim that RTI is effective at all levels has yet to be substantiated through research, it is not at all unusual for state departments of education to engage in Web-based cheerleading for new initiatives in efforts to build enthusiasm and gain momentum in participating districts. The Colorado effort began in March 2005 with a group of stakeholders who took on the task of creating a set of RTI readiness indicators for schools to use to determine resources and develop implementation action plans. The data from the readiness indicators were presented in April 2005 to the state Special Education Directors' Conference and from there to a statewide RTI Task Force convened by the Colorado Department of Education (CDE).

Material from the CDE task force posted on the department's Web site contained the following statement: "It is critical that educators view RTI as a schoolwide, multi-tiered prevention/intervention approach that is aimed at meeting the learning needs of ALL students, not just as part of the identification process for students with learning disabilities as referenced in IDEA 2004."

The repeated use of capitalization of the word ALL in these documents seems to reflect the need to say loudly, "This is not just a special ed thing!" One can surmise that as with the Kansas MTSS initiative, things that seem to be identified with special education at the outset often are found to be a hard sell with the general education establishment. This was certainly the case earlier when PBS made the leap from special education to general education in becoming schoolwide positive behavior support (SWPBS). To some principals and general education district-level administrators, RTI looks like SWPBS Part II.

Figure 9.5 reflects the 2008 version of the Colorado model for RTI: Multi-Tiered Model of Instruction and Intervention. Note that the Colorado schematic does not break out behavior and

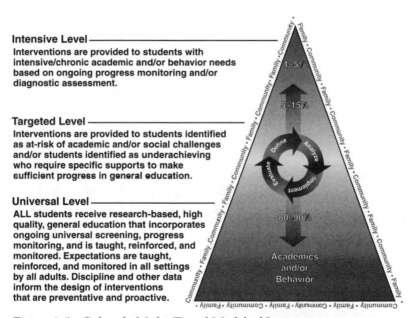

Colorado Multi-Tiered Model of Instruction & Intervention

Intensive Level
Interventions are provided to students with intensive/chronic academic and/or behavior needs based on ongoing progress monitoring and/or diagnostic assessment.

Targeted Level
Interventions are provided to students identified as at-risk of academic and/or social challenges and/or students identified as underachieving who require specific supports to make sufficient progress in general education.

Universal Level
ALL students receive research-based, high quality, general education that incorporates ongoing universal screening, progress monitoring, and is taught, reinforced, and monitored. Expectations are taught, reinforced, and monitored in all settings by all adults. Discipline and other data inform the design of interventions that are preventative and proactive.

Figure 9.5   Colorado Multi-Tiered Model of Instruction and Intervention

Source: Colorado Multi-Tiered Model of Instruction & Intervention, www.cde.state.co.us/Rfl/LearnAboutRtl.htm

academics as separate halves of the pyramid but rather integrates behavior and academics into a single conceptual model. An advantage of incorporating SWPBS within an overarching RTI model is that teachers are taught to interpret data from both sources simultaneously in order to make decisions concerning interventions. A fully integrated model would certainly be the goal for full RTI implementation. In some states, however, the two halves of schoolwide RTI may need to be conceptualized (and graphically represented) separately as teachers and administrators begin to learn the complexities of both sets of multitiered assessments and interventions. In other words, bringing the two halves of schoolwide RTI together may require two learning curves: one for SWPBS and one for RTI.

Colorado produced an RTI configuration map to enable districts and schools to self-assess their status at three levels—Awareness, Exploration, and Implementation—for each of six critical features of the state RTI initiative: data-driven decision making, collaboration, parent partnerships, problem-solving teams, three-tiered interventions, and research-based best practice.

For data-driven decision making at the Awareness level, assessment data from several sources are examined, shared with students and parents, and used to identify students who are not progressing in areas of the curriculum. At the Exploration level, data are examined collaboratively and used to develop agreement about linking research-based interventions for curriculum or behavior to measured student progress. At the Implementation level, the term *progress monitoring* is introduced as consistent documentation of the effectiveness of interventions.

For the critical feature of collaboration at the Awareness level, teachers share information about students informally, usually with minimal planning or structure, and only when a need arises. RTI language is seldom used. At the level of Exploration, formal mechanisms for collaborative meetings are put in place; meetings occur regularly, and RTI language and responsibilities are clarified. At the level of Implementation, the meetings are data driven, and teachers come to share responsibilities for the measured effectiveness of particular interventions.

For the critical feature of parent partnerships at the level of Awareness, teachers and administrators make some efforts to involve parents in educational planning and decision making. At the Exploration level, specific school structures such as teams are formalized at the school to provide parents with information needed to participate in decision making. Parent input is respected and valued. At the level of Implementation, a collaborative dialogue is established between school structures and parents to examine options for interventions. Parent partnerships are initiated by the school and then nurtured and sustained. The process is evaluated to assess the extent of positive experience on the part of parents.

> At the Exploration level, specific school structures such as teams are formalized at the school to provide parents with information needed to participate in decision making. Parent input is respected and valued.

The critical feature of problem-solving teams at the Awareness level has teachers learning to differentiate between problem solving and referral to special education, as well as learning to collect and report student progress data to use for decision making. At the Exploration level, problem-solving teams are in place, and the three-level RTI model is beginning to reflect intervention intensity with some progress monitoring. Student outcomes as a function of interventions are beginning to be assessed at the team level. At the level of Implementation, school problem-solving teams are consistently using progress monitoring data to assess student responsiveness to interventions. Schoolwide academic and behavioral data are reviewed by problem-solving teams to determine the extent to which interventions resulting from the data-based decision-making process are aligned with measured student needs.

The critical feature of three-tiered interventions at the Awareness level reflects conversations at the school concerning how RTI works and its purposes and requirements, and a consensus is emerging that to put a model into place is likely to be more effective for student achievement and a more efficient use of school resources. At the level of Exploration, interventions are organized into a three-level framework of intensity geared to student need. The community of practice of the school engages in discourse about steps to put RTI in place together with a comprehensive plan for staff and professional development. At the level of Implementation, all school personnel are informed about and knowledgeable of how the three-level RTI system is integrated into school problem-solving structures. Assessments and interventions are implemented at each level with progress monitoring for effectiveness assessment. Results are shared with parents, students, and the school community.

Finally, the critical feature research-based practice at the Awareness level has school personnel becoming familiar with what is meant by "evidence-based practices and interventions." It is expected that evidence-based practices are used inconsistently across the building. At the level of Exploration, school personnel are actively investigating and seeking out evidence-based practices and striving for a consensus on the identification and use of these practices. The effects on student achievement are analyzed and shared in order to further student achievement.

At the level of Implementation, school problem-solving teams consistently use progress monitoring to determine student responsiveness to interventions. Schoolwide data on both academics and behavior are reviewed by teams to ensure students are progressing. Interventions are aligned to student needs.

Family Involvement

The Colorado RTI initiative places emphasis on the full integration of SWPBS and academic interventions across the three levels. It brings parent and family participation much more prominently into focus by making it one of the model's critical features and evaluating family perspectives as they engage the process. Of all the states that have RTI processes and initiatives underway that I reviewed, Colorado was making the greatest effort to fully engage families in the process.

The Colorado RTI Web site (http://www.cde.stat.co.us/rti) contains a wealth of information for schools and districts in the state seeking to implement, although some of the information is rapidly becoming dated. (This is, of course, a problem with all Web sites serving a rapidly evolving system.) Next steps for CDE might include weaving all up-to-date Web-based information into an electronic manual, with regular updates so that all schools and districts will have the same information, with guidance from the state on their efforts to implement. A compilation of research documentation such as that provided by Kansas MTSS, for example, might also enhance Colorado's effort statewide, particularly since the state's model includes the critical feature of research-based best practice. Such a tool would be helpful to school problem-solving teams in seeking a consensus on evidence-based interventions.

New Hampshire Responds Model

The New Hampshire Responds model had its origins in a pilot project funded by an earlier state improvement grant. This project piloted RTI processes at four sites, including middle and high schools. Results from the pilot sites were incorporated into New Hampshire's State Personnel Development Grant Application in 2006, and approval of that application led to New Hampshire Responds, the state's RTI initiative.

New Hampshire Responds takes a different approach from the Kansas and Colorado models by embedding RTI in a broader plan of personnel preparation rather than making it the overarching agenda. As a comprehensive state personnel preparation plan, New Hampshire Responds is addressed to RTI applications to PBS and literacy, with a third component addressed to preparing personnel in the area of transition of special education students from secondary education to adult life.

The New Hampshire Responds Web site (http://www.ed. state.nh.us/education/doe/organization/instruction/SpecialEd/NH Responds.htm) states that its purpose is to

> improve pre-service and in-service personnel prepa-ration systems in order to improve the knowledge and skills of general and special education teachers, early intervention personnel, related services person-nel, paraprofessionals and administrators in designing, delivering and evaluating scientifically-based practices in two areas: (1) response to intervention (RtI) sys-tems of positive behavioral interventions and supports (PBIS) and literacy instruction (LI); and (2) intensive-level secondary transition supports (STS) for students with emotional/behavioral disorders (in participating high schools). We also aim to improve the systems for recruiting, hiring, and retaining education and related service personnel who are highly qualified in these areas.
>
> The ultimate goal of participation in NH RESPONDS is for schools to have a highly developed

integrated 3-tier system of academic and behavior support at the end of the grant period. In order for this to occur, school districts will have developed a coordinated system of district-wide and individual professional development plans and activities. The primary strategies for accomplishing these goals include intensive work with schools in five demonstration sites, workshops offered statewide, the creation of course work at the undergraduate and graduate levels, and the revision of education certification requirements in certain specialty areas.

Since the primary funding for the New Hampshire initiative comes from the state personnel development grant funds, the overall model and its administrative staff reflect a strong special education identity, although the RTI model is schoolwide in scope. To some extent, most of the state initiatives appear to be wrestling with the general education responsibility and implications of RTI on the one hand and start-up funding coming from special education sources on the other.

To some extent, most of the state initiatives appear to be wrestling with the general education responsibility and implications of RTI on the one hand and start-up funding coming from special education sources on the other.

Figure 9.6 illustrates the relationship of the three components of New Hampshire Responds. Note that the pyramid is essentially the same as the one provided in Chapter One of this book with the exception that it is inverted. Note that "Secondary Transition for High School" appears at the bottom of the figure and is separate from the behavior and literacy components, which are the subjects of RTI interventions.

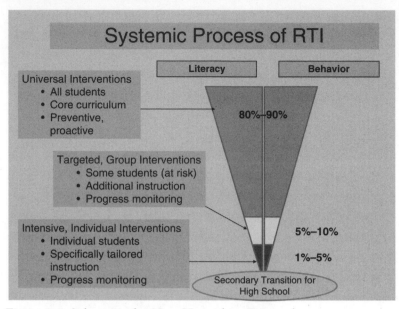

Figure 9.6 Schematic for New Hampshire Responds

State Request for Application

New Hampshire established in March 2008 a formal process for soliciting applications from its school districts to create demonstration sites for its RTI initiative. The New Hampshire Responds Request for Applications stated its purpose as addressing "children and youth in early childhood education (preschoolers), elementary, middle and high school, including students with a full range of mild, moderate, and severe disabilities through school demonstration sites in five (districts) throughout the state." Outcomes from the effort would include improved social and emotional skills, improved literacy knowledge and skills, reductions in problem behaviors (including school dropouts), and increased rates of graduation followed by competitive employment or enrollment in higher education.

To receive funding from the State Education Agency under New Hampshire Responds, each district application must identify one

K–12 school (any grade configuration) that can show evidence of 80 percent buy-in from the entire school staff to commit to RTI in literacy and PBS. High school applicants are required to show 70 percent buy-in. Second, the district must agree to identify at the end of the first year of funding two additional schools, including one early childhood education setting, that have also achieved the 80 percent buy-in rate. Third, the applicant district must establish a districtwide leadership team that will provide oversight of the process at the district level using data-based decision-making processes.

The request for application further states that applicant districts must be able to show that proposed demonstration site schools have already achieved implementation with measured fidelity on tier 1 RTI interventions and assessments in literacy, behavior, or both. Finally the request for application contains a note: "We are looking to select two high schools from the participating (districts) who commit to implementing secondary transition supports (STS) in addition to implementation of RTI in behavior and literacy."

Unique New Hampshire Responds Feature

Of the state RTI initiatives that I have reviewed, New Hampshire Responds is the first to offer incentive grants to districts to include early childhood preschool programs and high schools as model demonstration sites. RTI at the secondary level is just beginning to surface in conference presentations, and there are few models to observe. If New Hampshire can achieve model demonstration sites at the high school level, the state will have accomplished a remarkable feat.

The extension of RTI to preschool settings will also accomplish a major feat. Although there has been more published research on RTI processes with that age group, particularly assessments, there remain few examples of full RTI implementation, at least that I have been able to locate. Early childhood education settings present a different set of challenges for RTI implementation than high schools. These programs are less likely, for example, to be resistant to systems change initiation originating from special education than high schools. However, staff in these settings in my experience are often much more oriented to social development and "fun stuff" than to interventions with measured fidelity and data-based decision making. The challenge for early childhood settings will probably be embracing the scientific rigor that is required in RTI implementation.

Components of New Hampshire Responds

New Hampshire describes RTI as follows: "RTI is based on differentiated instruction and requires critical factors and components to be in place at the *universal* (Tier 1), *targeted* (tier 2), and *individual* (tier 3) levels." Tier 1 includes primary preventions for the whole population of the school and differentiated instruction to reach 80 to 90 percent of all students. Figure 9.7 presents the conceptual framework for RTI tier 1 of New Hampshire Responds.

Each RTI tier is guided by a team devoted to operations at that level. The tier 1 team is the site leadership team of the school, called the Universal School Leadership Team. Its members are administrators, the curriculum and assessment director, a general education teacher, a special education teacher, a psychologist or behavior specialist, a literacy specialist, the Title I coordinator, a paraeducator, and a family member. New Hampshire Responds is the only state initiative I have seen that calls for including paraeducators and parents on the school's leadership team. It is unclear whether parent participation would be compensated under the grant solicitation. One of the special roles of the tier 1 team is to "actively communicate with staff members and families regarding the activities of the school team." Having a parent (preferably paid) on

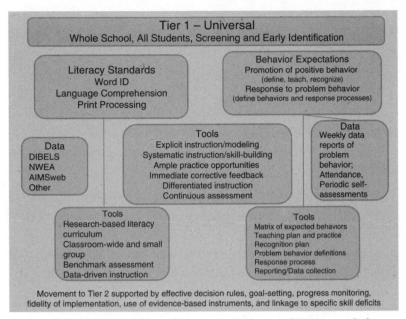

Figure 9.7   New Hampshire Responds Conceptual Framework for RTI Level 1

a school's RTI team can greatly facilitate parent-to-parent networking and communication regarding RTI processes, an important consideration when a substantial systems change effort is underway.

> *New Hampshire Responds is the only state initiative I have seen that calls for inclusion of paraeducators and parents on the school's leadership team.*

Identification of students for tier 2 interventions is geared to a percentage calculation of benchmark scores with a cutoff score, the results of screening for behavior disorders, and a cutoff number based on office disciplinary referrals. Tier 2 operations are defined as the "provision of additional time, strategies, approaches and tools." The approach also lists group interventions and targeted core instruction, with "increased monitoring of targeted skills to measure intervention progress."

Under *literacy*, assessment data are provided through DIBELS, AIMSweb, and other assessments, with interventions provided in small groups based on specific skill needs such as sight word recognition. Under *behavior*, assessments include "weekly data reports of problem behavior or pro-social behavior; progress monitoring of group interventions; and periodic self assessments." Interventions are listed as "social contracting; check-in, check-out; PASS (preparing and supporting self managers) and other group interventions and support."

Movement to tier 3 or 1 occurs when "supported by effective decision rules, goal setting, progress monitoring, fidelity of implementation, use of evidence-based instruments and linkage to specific skill defaults." Tier 2 operations are guided by a "targeted team." Specifications for team membership include essentially the same mix as the universal team except for a parent representative. Functions listed for the targeted team include "provides system of professional development and support for teachers" and "manage data to determine movement between and within tiers."

Tier 3 of New Hampshire Responds RTI "targets the 1–5% who are not responding to Tier I and Tier II efforts." In tier 3, intensive interventions are delivered in small groups or individually, in addition to core instruction. Students are individually monitored for progress at this tier. Interventions for behavior at this tier include a full functional behavioral assessment and PBS support plan with person-centered planning and crisis intervention strategies if needed. Wraparound is specified as available at this tier if required by student need. At the high schools, school-to-career planning is included as an option under transition planning. Data sources include individual progress monitoring and periodic self-assessments (if possible).

For tier 3 literacy, interventions include one-on-one tutoring and ample practice opportunities with immediate corrective feedback. In addition to data from DIBELS and AIMSweb, "diagnostic assessment" is listed, and "alternative education planning" is referred to as an intervention.

A tier 3 "intensive team" is specified under New Hampshire Responds, membership of which is individualized based on student need and includes specialists as needed. One of the functions of the tier 3 team is "evaluation and use of assistive technology and augmentative communication as needed."

New Hampshire Responds and Special Education

New Hampshire Responds does not directly mention special education referral in its published materials describing the model. One may assume that special educators participate at all three tiers since they are included on tier 1 and tier 2 teams. In addition, a "system for special education referral" is listed as one of five operations specified for tier 3 literacy. This puts the New Hampshire model a step ahead, in my view, of state models that envision tier 3 as requiring special education placement for either academic or behavioral deficiencies.

Finally the New Hampshire Responds RTI system includes at each site an RTI coach who has these qualities:

- Well respected
- A strong communicator
- Flexible in terms of developing schedules
- Highly skilled at building trusting relationships
- Ambitious about the change process
- Respectful of teachers and the demands of the classroom
- Skilled at working with data
- An effective problem solver

New Hampshire Responds clearly provides a rich mix of resources to be structured at each site, including an RTI coach and teams with a wide spectrum of multidisciplinary participation at all three tiers. Funds to get the process started are distributed through the state's SPDG grant to grantees in the various regions of the state. The recipients of these model demonstration grants are what New Hampshire, an intensely rural state, calls school administrative units, which may be a single district or a consortium of up to nine school districts.

> *New Hampshire Responds clearly provides a rich mix of resources to be structured at each site, including an RTI coach and teams with a wide spectrum of multidisciplinary participation at all three tiers.*

To Sum Up

This chapter is concerned with the "runaway train" argument that often comes up in discussion of RTI. Coming out of research in special education focused on disability determinations, RTI has unquestionably run far ahead of its basis in research for demonstrated efficacy. By making the leap to general education, problem-solving or schoolwide RTI is witnessing an explosion in policy- and resource-driven initiatives at all levels of public education.

To consider the perspective of state education agencies and, in particular, state RTI initiatives, I examined three states in some detail: Kansas, Colorado, and New Hampshire. Each of these state initiatives to some extent follows a common template that can be seen across most of the state initiatives, yet each addresses the extensive systems change process differently.

I reviewed the Kansas MTSS initiative, which is schoolwide RTI lodged administratively under the state director for special education. As with most of the other state RTI initiatives, there is a distinct special education flavor to MTSS, yet it is structured to have an impact on all students at each of three tiers of assessment and intervention. The Kansas system links SWPBS to academics in an integrated RTI model. One of the distinguishing characteristics of MTSS is the careful documentation of the published research base for each of its critical features. MTSS also includes a self-assessment system for schools, and the state provides technical assistance and professional development to districts that volunteer to undertake the model, through regionalized special education resources.

Colorado's Multi-Tiered Model of Intervention and Instruction initiative is similar to that in Kansas in many ways but places a great deal of emphasis on fully integrating SWPBS and academics at each RTI tier. The Colorado model also repeatedly stresses the word "ALL," always in caps in its material, to indicate the state's intent that its RTI model is not just about special education but is schoolwide. As with the Kansas initiative, Colorado also provides a configuration map to enable districts and schools to self-assess on a three-point scale from "awareness" to "implementation." Narrative indicators are provided for each of the model's critical features at each stage in the configuration map. Colorado has a strong parent and family participation component, which sets it apart from many state initiatives.

New Hampshire Responds, the RTI initiative, differs from those in Kansas and Colorado by restricting itself to PBS and literacy and having a distinct special education flavor. It has the unique strengths of bringing RTI into early childhood education settings and high schools. It also provides incentives for schools to implement school-wide RTI through within-state grants funded by the state's SPDG program. By requiring 80 percent buy-in from all staff at schools within state administrative units, the state hopes to move from the special education focus required for state funding to a whole school focus in implementation. The grants are intended to create model RTI demonstration sites in various regions of the state, which can then be used later on to scale up within districts.

In reviewing all of the state initiatives on RTI, it became clear to me that the funding and policy split that exists at the federal level between special education and general education directly affects and greatly complicates the process of moving schoolwide RTI toward scale within the states. With resources and finances concentrated administratively within special education systems, schoolwide RTI is somewhat of a hard sell to the general education establishment. Yet the movement in 2009 clearly has legs.

10

The Shape of Schools to Come

Although this book is really about all schools, my particular turf is the inner city. In my view, if we can put urban education on a sound track, the procedures followed will benefit all schools. *Urban education* is a broad term. The Kansas City metropolitan area, for example, is classed as urban but includes a large variety of neighborhoods, some of which could as easily be classified as suburban. When I write of urban schools, I mean the inner core. In most American big cities, the inner core is or has been negatively affected by poverty, with its mix of white flight, homelessness, unemployment, decimated family structure, drug abuse, and violent crime. Low-performing schools can also be added to the mix. Although there are interesting exceptions here and there, America's big city inner-core schools are broken for the most part and in serious need of physical, psychological, and educational repair.

> *Although there are interesting exceptions here and there,,*
> *America's big city inner-core schools are broken for the most*
> *part and in serious need of physical, psychological, and edu-*
> *cational repair.*

No Child Left Behind and Adequate Yearly Progress

The George W. Bush administration, through No Child Left Behind (NCLB), chose to address the problem by setting a rising bar of required pupil progress as measured by annual, standardized grade-level state assessments and then holding schools accountable for adequate yearly progress (AYP). Schools that fall far enough behind the 5 percent annual increase in the rising bar come under punitive sanctions, often with exclusionary tactics. When a school in some cities, for example, is chronically low performing, parents in that school are offered vouchers equal to an amount calculated to reflect the annual cost of educating the student in that school. Parents are told that they can enroll their child in a higher-performing public school or take their child to a local private school that agrees to accept the vouchers as part or whole tuition for enrollment.

A Privatization Agenda?

Research has repeatedly shown that the private, often religious, schools that sprout like mushrooms in the inner city to receive these students perform at an even lower level than the public schools that supplied their enrollment. The May 2008 issue of *Phi Delta Kappan* published an article by Christopher Lubienski, Corinna Crane, and Sarah Lubienski, *What Do We Know About School Effectiveness?* that followed up on a 2005 article by Sarah Lubienski and Christopher Lubienski comparing the results of students in grades 4 and 8 on measured academic achievement. Lubienski, Crane, and Lubienski stated:

> Like most people, we had assumed that the higher average scores in private schools meant that private schools were more effective—an assumption that undergirds much of the current thinking surrounding education policies and reforms. But to our surprise, the data on the nationally representative sample of 30,000 students in fourth and eighth grades showed public schools to be outperforming private schools in mathematics achievement

after   student   background   factors   were   considered [p. 689].

The researchers then followed up the 2000 study with a second sample of 345,000 students in response to criticism that their sample was too restrictive. They again found, counter to their expectations, that public schools outperformed both private and charter schools. In their 2008 publication, the authors reported a third study that looked at student gains over time rather than at static snapshots of test scores at a single grade level. They again found essentially the same results, concluding, "In view of the inherent limitations of relying on any single type of methodological approach, the fact that we are seeing similar patterns in different types of data—and from comprehensive and trusted datasets— suggests that old assumptions about the inherent superiority of private schools—the 'private school effect'—may no longer hold true" (p. 694).

From the viewpoint of an academic working with inner-city schools, the goal of NCLB can look at times like a thinly disguised privatization agenda. The logic is to set a rising bar of measured pupil academic progress; hold schools accountable each year for chasing the bar; and then encourage vouchers, charters, and transfers for those that cannot clear the bar. In my own work, I have interviewed numerous parents given the transfer option who reported that after spending countless hours and going to great expense, they could not find another public school that would accept their child. The usual reason given was, "We are overenrolled." When they found they could not afford schools in the Catholic diocese and other good private schools, they were left with no choice but to enroll their children in relatively new private schools that would accept their vouchers as payment. The Illinois studies, as well as others, now show their children would likely have gotten a better education in what had been deemed a "chronically low-performing school."

From the viewpoint of an academic working with inner-city schools, the goal of NCLB can look at times like a thinly disguised privatization agenda. The logic is to set a rising bar of measured pupil academic progress; hold schools accountable each year for chasing the bar; and then encourage vouchers, charters, and transfers for those that cannot clear the bar.

When you consider the amount of wealth being transferred from the public education sector to the private sector—funds that are desperately needed to improve or at least hold the line in high-poverty-area public schools—then you can only conclude that we have a crisis situation confronting inner-city public education. If research continues to show that inner-city students are academically worse off in their private or charter school alternatives, then we have clear evidence of a broken system that must be repaired.

My intent here is not to belabor the myriad problems affecting mainly blacks and Latino/as in broken schools in broken communities. Jonathan Kozol has done that job with tremendous eloquence in *Savage Inequalities* and his other books. The issue I want to address is what we can do, given all of the constraints imposed by discriminatory public policy, inadequate funding, negative media attention, and real estate practices, to ensure that inner-city children get an education of comparable quality to children in largely white, more affluent suburban areas. We know from published research that inner-city students achieve academic parity under conditions of good instruction and systemic improvements in the teaching-learning process. I have seen examples of inner-city schools where the students outperform the affluent community schools on the outskirts of the city.

The issue I want to address is what we can do, given all of the constraints imposed by discriminatory public policy, inadequate funding, negative media attention, and real estate practices, to ensure that inner-city children get an education of comparable quality to children in largely white, more affluent suburban areas.

The question, then, which this book has addressed, is, "What does it take?" I have argued that the medical model for American education, from an earlier age of specialization, has outlived its usefulness and, given existing constraints and demographic changes, cannot get the job done. I would take the argument a step further and suggest that the medical model may now be contributing to the problem.

In the postwar age of specialization, it was felt that if we divided a unit, say, the human body, into smaller chunks, say, the heart, lungs, ear/nose/throat, feet, and so on, and if we trained highly specialized physicians to treat only those chunks, overall health care would benefit as a result. In education, it was similarly felt that if we looked at problems of learning as chunks of deficiencies within students, such as non-English speaking, disabled, needing free or reduced lunch, chronic health care needs, the gifted, and so on, and if we created systems of specialization to address these issues, American education would improve.

Many in medicine will argue that the medical model of specialization has run its course in that profession. New models of holistic medicine and integrated health care are emerging and gaining ground each year. In education, we should follow suit. That is what I mean by desiloization. We need to finally heed the advice of Canadian scholar Michael Fullan and create a holistic system of education, particularly in the inner city, where young people need the benefit of all available expertise and participation in the teaching-learning process.

Response to Intervention

In my opinion, RTI is the most promising systems-level set of processes with which to replace medical model thinking. It offers, for the first time, a clear pathway from ongoing scientific research into teaching practice. Under the medical model, the school psychologist, together with the school nurse and social worker, was the agent of interpretation from scientific investigation to classroom practice.

Now, under RTI, those informed points of decision are shifted to multidisciplinary teams where teachers are becoming the primary interpreters of scientific data and, assisted by specialists, are empowered to make decisions about what resources should be matched to measured student need to solve problems of learning.

Does this mean that the answer to the question, "What does it take?" is RTI alone? Another related question is, "Is RTI the magic bullet?" Unfortunately, the answer is no. There is no magic bullet to fix broken schools and school systems. There are, however, interesting conceptual breakthroughs, like problem-solving RTI, that can set the stage for a vastly improved play to be performed. RTI is about moving science more comprehensively into the teaching-learning process. But science alone, as a purely rational-technical enterprise, can do only so much. There are times when science looks surprisingly like religion: something we do not question and should be content to take on faith. In Kansas a few years ago, we watched the spectacle of scientists and religious conservatives yelling at each other on public television over whether humans evolved from apes or appeared on earth intact around five thousand years ago. The debate would have been laughable except that it was the basis for Kansas State Board of Education policy on teaching science in public school classrooms. What was interesting to me was not so much the content of the debate—Darwinian evolution versus creationism—but the disrespectful ad hominem styles of the opposing sides. The gist of the statements were of the form, "How could you be so stupid as to not recognize that we were created in the image of God?" versus "How could you be so stupid as to not recognize the body of scientific evidence in support of evolutionary biology?"

> *There is no magic bullet to fix broken schools and school systems. There are, however, interesting conceptual break-throughs, like problem-solving RTI, that can set the stage for a vastly improved play to be performed.*

The Kansas debates showed that under certain circumstances, religious conservatives will behave like scientists and scientists will behave like true believers. That caveat aside, the infusion of science into teaching practice and school structures is a welcome breakthrough. Alone, it is not enough.

Three Facets of Teaching

For the past five years, I have spent time in urban classrooms watching teachers teach and trying to understand why some are so successful relative to others. My conclusion for now is that there are three critical domains of teaching and that if sufficient elements of all three are in place, the class will do well. All assumptions about what constitutes good teaching are, of course, arguable, and existing research on classroom teaching tends to be focused on specific practices such as differentiated instruction rather than on more teacher-specific or personal variables. Nevertheless, if I were asked to evaluate classroom teachers to see who should get the biggest raise, my checklist for classroom observations would include indicators of the three domains and some estimate of class progress gleaned from curriculum-based measures.

The three domains of teaching effectiveness are science, relationships, and inspiration. When I reflect on the most effective teachers across all of the schools that we work with through the Schoolwide Applications Model (SAM) process and at our research sites, I consistently see elements of the three domains within each teacher. Some are long on one or two domains relative to others, but all three are clearly observable and, perhaps, eventually measurable in each person's teaching practice.

Science

The first domain of effective teaching is really the central topic of this book. RTI is the first substantive systems change effort in American education that brings scientific elements of teaching into day-to-day professional practice. Four characteristics of the scientific teacher can be readily determined from classroom observation and interview data: skepticism, use of evidence-based practices, concern for fidelity of intervention, and a focus on data reflecting pupil progress to make decisions about intensity or interventions.

Scientific skepticism comes down to approaching one's professional work with a questioning attitude. Among good scientists, there are no true believers when approaching subject matter for study. A scientific teacher approaches all sources of new knowledge and published curricula with a show-me attitude. If a teacher is 100 percent convinced that a Reading First curriculum is all that is needed to improve literacy skills in the class, that teacher scores low on scientific skepticism. If a teacher instead reacts to a new packaged curriculum with, "Okay, let's put this to the test," and then uses data from students to determine its effectiveness, that teacher scores high on the characteristic of scientific skepticism.

The scientific teacher searches for sources of evidence that a particular teaching practice, structural enhancement, or curriculum element is as good as its proponents claim. Some of the most effective teachers I know regularly use the Internet to find published reports of evidence for the effectiveness of consultants and materials that they, their school, and their district are considering. Taking the trouble to seek out and use evidence-based practices or using the mechanisms provided through grade-level teams and the general team structure of the school to raise questions about materials and practices for which there is no credible evidence is one of the hallmarks of a scientific teacher. Teaching is too important a professional endeavor, and teaching time is too short to waste any of it on processes and practices that do not contribute to students' academic achievement.

Concern for fidelity of implementation is a quality of the scientific teacher that is closely related to the quality of seeking evidence for specific practices. I became concerned with this issue when I began observing teachers implementing Reading First programs. Some of these recommended programs have a pretty solid initial base of effectiveness research. The data on their effectiveness, however, are closely tied to the issue of fidelity of implementation. The program must be taught in the same way that it was taught when its efficacy data were collected. When I see teachers selecting bits and pieces of the total curriculum package while discarding others or failing to master the computer skills needed to fully implement the program, then I am concerned with the fidelity of intervention quality of the scientific teacher. If the approach or program has no scientific evidence behind it, fidelity does not matter. If it does, then fidelity of intervention is critical; otherwise, there is no basis to evaluate its relationship to changes in levels of student performance.

The scientific teacher is usually well on the way to understanding the power and use of data. Teachers I have worked with were initially resistant to the RTI requirement of collecting screening and progress monitoring data and then using those data to make important decisions about levels of interventions, types of interventions, and accessing services and supports such as special education. But when we showed teachers observational data on time they spent in various task categories throughout the school day and asked them to rate the extent of likely impact on student achievement of each category, they acknowledged that some categories probably could be revised or replaced to create time for additional assessments. My experience has been that teachers who collect and use data to make decisions as a matter of course will ultimately say that they would never give up data collection as an element in their professional practice. They have adopted a critical element in becoming a scientific teacher.

Relationships

The second domain of effective teaching is the ability to connect with the students. In some of the episodes of the fourth season of HBO's celebrated TV series *The Wire*, a middle school teacher, Prez, a white man, is featured as he attempts to make the transition from being a Baltimore policeman to being a middle school teacher in one of the city's inner-core schools. His unruly students are all black, and Prez stumbles from humiliation to despair as he seeks a way to connect with his students in any manner that will further their education. He ultimately succeeds by engaging the students in unorthodox methods reflective of their own street culture. He essentially "tricks" the students into learning when they think they are just goofing off because their teacher has given up on them. Eventually the students, surprised at their own success in mastering math concepts, become interested in furthering their skill attainment, and the classroom slowly begins to resemble a proper middle school math class.

There is relatively little research on relationship factors in teaching, but a sizable body of evidence exists from the fields of educational sociology and anthropology. The issue of relationship building, or connecting with individual students and a class, takes on exceptional meaning in inner-city schools. Few things upset me more than when I go into urban core schools and see teachers yelling at the kids and warning them of a litany of punitive circumstances that will occur if they do not behave. Yet I understand the impulse. Young people who spend a lot of time on the mean streets of the city are going to reflect that subculture and its antisocial norms in the schools.

Few things upset me more than when I go into urban core schools and see teachers yelling at the kids and warning them of a litany of punitive circumstances that will occur if they do not behave. Yet I understand the impulse.

Readers interested in pursuing more information on ethnicity and its implications would do well to examine two books by Pedro Noguera: *The Trouble with Black Boys: And Other Reflections on Race, Equity, and the Future of Public Education;* and *Unfinished Business: Closing the Racial Achievement Gap in Our Schools.* Noguera is an urban sociologist who has spent much of his professional career engaged in the study of urban core schools. His work offers insights into complex problems confronting teachers in these schools, particularly as they bear on forming relationships with students that enhance their educational outcomes. As a Latino, Noguera brings the perspective of the student into focus with this personal anecdote:

> As a high school student, I had coped with the isolation that comes from being one of the few students of color in my advanced classes by working extra hard to prove that I could do as well as or better than my white peers. However, outside the classroom, I also worked hard to prove to my less studious friends that I was cool or "down," as we would say. For me this meant playing basketball, hanging out, fighting when necessary, and acting like "'one of the guys." I felt forced to adopt a split personality: I behaved one way in class, another way with my friends, and yet another way at home [pp. 4–5].

The connected teacher is knowledgeable about and sensitive to the conditions affecting the lives of his or her students. I can say that I have never known an effective teacher who was not also a connected teacher. Sadly, I can also say that I have known inner-city teachers who were low on the relationship domain and some who were high and connected but lacked the other two characteristics of effective teaching.

The connected teacher is knowledgeable about and sensitive to the conditions affecting the lives of his or her students. I

*can say that I have never known an effective teacher who was
not also a connected teacher.*

I remember one teacher whose students loved her and whose
class always seemed to be having fun. When I looked at
the curriculum-based measures (CBM) performance record of
her classes over a three-year period, however, it was clear that good
relationships and fun were not getting it done. This teacher's biggest
problem appeared to be inconsistency. She was continually trying
new things to keep her students interested and enjoying the classroom experience. Lack of attention to evidence that some of these
activities would enhance learning worked against her over time.
The students enjoyed the activities but were not inspired to take
on more challenging work as a result.

I have known other teachers who felt, and in some cases strongly,
that the lives of their students outside the classroom were none of
their business. One teacher told me, "What these kids do outside
of this classroom is someone else's problem, not mine. My job is
to teach my lesson plan, and those who pay attention I expect to
do just fine. Those who don't may need to be taught elsewhere by
someone else." Her three-year CBM data were pretty dismal.

The relationship factor in effective teaching is a form of culture
building in this sense—the culture of the classroom. One measure
of a strong, positive culture is school and classroom estimates of
climate. When measures of classroom climate show steady increases,
student achievement increases as a correlated factor. Many inner-
city kids get yelled at a lot. Circumstances of poverty and associated
community and family stress can put just about everyone on edge.
The street culture often reflects this atmosphere of meanness such
that kids disrespect each other and, ultimately, themselves.

Effective teaching requires a measure of self-esteem building.
Putting up with a difficult and disrespectful student until a way
can be found to reach that student may pay dividends later, when
the student begins to show and learn what he is capable of doing
academically. That is one of the reasons that the schoolwide RTI

model engages positive behavior support as its approach to teaching social and behavioral skills. Schoolwide PBS provides an excellent pathway to relationship building for teachers.

The last key indicator for the relationships domain of effective teaching is the welcoming spirit. When Ravenswood City School District began integrating its special education students into general education classrooms as it phased out its special classes, grade-level teachers were asked if they would be willing to add a student with an individualized education program to their class roster in midterm. In general, the teachers who volunteered and welcomed their new students produced the highest-performing classes in their schools. These connected teachers knew that there would be educational benefits to all of the students in welcoming a new student with some challenges into the classroom. And when some of these new students were at the low end of the spectrum on intellectual ability and perhaps had other problems affecting learning, connected teachers knew that they would not be holding these students to the same benchmark performance levels as their more typical students.

Inspiration

Inspiration is the least understood component of effective teaching. There is scant research to draw from in seeking to pinpoint the characteristics of the inspiring teacher. As a researcher, I know it when I see it, but I do not yet know how to measure it. Most school-wide RTI research is focused on teaching practices, assessments, and curriculum, but with little attention paid to the question of what causes a child to seek opportunities to engage material that is at a level above that child's current performance. We know that children who routinely do that turn in stronger progress records of academic achievement than those who do not.

Furthermore, we know that the tendency for students to seek out and engage more challenging material is directly tied to teaching interventions and teacher factors in general, but we do not know for sure what those qualities and interventions consist of. I suggest that the answer lies in a rather complex package of teaching-learning issues. The curriculum is certainly at issue. The inspiring teacher who gets students excited about learning an otherwise dull and boring subject matter is certainly deserving of high scores on the inspiration dimension.

> *The inspiring teacher who gets students excited about learning an otherwise dull and boring subject matter is certainly deserving of high scores on the inspiration dimension.*

My Fourth-Grade Teacher

By fourth grade, I was beginning to hate school and becoming a very difficult student. As the third-grade class clown, I had succeeded in driving my third-grade teacher to the point where she had recommended to my mother that I be placed in a private residential school. My fourth-grade teacher, however, reacted to my antics with patient bemusement. Instead of sending me to the principal's office, she would seek me out at recess and begin to get to know me while sharing her snacks with me. A high point in the relationship came when she intervened in a fight that I was about to lose in a big way, and thus she became my rescuer as well as my friend. As the weeks passed, she would see me after class and put books in my hand. Those books not only inspired me; they lit a fire of passion for reading that has never let up. She would say things like, "Wayne, I know this book is at a higher grade level, but if you can understand it, I think you will enjoy it." These comments would make me determined to understand and to show her that I could master the more advanced material.

In retrospect, I think my fourth-grade teacher sort of tricked me into becoming an active, engaged learner, and in doing so, she may have rescued me in more ways than one.

My experience working with White Church Elementary in Kansas City, Kansas, has me thinking that a critical mass of inspiring teachers at a school may lead to the interesting phenomenon of an inspirational school. There were days when I walked through the school and had to step around groups of children sitting in circles in the hallways working on projects so that they would not be distracted by other groups working in the classroom. These spontaneous work groups were self-originated and self-directed. The teachers were simply facilitating the process. White Church, an early example of an RTI school, of course could not have become the top-performing public elementary school in Kansas on inspiration alone. Its teachers had a strong blend of science, relationship building, and inspirational teaching to enable a strong learning community to emerge and come to fruition.

A Framework, Not a Magic Bullet

RTI is not a magic bullet that will fix broken schools. It does, however, create a framework for introducing scientific educational practices into the school. The RTI model proposed in this book suggests going further than simply introducing scientific practices in a three-tiered prevention model. Attention must also be paid to factors affecting school climate and school organization so that resources can be coordinated in such a way that all of the students can benefit, particularly those in urban, inner-core schools.

RTI for the Endangered School

Richard Elmore's central thesis on school reform, set out in his book *School Reform from the Inside Out*, captured in part in the following quotation, is that the core of the teaching-learning process of American education is solid:

> Asking teachers and administrators to increase academic performance for students without fundamentally

altering the conditions under which they failed to produce student learning in the first place is a dead end.
Teachers and administrators generally do what they
know how to do—they do not deliberately engage in
actions they know will produce substandard performance, nor do they intentionally withhold knowledge
that they know might be useful to student learning. If
schools are not meeting expectations for student learning, it is largely because *they do not know what to do*. And,
given the longstanding disconnect between policy and
practice, neither do policymakers [p. 217].

American schools have good foundational curricula, teachers
who for the most part have been well trained and know how to
teach, and reasonable processes for assessing pupil progress. What
we lack are structural processes that allow this mix to work its magic.

Schoolwide RTI is significant structural reform, so if we put it
into place in our most struggling schools with fidelity, we can put
it to the test. Those students deserve a shot. A just society should,
at the very least, strive to create circumstances through education
that hold out the possibility of a ticket out of poverty and a chance
to participate in the American dream.

*A just society should, at the very least, strive to create cir-
cumstances through education that hold out the possibility
of a ticket out of poverty and a chance to participate in the
American dream.*

Note that I used that word *fidelity*. As with all other reforms
grounded in big ideas, RTI can be misinterpreted, misused, and
misapplied. When substantive reforms are introduced into any stable system, that system will experience disequilibrium and periods
of oscillation. Forces will exist in the system from early on that will
tend to return a changing system to its former (static) state. Systems

behave a bit like chemistry experiments. Say you want to change a liquid compound into a different liquid compound, one with a different molecular structure. You introduce a catalytic agent to start the process. The chemical reaction enters a period of instability (oscillation), and if the experiment is not conducted with care, it may return to its former state. Putting RTI into place in a school with fidelity in accordance with a carefully planned set of steps and processes will help to ensure that the school will survive the period of instability and oscillation.

My recommendation for school districts is to start slowly: work with the most difficult schools, and then build on the success of early cohorts of schools in starting up with later cohorts. In my group's work with putting our RTI model, SAM, into place in some Washington, D.C., school district's schools, we began with identifying clusters of four schools each. For the first cohort of schools to be provided technical assistance and professional and staff development, we partnered with the district to identify two clusters. The district wisely proceeded by arranging for a large number of schools to learn about the model and have the opportunity to engage in discussions within the community of practice of each school. Following the information phase, the district asked for schools to volunteer.

Schools behaved predictably, with lots of questions, particularly concerning whether the district would support the conversion process by providing reasonable resources if the school could make its case for necessity in order to implement the model. Through this process of negotiation and information sharing, eight elementary schools were identified to begin the systems change venture in the 2008–2009 academic year. Two new clusters of four elementary schools each have now been identified for the 2009–2010 academic year. As this book is being written, the schools' communities of practice show every indication of being excited about engaging the process. The cohort one school year is winding down with a sense of momentum mixed with a bit of apprehension concerning the implications of the changing school culture.

There are many ways to start an RTI initiative, but some may offer important advantages over others. The principles of buy-in and empowerment are important considerations in getting started. If the RTI conversion process is mandated from on high, some schools will defend against the initiative and may never make it into the phase of oscillation. If these schools become documented failures, RTI runs the risk of becoming yet another big idea that became a failed policy initiative.

> *There are many ways to start an RTI initiative, but some may offer important advantages over others. The principles of buy-in and empowerment are important considerations in getting started.*

All troubled school districts seek a magic bullet cure. There is a palpable sense of desperation in some urban school districts, and if a new big idea looks promising, that desperation could lead to decisions around implementation that will work against success. Administrators need to carefully consider the importance of buy-in at the level of the start-up schools and the equal importance of scaling up slowly. RTI is *not* a magic bullet so letting the process of systems change run its course over time by taking it on in reasonable chunks and transferring knowledge gained from the experience of early cohorts to later cohorts will help to ensure the success of the transformation.

Capacity Building and Sustainability

Major systems change efforts are usually accomplished with some form of outside assistance. School districts usually lack the internal capacity to advise, assist, and train schools to put the pieces of the puzzle together using their own resources. In Kansas, for example, the MTSS initiative is linked to professional development and technical assistance provider systems funded by the state. These systems function as early catalytic interveners to get processes started, before they need to move on to other schools and districts that are eager to get started. We know, however, that major systems change involves destabilization and periods of oscillation.

Sustainability of systems change is the explicit or implicit goal of the upfront investment in the process, so careful attention needs to be paid early on to issues affecting sustainability. We know from research that critical factors in achieving sustainable systems change are leadership, stability of workforce, and local capacity to take on professional and staff development and technical assistance functions provided by outside systems required to get the process started.

Leadership

Stable leadership at the school level is critical to sustainability. I am familiar with schools that undertook systems change efforts and witnessed strong gains in measured student achievement early in the process as a result. When district administrators saw the results, however, they attributed the student gains to the quality of leadership alone, and on that basis transferred two principals and members of their leadership teams to other low-performing schools so that they could replicate their magic in other needy settings. The result was meltdown of the critical features of the systems change venture in the original school and a corresponding decrease in measured pupil performance. Once a school has moved beyond the period of instability and oscillation, so that the new structures have become business as usual at the school, then the new processes will likely survive a change in leadership.

Stability

Stability in the teaching community of a school can also affect sustainability. Teacher and staff turnover is a chronic problem in urban core schools and can significantly impair the progress of innovative practices. Many of the initial staff and professional development activities occur in the first one or two years of implementation in systems change. If a large segment of the teaching force that received those interventions is replaced by others who have not received comparable training, the school becomes mired in oscillation. Stability of workforce issues is a thorny problem, particularly for school districts serving low-income areas. Teachers can often easily get new jobs in higher-paying districts, and usually with more benefits, particularly when there are serious teacher shortages. Districts may wish to consider creating teacher incentives in the early stages of putting schoolwide RTI into place to attempt to counteract turnover.

Districts may wish to consider creating teacher incentives in the early stages of putting schoolwide RTI into place to attempt to counteract turnover.

Capacity

Local capacity to nurture a systems change initiative toward scaleup is a matter of aligning the culture of the district with the changing culture of the schools. Schoolwide RTI schools will find themselves interacting with their district central offices in very different ways than they did before undergoing the conversion.

The changing relationship of special education to general education is an area that I have seen become quickly problematic in RTI initiatives. If the district responds to changing communications from the school in the old ways, the school may not emerge from oscillation and may revert to its traditional way of doing business. In my view, conversion to schoolwide RTI requires a continuous dialogue between leadership teams at the school sites and district-level administration. The culture of the district needs to undergo a similar transformation as that reflected by the schools; however, the district will face some challenges that the schools do not. If the district is scaling up RTI in cohorts as recommended, then it will have one set of responses for RTI schools and a different set for its traditional schools. One way to solve the problem is to create a special unit at the district level to work with the schools undergoing systems change.

A district relying on external systems by contracting with private entities, partnering with universities, or accessing systems provided through the state must require its external providers to build capacity at the district level into its arrangements. A cadre of personnel at the district level will ultimately need to learn to provide the same functions for sustaining the processes in early cohorts of schools and getting new cohorts started consistent with its scale-up plan. External providers often have a vested interest in keeping their business plans viable by moving on to new innovations and seeking new contracts with other districts. Becoming dependent on external systems to scale up systems change efforts over the long run can work against sustainability.

Potential Traps in Implementing RTI

As my colleagues around the country and I have been engaged in implementing our schoolwide RTI model, SAM, in various school districts, we have encountered some varied and unanticipated obstacles that we collectively have come to think of as school reform scale-up traps. We look now at some of these more prominent traps.

Multilevel Sets of Interventions

The first potential trap that schools tend to fall into, particularly in the oscillation phase, is applying old ways of thinking about students that are no longer applicable to new methods of education. We humans tend to behave categorically in coping with our world, particularly when it comes to dealing with others. Race is an obvious case in point.

In my group's work in implementing SAM, we encountered this trap so frequently that we now come to anticipate it in the early stages of RTI implementation. Tiers of RTI become attributes of students rather than considerations of instructional intensity and types of interventions, as in, "Here comes DeShaun. He's one of our tier 3 kids." Another variant on the multilevel trap is to think of RTI as places for interventions to occur rather than levels of intensity. I regularly get taken to "our tier 2 room" in schools in the early stages of implementing RTI. One school simply mapped RTI lingo over its traditional structures. General education grade-level classrooms had "tier 1 students," the old resource room for special education became the "tier 2 room," and the special education classroom was referred to as the "tier 3 room." The challenge for this school was how to rethink special education as a source of specialized interventions and how to reconceptualize its space to maximize gains from interventions at all three levels.

> *The challenge for this school was how to rethink special education as a source of specialized interventions and how to reconceptualize its space to maximize gains from interventions at all three levels.*

Screening

Screening, an essential function of RTI, can be a trap similar to the multilevel categorization. The purpose of screening is to determine the risk for needing more intensive interventions. It is not to provide the basis for a decision to engage tier 2 or tier 3 interventions. Furthermore, screening is not a basis for referral for evaluation for special education. Often students who turn up as "at risk" respond positively to differentiated instruction, a tier 1 intervention, and data from progress monitoring and periodic assessments reflect benchmark performance.

The most dangerous trap linked to screening, at least in my experience, is akin to profiling. A teacher who views data from, say, SSBD or DIBELS as a way to find out "who my problem children are" may be engaging in efforts to screen out rather than screen for risk and for a potential change in level of intensity of intervention. Some charter schools in my experience have used screening data to counsel families to seek alternative placements for their students.

Progress Monitoring

The most frequent trap I encounter in schools beginning to implement RTI concerning progress monitoring is a variant of what I think of as the "data wall" phenomenon. One school papers the walls of its central hallway with DIBELS charts. When I raise questions about the implications of some of the charts in discussions with grade-level teams, I discover that the function of the data wall is more cosmetic than providing an incentive to respond to the implications or even to celebrate progress.

Progress-monitoring data walls can be helpful to the school-wide RTI process, but the wall should be in a place where teachers congregate, say, the room used for grade-level team meetings, and should be a basis for discourse and decision making. If the intent of the data wall is to motivate students, then the wall should be classroom based, and the students should understand what the charts are showing and how close they are coming to meeting classroom goals, which they participate in setting.

Another progress monitoring trap, and the one I see most frequently in the early stages of RTI, is collecting data for the sake of collecting data. For some, RTI can be sized up as "more stuff we have to do," one element of which is data collection. Progress monitoring data are collected in accordance with an RTI plan but then filed away and not used until required in some meeting. By the time the data are deemed relevant, the window of opportunity to adjust interventions has closed, and student progress remains level or deteriorates.

Progress monitoring data are a cornerstone in the data-based decision-making process at the heart of schoolwide RTI. They are particularly important in arriving at any decision to engage a different level of intensity from among levels 1, 2, or 3. Grade-level teams and coaches have a particular responsibility under RTI to work with classroom teachers, grade level or specialized, to interpret the data and advise the teacher on possible changes in interventions or levels of intensity.

Interventions

As with all other school reform measures, RTI comes with its own unique lingo. Schoolwide RTI is grounded in scientific rigor, so what some would call lesson plans, curricular modules, or teaching techniques, RTI calls "interventions." The term came into play as a way to put a spotlight on measurable outcomes arising from specific alterations in ongoing teaching practices. If, for example, classroom management is a problem as revealed by tier 1 behavioral data, then a possible intervention might be for the teacher to incorporate instruction in school expectations of behavior into content instruction. "Carlos, there is that word *expectation*. Can you think of one of the school's expectations for behavior? Good. Can you think of an example of being responsible?" Teaching SWPBS expectations is an intervention if it was not previously part of the teaching day for that teacher. The effects of the intervention can be ascertained through ongoing data collection on tier 1 applications.

> *Teaching SWPBS expectations is an intervention if it was not previously part of the teaching day for that teacher. The effects of the intervention can be ascertained through ongoing data collection on tier 1 applications.*

A trap implied in the term *intervention* can be to simply substitute the new buzzword for the same old teaching practices ("Eight thirty to nine thirty is reading interventions time"). Teachers in the early stages of implementing schoolwide RTI may need assistance learning to distinguish interventions from standard teaching practices. Interventions are measurable teaching enhancements, and their effects can be estimated from changes in measured student performance. A related trap is to think of any new teaching enhancement as an intervention. But interventions under RTI models are, by definition, evidence based. Any decision to adopt a particular intervention should be preceded by verification that scientific evidence supports its efficacy in situations that closely resemble the teaching situation at hand.

> *Interventions are measurable teaching enhancements and their effects can be estimated from changes in measured student performance. A related trap is to think of any new teaching enhancement as an intervention. Interventions under RTI models are, by definition, evidence-based.*

Fidelity

If a curriculum component or a specific intervention has a solid base of evidence to back it up, it still may fail to deliver as promised if the circumstances in which it is used differ significantly from the circumstances in place when the scientific evidence was obtained. Two types of fidelity are important to RTI implementation: implementation fidelity and intervention fidelity. The difference is largely one of scope. Trophies is a reading curriculum. Evidence for its effectiveness came through controlled experiments consistent with the NCLB Reading First initiative. Fidelity of implementation of Trophies requires adopting the curriculum in schools that do not differ widely from the range of schools in which the curriculum was tested. In addition, teachers must be thoroughly trained in its implementation so that different classrooms of a particular grade level can be assumed to be producing equivalent progress monitoring data for purposes of determining particular interventions.

Fidelity of interventions requires that a specific change in teaching practice for which there is a basis in evidence be carried out the same way whenever and by whomever it is employed. Again, the purpose is to be able to reliably gauge its impact on measured student performance. Check-in/check-out (CICO) is an evidence-based intervention available for tier 2 applications when behavioral progress monitoring has led to a decision to employ it. Failure to employ CICO with fidelity would occur if the procedure was undertaken inconsistently and piecemeal rather than daily.

The trap with which I am most familiar concerning fidelity is when it comes into conflict with flexibility. Both are characteristics of good schoolwide RTI models. When, for example, Madison Elementary School in Kansas adopted portions of the Open Court Reading Curriculum to use for specific interventions at tiers 1 and 2 of RTI, the issue of implementation fidelity was moot because the school was using a different curriculum. The fidelity, however, with which teachers at the school carry out the "flexible" intervention becomes important, particularly for evaluating its results in terms of student performance across classrooms. The "trap" is to sacrifice flexibility in teacher-directed interventions in order to adhere to implementation fidelity where it is not a critical issue.

The Undeniable Thrill of Success

Even with all of the struggles and hardships in getting beyond the traps, success is never all that far away if a committed community of practice in the school and a supportive district come together to work out the bugs. White Church Elementary in Kansas overcame every conceivable obstacle, including a tornado that ravaged its neighborhood and rearranged its demographics, to become a consistently high-performing school. Cesar Chavez Academy in California, a mostly Latino/a school with high student turnover and significant second-language issues, is well on track to become a high-performing school.

Each of these schools, and many others like them around the country, have successfully navigated the winds of substantive change in fully implementing school reform processes reflecting schoolwide RTI practices. The positive climate of these schools is palpable. The teachers love their jobs, at least the ones I know, and the students are fully engaged learners. Bringing about a difficult cultural change like that embodied in schoolwide RTI is not for the faint of heart, but it can be an unforgettable experience that is like the proverbial gift that keeps on giving.

To Sum Up

This concluding chapter addressed the necessity for and challenges associated with implementing schoolwide RTI. I briefly reviewed some of the school reform efforts that have been tried mainly in urban settings such as charter schools and voucher-linked private schools and concluded that none of these has yet been successful. The central question here is what it takes to have inner-city schools perform at a level comparable to or exceeding schools in more affluent areas. Response to intervention was discussed as having some unique features that hold potential for reengaging the teaching-learning process in all schools, but particularly in low-performing schools.

In this context, I discussed three facets, or domains, of teaching that I deem essential for powering a schoolwide RTI model: science, relationships, and inspiration. Science in teaching is concerned with selecting evidence-based practices, intervening with fidelity at each of the three levels of RTI, and using reliable and valid data to make intervention decisions. Relationships have to do with building a positive culture in the classroom and across the rest of the school. It has to do with connecting with the class and with individual students to make schooling a positive experience. It is also about forming bonds of trust among teachers and administrators to create a positive school climate. Inspiration is the part of teaching that motivates students to do the hard work of learning. Inspirational teaching is helping students to engage the curriculum in a way that has meaning for them and makes the process worthwhile. It is about helping students to get excited about learning.

Next, this chapter was concerned with the relationship of structural elements of school reform and the special considerations posed by inner-city schools. The manner in which schoolwide RTI is started in urban school districts may be a critical factor in its success as a major systems change initiative. The initial processes can particularly affect the sustainability of the effort over time. In this context, I discussed the need to build internal capacity within the district to nurture and help sustain the RTI practices.

Next, I discussed some of the potential traps that schools can fall into during the initial stages of RTI implementation. Most of these have to do with embracing RTI as a language system rather than changing actual practices of the teaching-learning process.

The chapter concluded with a reflection on the exhilaration of success when a low-performing school transforms itself through schoolwide RTI into a high-performing school, and the whole difficult endeavor becomes worthwhile for all involved in the transformation process.

Sources and Additional Resources

Chapter 1

Sources

Benson, L., Harkavy, I., & Puckett, J. (2007). *Dewey's dream: Universities and democracies in an age of education reform.* Philadelphia: Temple University Press.

Bergan, J. R., & Kratochwill, T. R. (1990). *Behavioral consultation and therapy.* New York: Plenum.

Bradley, R., & Danielson, L. (2004). The Office of Special Education Program's LD Initiative: A context for inquiry and consensus. *Learning Disability Quarterly*, 27(4), 186–188.

Bradley, R., Danielson, L., & Doolittle, J. (2007). Responsiveness to intervention: 1997 to 2007. *Teaching Exceptional Children*, 39(5), 8–12.

Brown-Chidsey, R., Loughlin, J. E., & O'Reilly, M. J. (2004, April). *Using response to intervention methods with struggling learners.* Presentation at the annual meeting of the National Associate of School Psychologists, Dallas, TX.

Brown-Chidsey, R., & Steege, M. W. (2005). *Response to intervention: Principles and strategies for effective practice.* New York: Guilford Press.

Eber, L., Hyde, K., Rose, J., Breen, K., McDonald, D., & Lewandowski, H. (2008). Completing the continuum of school-wide positive behavior support: Wraparound as a tertiary level intervention. In E. Walker & M. Roberts (Series Eds.) & W. Sailor, G. Dunlap, G. Sugai, & R. Horner (Eds.), *Handbook of positive behavior support.* New York: Springer Publishing Company.

Fernley, S. A., LaRue, S. D., & Norlin, J. W. (2007). *What do I do when . . . the answer book on RTI.* Danvers, MA: LRP Publications.

Fuchs, D., Mack, D., Morgan, P. L., & Young, C. L. (2003). Responsiveness-to-intervention: Definitions, evidence, and implications for the learning disabilities construct. *Learning Disabilities Research and Practice*, 18(3), 157–171.

Johnson, E., Mellard, D. F., Fuchs, D., & McKnight, M. A. (2006). *Responsiveness to intervention (RTI): How to do it.* Lawrence, KS: National Research Center on Learning Disabilities.

Knight, J. (2007). *Instructional coaching.* Thousand Oaks, CA: Corwin Press.

McCook, J. E. (2006). *The RTI guide: Developing and implementing a model in your schools.* Horsham, PA: LRP Publications.

Mellard, D. F., & Johnson, E. (2008). *RTI: A practitioner's guide to implementing response to intervention.* Thousand Oaks, CA: Corwin Press and National Association of Elementary School Principals.

National Association of State Directors of Special Education. (2006). *Response to intervention: Policy considerations and implementation.* Alexandria, VA: Author.

National Research Center on Learning Disabilities. (2006). *Responsiveness to intervention (RTI): How to do it.* Washington DC: Office of Special Education Programs.

Noguera, P. A. (2008). *The trouble with black boys: And other reflections on race, equity, and the future of public education.* San Francisco: Jossey-Bass.

Recovery School District. (2007). *Response to intervention (RTI) in the Recovery School District, 2007–2008.* New Orleans: Author.

Sailor, W., Doolittle, J., Bradley, R., & Danielson, L. (2008). Response to intervention (RTI) and positive behavior support. In W. Sailor, G. Dunlap, G. Sugai, & R. Horner (Eds.), *Handbook of positive behavior support* (pp. 729–753). New York: Springer Publishing Company.

Sailor, W., Dunlap, G., Sugai, G., & Horner, R. (2008). *Handbook of positive behavior support.* New York: Springer Publishing Company.

Sailor, W., & Roger, B. (2003). *SAMAN: An instrument for the analysis of critical features of the Schoolwide Applications Model (SAM).* Unpublished research instrument.

Sailor, W., & Roger, B. (2005). Rethinking inclusion: Schoolwide applications. *Phi Delta Kappan*, 86(7), 503–509.

Shores, C., & Chester, K. (2009). *Using RTI for school improvement: Raising every student's achievement scores.* Thousand Oaks, CA: Corwin Press.

Sprague, J., Cook, C. R., Browning Wright, D., Sadler, C. (2008). *RTI and behavior: A guide to integrating behavioral and academic supports.* Horsham, PA: LRP Publications.

Additional Resources

Council of Administrators of Special Education, http://www.casecec.org/rti.htm.

Hawken, L. S., Vincent, C. G., & Schumann, J. (2008). Response to intervention for social behavior: Challenges and opportunities. *Journal of Emotional and Behavioral Disorders*, 16(4), 213–225.

Johnson, E., Mellard, D. F., Fuchs, D., & McKnight, M. A. (2006). *Responsiveness to intervention (RTI): How to do it.* Available at National Research Center on Learning Disabilities, www.nrcld.org.

National Center on Response to Intervention, http://www.rti4success.org.

Chapter 2

Sources

American Psychiatric Association. (2000). *Diagnostic and statistical manual of mental disorders.* Washington, DC: Author.

Bolman, L., & Deal, T. (2002). *Reframing the path to school leadership: A guide for teachers and principals.* Thousand Oaks, CA: Corwin Press.

Deal, T., Purrinton, T., & Waetzeos, D. (2009). *Making sense of social networks in schools.* Thousand Oaks, CA: Corwin Press.

Dewey, J. (1915). *The school and society.* Chicago: University of Chicago Press.

Finn, Jr., C. E., Rotherham, A. J., & Hokanson Jr., C. R. (Eds.). (2001). *Rethinking special education for a new century.* Washington, DC: Thomas B. Fordham Foundation and Progressive Policy Institute.

Hardcastle, B., & Justice, K. (2006). *RTI and the classroom teacher: A guide for fostering teacher buy-in and supporting the intervention process.* Horsham, PA: LRM Publications.

Knight, J. (2007). *Instructional coaching.* Thousand Oaks, CA: Corwin Press

Lyon, G. R., Fletcher, J. M., Shaywitz, S. E., Shaywitz, B. A., Torgesen, J. K., Wood, F. B., et al. (2001). Rethinking learning disabilities. In C. E. Finn Jr., A. J. Rotherham, & C. R. Hokanson Jr. (Eds.), *Rethinking special education for a new century* (pp. 259–286). Washington, DC: Thomas B. Fordham Foundation and the Progressive Policy Institute.

McCook, J. E. (2006). *The RTI guide: Developing and implementing a model in your schools.* Horsham, PA: LRP Publications.

Mellard, D. F., & Johnson, E. (2008). *RTI: A practitioner's guide to implementing response to intervention.* Thousand Oaks, CA: Corwin Press and National Association of Elementary School Principals.

Noguera, P. A. (2008). *The trouble with black boys: And other reflections on race, equity, and the future of public education*. San Francisco: Jossey-Bass.

P.J. et al v. State of Connecticut, Board of Education, et al Civil Action No: 291CV00180(RNC)

Sailor, W., Dunlap, G., Sugai, G., & Horner, R. (2008). *Handbook of positive behavior support*. New York: Springer Publishing Company.

Additional Resources

Applebaum, M. (2009). *Implementing RTI*. Thousand Oaks, CA: Corwin Press

Bender, W. N., & Shores, C. (2007). *Response to intervention. A practical guide for every teacher*. Thousand Oaks, CA: Corwin Press.

Brown-Chidsey, R., & Steege, M. W. (2005). *Response to intervention: Principles and strategies for effective practice*. New York: Guilford Press.

Curriculum Based Measurement Support for K-12, www.cbmnow.com.

Enhancing Access to the General Education Curriculum for Students with Disabilities, www.K8accesscenter.org.

Hall, S. L. (2008). *Implementing response to intervention: A principal's guide*. Thousand Oaks, CA: Corwin Press.

Intervention Central, www.interventioncentral.org.

Iris Center, http://iris.peabody.vanderbilt.edu/index.html.

National Center on Response to Intervention, www.rti4success.org.

National Center on Student Progress Monitoring, www.studentprogress.org.

Shores, C., & Chester, K. (2009). *Using RTI for school improvement: Raising every student's achievement scores*. Thousand Oaks, CA: Corwin Press.

Universal Design for Learning, www.cast.org.

Chapter 3

Sources

Benson, L., Harkavy, I., & Puckett, J. (2007). *Dewey's dream: Universities and democracies in an age of education reform*. Philadelphia: Temple University Press.

Dewey, J. (1915). *The school and society*. Chicago: University of Chicago Press.

Dunlap, G., Sailor, W., Horner, R. H., & Sugai, G. (2008). Overview and history of positive behavior support. In W. Sailor, G. Dunlap, G. Sugai, & R. Horner (Eds.), *Handbook of positive behavior support* (pp. 3–16). New York: Springer Publishing Company.

Kirst, M. W., & Kelley, C. (1995). Collaboration to improve education and children's services: Politics and policy making. In L. C. Rigsby, N. C. Reynolds, & M. C. Wang (Eds.), *School-community connections: Exploring issues for research and practice* (pp. 21–44). San Francisco: Jossey-Bass.

Noguera, P. A. (2008). *The trouble with black boys: And other reflections on race, equity, and the future of public education.* San Francisco: Jossey-Bass.

Sailor, W., Doolittle, J., Bradley, R., & Danielson, L. (2008). Response to intervention and positive behavior support. In W. Sailor, G. Dunlap, G. Sugai, & R. Horner (Eds.), *Handbook of positive behavior supports* (pp. 729–753). New York: Springer.

Sailor, W., Dunlap, G., Sugai, G., & Horner, R. (Eds.). (2008). *Handbook of positive behavior supports.* New York: Springer.

Sailor, W., Wolf, N., Choi, H., & Roger, B. (2008). Sustaining positive behavior support in a context of comprehensive school reform. In W. Sailor, G. Dunlap, G. Sugai, & R. Horner (Eds.), *Handbook of positive behavior supports.* (pp. 633–669). New York: Springer.

Shorr, L. B. (1998). *Common purpose.* New York: Bantam Dell.

Slavin, R. E., Madden, N. A., Dolan, L. J., & Wasik, B. A. (1993). *Success for all: Evaluations of national replications.* Baltimore: Johns Hopkins University, Center for Research on Effective Schooling for Disadvantaged Students.

Additional Resources

Applebaum, M. (2009). *The one stop guide to implementing RTI: Academic and behavioral interventions, K-12.* Thousand Oaks, CA: Corwin Press.

Brown-Chidsey, R., & Steege, Mark W. (2005). *Response to intervention: Principles and strategies for effective practice.* New York: Guilford Press.

Chandler, L. K., & Dahlquist, C. M. (2006) *Functional assessment: Strategies to prevent and remediate challenging behavior in school settings* (2nd ed.). Upper Saddle River, NJ: Merrill Prentice Hall

Cook, S. R., Sprague, J., Browning Wright, D., & Sadler, C. (2007). RTI and behavior. In S. A. Fernley, S. D. LaRue, & J. W. Norlin (Eds.), *What do I do when . . . the answer book on RTI* (pp. 4:1–4:17). Danvers, MA: LRP Publications.

Crone, D. A., & Horner, R.H. (2003). *Building positive behavior support systems in schools.* New York: Guilford Press.

"Effective Behavior Support," DVD available from www.forumoneducation.org.

Forum on Education, www.forumoneducation.org.

Hawken, L. S., Vincent, C. G., & Schuman, J. (2008). Response to intervention for social behavior. *Journal of Emotional and Behavior Disorders*, 16(4), 213–225.

Intervention Central at www.interventioncentral.org.

National Association for Positive Behavior Support, www.APBS.org.

National Technical Assistance Center on Positive Behavior Support, www.pbis.org.

"Toward a Unified Educational System," DVD available from www.forumoneducation.org.

Schoolwide Information System, www.swis.org.

Chapter 4

Sources

Fernley, S. A., LaRue, S. D., & Norlin, J. W. (2007). *What do I do when . . . the answer book on RTI*. Horsham, PA: LRP Publications.

Hall, S. L. (2008). *A principal's guide: Implementing response to intervention*. Thousand Oaks, CA: Corwin Press.

McCook, J. E. (2006). *The RTI guide: Developing and implementing a model in your schools*. Horsham, PA: LRP Publications.

Mellard, D. F., & Johnson, E. (2008). *RTI: A practitioner's guide to implementing response to intervention*. Thousand Island, CA: Corwin Press.

Open Court Reading—see www.opencourtresources.com

Walker, H. M., & Severson, H. H. (1992). *Systematic screening for behavior disorders (SSBD)* (2nd ed.). Eugene: Oregon Research Institute.

Wright, J. (2007). *RTI toolkit: A practical guide for schools*. Port Chester, NJ: Dude Publishing.

Additional Resources

AIMSweb, www.aimsweb.com, www.cbmnow.com.

Brown-Chidsey, R., & Steege, Mark W. (2005). *Response to intervention: Principles and strategies for effective practice*. New York: Guildford Press.

Compton, D. L., Fuchs, D., Fuchs, L. S., & Bryant, J. D. (2006). Selecting at risk readers in first grade for early intervention: A two-year longitudinal study of decision rules and procedures. *Journal of Education Psychology*, 98, 394–409.

Edcheckup, www.edcheckup.com.

Intervention Central, www.interventioncentral.org.

Shores, C., & Chester, K. (2009). *Using RTI for school improvement: Raising every student's achievement scores*. Thousand Oaks, CA: Corwin Press.

Sopris West, www.sopriswest.com.

University of Oregon Center on Teaching and Learning. https://dibels.uoregon
.eduSystem to Enhance Education Performance, www.iSTEEP.com.

Chapter 5

Sources

AIMSweb, (2008). retrieved August 11, 2008, from www.aimsweb.com.

Brown-Chidsey, R., & Steege, M. W. (2005). *Response to intervention: Principles
and strategies for effective practice*. New York: Guilford Press.

Darling-Hammond, L. (2006). No child left behind and high school reform. *Harvard Educational Review, 26*(4), 642–667.

Eber, L., Hyde, K., Rose, J., Breen, K., McDonald, D., & Lewandowski, H.
(2008). Completing the continuum of schoolwide positive behavior support: Wraparound as a tertiary-level intervention. In W. Sailor, G. Dunlap,
G. Sugai, & R. Horner (Eds.), *Handbook of positive behavior support* (pp.
667–700). New York: Springer.

Friend, M. (2005). *The power of two, second edition.* [DVD]. Indianapolis: Indiana
University and Forum on Education. www.forumoneducation.org.

Hall, S. L. (2008). *A principal's guide: Implementing response to intervention*. Thousand Oaks, CA: Corwin Press

Johnson, E., Mellard, D. F., Fuchs, D., & McKnight, M. A. (2006). *Responsiveness to intervention (RTI): How to do it.* Nashville, TN: National Research
Center on Learning Disabilities and the U.S. Office of Special Education
Programs.

McCook, J. E. (2006). *The RTI guide: Developing and implementing a model in your
schools*. Horsham, PA: LRP Publications.

Mellard, D. F., & Johnson, E. (2008). *RTI: A practitioner's guide to implementing
response to intervention*. Thousand Island, CA: Corwin Press.

National Association of State Directors of Special Education. (2006). *Response
to intervention: Policy considerations and implementation*. Alexandria, VA:
Author.

O'Day, J. A. (2002). Complexity, accountability, and school improvement. *Harvard
Educational Review, 72*, 293–329.

School Social Behavior Scales (2nd ed.). (2002). Baltimore, MD: Brookes Publishing.

Sprague, J., Cook, C. R., Browning Wright, D., & Sadler, C. (2008). *RTI and
behavior: A guide to integrating behavioral and academic supports*. Horsham,
PA: LRP Publications.

University of Oregon Center on Teaching and Learning. *DIBELS*. Retrieved August 3, 2008, from https://dibels.uoregon.edu/.

Walker, H. M., & Severson, H. H. (1992). *Systematic screening for behavior disorders (SSBD)* (2nd ed.). Eugene: Oregon Research Institute.

Wraparound—for more information see: Illinois PBIS Network, http://www.pbisillinois.org.

Additional Resources

Bender, W. N., & Shores, C. (2007). *Response to intervention: A practical guide for every teacher*. Thousand Oaks, CA: Corwin Press.

Curriculum-Based Measures, www.cbmnow.com.

Ed Formation, http://edformation.com.

Edprogress, www.edprogress.com (measurement tools).

Griffith, A-J., Parsons, L. B., Burns, M. K., VanDerHeyden, A., and Tilly, W. D. (2007). *Response to Intervention Research for Practice*. Alexandria, VA: NASDSE

Hawken, L. S., Vincent, C. G., & Schumann, J. (2008). Response to intervention for social behavior: Challenges and opportunities. *Journal of Emotional and Behavioral Disorders* 16(4), 213–225.

Institute of Education Sciences, www.ies.ed.gov/ncee/wwc (evidence-based practices).

Intervention Central, www.interventioncentral.org (CBMs and interventions).

Journal of Evidence-Based Practices, www.rowmaneducation.com/Journals/JEBP/index.shtml.

National Association of State Directors of Special Education, Inc. (2008). *Response to Intervention Blueprints for Implementation*. *District Level*. Alexandria, VA: Author.

National Center for Student Progress Monitoring, www.studentprogress.org.

Offfice of Special Education Programs, www.osepideasthatwork.org (special education toolkit for RTI).

Pro-ed. www.pro-ed.com (reading and math basic skills measurement).

Resources and Research on iSTEEP and RTI, www.joewitt.org [Universal CBM (isteep)].

Schoolwide Information System (SWIS), www.swis.org.

Sopris West, www.sopriswest.com.

System to Enhance Education Performance, www.isteep.com (isteep CBM and total process).

Chapter 6

Sources

Education Alliance at Brown University. (2001, March). *English language learners, the comprehensive school reform demonstration project, and the role of the state departments of education*. Retrieved August 16, 2008, from www.alliance.brown.edu/pubs/csrd/ELLCSRD_rpt.pdf.

Fetterman, D. M., Kaftarian, S. J., & Wandersman, A. (Eds.). (1996). *Empowerment evaluation. Knowledge and tools for self-assessment and accountability*. Thousand Oaks, CA: Sage.

Fullan, M. (2001). *The new meaning of educational change*. New York: Teachers College Press.

Horner, R. H., Todd, A. W., Lewis-Palmer, T., Irvin, L. K., Sugai, G., & Boland, J. B. (2004). The School-Wide Evaluation Tool (SET): A research instrument for assessing school-wide positive behavior support. *Journal of Positive Behavior Interventions*, 6, 3–12.

Levin, H. M. (1987). Accelerated schools for disadvantaged students. *Education Leadership*, 44(6), 19–21.

Levin, H. M. (1996). Accelerated schools after eight years. In L. Schauble & R. Glaser (Eds.), *Innovations in Learning: New environments for education* (pp. 329–352). Mahwah, NJ: Erlbaum.

National Commission on Excellence in Education. (1983). *A nation at risk: The imperative of educational reform*. Washington, DC: U.S. Government Printing Office.

Rose, D. H., Sethuraman, S., & Meo, G. J. (2000). Universal design for learning. *Journal of Special Education Technology*, 15, 56–60.

Sailor, W., & Roger, B. (2003). *SAMAN: An instrument for the analysis of critical features of the Schoolwide Applications Model (SAM)*. Unpublished research instrument.

Sailor, W., & Roger, B. (2004). *Creating a unified system integrating general and special education for the benefit of all students* [Video]. Produced by Forum on Education. available at www.forumoneducation.org

Sailor, W., & Roger, B. (2005). Rethinking inclusion: Schoolwide applications. *Phi Delta Kappan*, 86(7), 503–509.

Sailor, W., & Roger, B. (2006). PBS in the urban core. *TASH Connections*, 32(1/2), 23–24.

Sailor, W., Zuna, N., Choi, J. H., Thomas, J., McCart, A., & Roger, B. (2006). Anchoring schoolwide positive behavior support in structural school reform. *Research and Practice for Persons with Severe Disabilities*, 31(1), 18–30.

Slavin, R. E., Madden, N. A., Dolan, L. J., & Wasik, B. A. (1993). *Success for all: Evaluations of national replications.* Baltimore: Johns Hopkins University, Center for Research on Effective Schooling for Disadvantaged Students.

Additional Resources

Burrello, L., Hoffman, L., & Murray, L. (2005). *School readers building capacity from within.* Thousand Oaks, CA: Corwin Press.

Burrello, L., Lashley, C., & Beatty, E. E. (2001). *Educating all students together. How school leaders create unified systems.* Thousand Oaks, CA: Corwin Press.

Fullan, M. (2001). *The new meaning of educational change.* New York: Teachers College Press.

Goldenber, C. (2004). *Successful school change. Creating settings to improve teaching and learning.* New York: Teachers College Press.

Katzenmeyer, M., & Moller, G. (2001). *Awakening a sleeping giant: Helping teachers develop as leaders.* Thousand Oaks, CA: Corwin Press.

Marzano, R. J., Water, T., & McNulty, B.A. (2005). *School leadership that works.* Alexandria, VA: Association for Supervision and Curriculum Development, and Aurora, CO: Mid-continent Research for Education and Learning.

Read 180, http://teacher.scholastic.com/products/read180/overview/.

Chapter 7

Sources

Bauwend, J., Houracade, J., & Friend, M. (1989). Cooperative teaching: A model for general and special education integration. *Remedial and Special Education* 10(2), 17–22.

Fountas and Pinnell, www.fountasandpinnell/benchmarkassessment.com.

Friend, M. (2005). *The power of two, second edition.* [DVD]. Indianapolis: Indiana University and Forum on Education. www.forumoneducation.org.

Kruel, M. Guided Reading. in the primary classroom, retrieved August 5, 2008, from http://content.scholastic.com/browse/article.jsp?id=4343.

Knight, J. (2007). *Instructional coaching: A partnership approach to improving instruction.* Thousand Oaks, CA: Corwin Press.

Kohn, A. (1999). *The schools our children deserve.* Boston: Houghton Mifflin.

Kohn, A. (1999). *Punishment with rewards: The trouble with gold stars, incentive plans, A's, praise, and other bribes.* Boston: Houghton Mifflin.

Marzano, R. J., Waters, T., & McNulty, B. A. (2005). *School leadership that works.* Alexandria, VA: ASCD.

Open Court Reading. Retrieved July 30, 2008, from www.opencourtresources.com.

Read Naturally, quick Phonics Screener. retrieved August 2, 2008 from www .readnaturally.com/products/qps.htm

Skrtic, T. (1995). *Disability and democracy. Reconstructing (special education for postmodernity.* New York: Teachers College Press.

Additional Resources

Applebaum, M. (2009). *The one stop guide to implementing RTI: Academic and behavioral interventions, K-12.* Thousand Oaks, CA: Corwin Press.

Bender, W. N., & Shores, C. (2007). *Response to intervention: A practical guide for every teacher.* Thousand Oaks, CA: Corwin Press.

Gravois, T. A., & Rosenfield, S. (2002). A multi-dimensional framework for evaluation of instructional consultation teams. *Journal of Applied School Psychology,* 19(1), 5–29.

Hall, S. (2008). *Implementing response to intervention: A principal's guide.* Thousand Oaks, CA: Corwin Press.

Mankins, M. C. (2004). Stop wasting valuable time. *Harvard Business Review,* 82(9), 58–65.

Rosenfield, S., Silva, A., & Gravois, T. (2008). Bringing instructional consultation to scale: Research and development of IC and IC Teams. In W. Erchul & S. Sheridon (Eds.), *Handbook of research in school consultation: Empirical foundations for the field* (pp. 203–224). Mawah, NJ: Erlbaum.

Chapter 8

Sources

Brown-Chidsey, R., & Steege, M. W. (2005). *Response to intervention: Principles and strategies for effective practice.* New York: Guilford Press.

Cuban, L., & Usdan, M. (Eds.). (2003). *Powerful reforms with shallow roots. Improving America's urban schools.* New York: Teachers College Press.

Education and Community Supports. (2008). *School-wide information system (SWIS).* Retrieved August 3, 2008, from http://www.swis.org.

Lawson, H., & Sailor, W. (2000). Integrating services, collaborating, and developing connections with schools. *Focus on Exceptional Children,* 3(2), 1–22.

Marzano, R. J., Waters, T., & McNulty, B. A. (2005). *School leadership that works: From research to results*. Alexandria, VA: ASCD.

Matzke, L., & Neumiller, T. L. (2008). *RTI in Title I: Tools and guidance to get it right*. Horsham, PA: LDP Publications.

McCook, J. E. (2006). *The RTI guide: Developing and implementing a model in your schools*. Horsham, PA: LRP Publications.

National Association of State Directors of Special Education. (2006). *Response to intervention: Policy considerations and implementation*. Alexandria, VA: Author.

New Bay Media. (2003). *Benchmark assessment system teacher user guide*. Retrieved August 3, 2008, from www.techlearning.com/techlearning/pdf/events/techforum/ny03/vault/MiningData_Handout.pdf.

Recovery School District. (2007). *Response to intervention (RTI) in the recovery school district*. New Orleans: Author.

Scholastic. *Read 180 reading intervention program: A comprehensive reading intervention solution*. Retrieved August 2, 2008, from http://teacher.scholastic.com/products/read180/overview/.

Scholastic. (2007). *FASTT*. Retrieved August 3, 2008, from www.tomsnyder.com/fasttmath/tour.html.

Tyack, D., & Cuban, L. (1995). *Tinkering toward utopia*. Cambridge, MA: Harvard University Press.

University of Oregon Center on Teaching and Learning. *DIBELS*. Retrieved August 3, 2008, from https://dibels.uoregon.edu/.

Voyager Expanded Learning. Retrieved August 3, 2008, from http://www.voyagerlearning.com/prj/assessment.jsp.

Additional Resources

Hilton, A. (2007). Response to intervention: Changing how we do business. *Leadership*, 36(4), 16–19.

Marzano, R. J. (2003). *What works in schools: Translating research into action*. Alexandria, VA: Association for Supervision and Curriculum Development.

McCook, J. D. (2006). *The RTI guide: Developing and implementing a model in your schools*. Horsham, PA: LRP Publications.

Shores, C., & Chester, F. (2009). *Using RTI for school improvement: Raising every student's achievement scores*. Thousand Oaks, CA: Corwin Press.

Sindelar, P. T., Shearer, D. K., Yendol-Hoppey, D., & Liebert, T. W. (2006). The sustainability of inclusive school reform. *Exceptional Children*, 72(3), 317–331.

Wright, J. (2007). *RTI toolkit: A practical guide for schools*. Port Chester, NY: Dude Publishing.

Chapter 9

Sources

Brown-Chidsey, R., & Steege, M. W. (2005). *Response to intervention: Principles and strategies for effective practice*. New York: Guilford Press.

Center for Accelerating Student Learning. Retrieved August 21, 2008, from http://kc.vanderbilt.edu/casl.

Colorado Multi-Tiered Model of Interventions and Instruction. Retrieved August 21, 2008, from http://www.cde.state.co.us/RtI/LearnAboutRtI.htm.

Dunlap, G. (2007). Response to intervention: Issues related to its implementation in settings for young children [Special issue]. *Topics in Early Childhood Special Education, 24*(4).

Hall, S. L. (2008). *Implementing response to intervention: A principal's guide*. Thousand Oaks, CA: Corwin Press.

Kansas Multi-Tiered System of Supports Innovation Configuration Matrix (ICM). Retrieved April 3, 2009, from www.kansasmtss.org.

Mellard, D. F., & Johnson, E. (2008). *RTI: A practitioner's guide to implementing response to intervention*. Thousand Oaks, CA: Corwin Press and National Association of Elementary School Principals.

National Association of State Directors of Special Education. (2006). *Response to intervention: Policy considerations and implementation*. Alexandria, VA: Author.

New Hampshire Department of Education. *NH Responds: Professional development for excellence in education*. Retrieved August 18, 2008, from http://www.ed.state.nh.us/education/organization/instruction/SpecialEd/NHResponds.htm.

Sailor, W., Doolittle, J., Bradley, R., & Danielson, L. (2008). Response to intervention and positive behavior support. In W. Sailor, G. Dunlap, G. Sugai, & R. Horner (Eds.), *Handbook of positive behavior supports* (pp. 729–753). New York: Springer.

Sailor, W., Dunlap, G., Sugai, G., & Horner, R. (2008). *Handbook of positive behavior support*. New York: Springer Publishing Company.

Samuels, C. A. (2008, Jan. 23). RTI sparks interest, questions. *Education Week*.

Shawnee Mission School District. Retrieved August 18, 2008, from http://www.smsd.org.

Shores, C., & Chester, F. (2009). *Using RTI for school improvement: Raising every student's achievement scores*. Thousand Oaks, CA: Corwin Press.

What Is a Multi-Tiered System(s) of Support (MTSS)? Retrieved August 17, 2008, from http://www.ksde.org/Default.aspx?tabid=2004.

Additional Resources

Mississippi RTI Model, www.mde.k12.ms.us/acad1/programs/tst/faqtst.doc.

New Mexico Public Education Department, SAT manual, www.sde.state.nm.us/resources/downloads/sat.manual.html.

RTI Resources, www.interventioncentral.org.

Shinn, M. R. (2007). Implementation in secondary schools. In S. A. Fernley, S. D. LaRue, & J. W. Norlin (Eds.). *What do I do when . . . the answer book on RTI* (pp. 7-1 to 7-12). Danvers, MA: LRP Publications.

Vanderheyden, A. M. (2007). Implementation in preschool settings. In S. A. Fernley, S. D. LaRue, & J. W. Norlin (Eds.), *What do I do when . . . the answer book on RTI* (pp. 7-1 to 7-12). Danvers, MA: LRP Publications.

Vanderheyden, A. M., Snyder, P., Broussard, C., & Ransdell, K. (2007). Meaningful response to early literary intervention with preschoolers at risk. *Topics in Early Childhood Special Education*, 27, 232–249.

Wright, J. (2007). *RTI toolkit: A practical guide for schools*. Port Chester, NY: Dude Publishing.

Chapter 10

Sources

Elmore, R. F. (2006). *School reform from the inside out: Policy, practice, and performance*. Cambridge, MA: Harvard Education Press.

Fullan, M. (2008). *The six secrets of change: What the best leaders do to help their organizations survive and thrive*. Hoboken, NJ: Wiley.

Hawken, L. H. (2003). Evaluation of a targeted intervention within a schoolwide system of behavior support. *Journal of Behavioral Education*, 12(3), 225–240.

Kohn, A. (1999). *The schools our children deserve*. Boston: Houghton Mifflin.

Kozol, J. (1992). *Savage inequalities*. New York: HarperCollins.

Kozol, J. (1995). *Amazing grace*. New York: Crown.

Lubienski, C., Crane, C., & Lubienski, S. T. (2008). What do we know about school effectiveness? *Phi Delta Kappan*, 89(9), 689–696.

Lubienski, S. T., & Lubienski, C. (2005). A new look at public and private schools: Student background and mathematics achievement. *Phi Delta Kappan*, 86(9), 696–699.

Noguera, P. A. (2006). *Unfinished business: Closing the racial achievement gap in our schools*. San Francisco, CA: Jossey-Bass.

Noguera, P. A. (2008). *The trouble with black boys: And other reflections on race, equity, and the future of public education*. San Francisco: Jossey-Bass.

Sailor, W., & McCart, A. (2004). *Creating a unified system integrating general and special education for the benefit of all students* [Video]. Forum on Education. www.forumoneducation.org.

Todd, A. W., Campbell, A. L., Meyer, G. G., & Horner, R. H. (2008). The effects of a targeted intervention to reduce problem behaviors: Elementary school implementation of check in-check out. *Journal of Positive Behavior Interventions*, 10(1), 46–56.

Additional Resources

Burrello, L., Hoffman, L., & Murray, L. (2005). *School leaders building capacity from within*. Thousand Oaks, CA: Corwin Press.

Coulter, A. (2007). *RtI: Create your own response to intervention* [DVD]. Indianapolis: Indiana University and Forum on Education.

Forum on Education, www.forumoneducation.org.

Hume, K. (2006). *Catch a moving train: H.S. transformation and special education* [DVD]. Indianapolis: Indiana University and Forum on Education.

Schoolwide Applications Model, www.samschools.org.

Index